Collected

Gra

"At a time when the meaning of America is up for grabs, Cody Keenan's new book chronicles ten days that tested us and ultimately showed us at our best. It's a captivating story about what's worth fighting for, an antidote to cynicism that will make you believe again."

—President Barack Obama, via Twitter

"*Grace* is a beautifully written, gripping tale of a monumental week in the life of America. As a political memoir, it is a masterpiece, rendering the White House's characters—including President Barack Obama—in deeply human terms, with unforgettable behind-the-scenes accounts of how history was made. But in *Grace*, Cody Keenan does something even deeper by opening up the chilling rise of white supremacism, delving into the horrific costs of racial injustice in America, and showing how—with courage, decency, and a rich, expansive form of patriotism—our better angels can prevail."

—Samantha Power, Pulitzer Prize–winning author of *A Problem from Hell* and former U.S. ambassador to the United Nations

"*Grace* is an exuberant love letter to public service and a beautifully written record of how a president and his speechwriter faced down the darkest demons of American identity to offer a better, truer story of who we can be. At a time when cynicism and apathy endanger democracy, Cody Keenan lets us all experience how it felt to be in the room and reminds us of the things that are worth fighting for."

—Ben Rhodes, author of *The World as It Is*

"Cody Keenan's *Grace,* like the speeches he wrote with President Obama, is a compelling force. People of faith will know the 'grace' of which Keenan and Obama speak; political and history buffs will appreciate the look inside these tragic, triumphant moments; and all Americans will be moved to tears of sorrow and joy through Keenan's retelling. Grace is what's needed in our country right now, and Keenan's *Grace* is likewise a needed, essential read."

—Joshua DuBois, spiritual advisor to President Obama and author of *The President's Devotional*

"Cody Keenan has the heart of a novelist, the agile mind of an historian, and the acuity of someone who knows politics inside out. This remarkable book speaks in epic ways to the beauty and turmoil of the intimate moments that shape our lives. This is a hero's journey, told with humility, insight, and, of course, grace."

—Colum McCann, National Book Award–winning author of *Let the Great World Spin*

"At a time when cynicism permeates every ounce of our news and our politics, reading this hopeful, inspiring, gorgeous book is as refreshing as skinny-dipping in a mountain lake. *Grace* is an invigorating reminder of the power each of us has to change the things for the better. Read this book! And then buy another one for your friend who thinks nothing matters and the world is doomed."

—Kal Penn, author of the national bestseller *You Can't Be Serious*

"An absorbing book debut with an insider's view of the pressured, often 'fucking terrifying' workings within the White House. . . . A moving portrait of a presidency and its top speechwriter."

—*Kirkus Reviews* (starred review)

"A compelling memoir. . . . [Keenan] offers a candid slice of life in a West Wing characterized by camaraderie, integrity, and hard work."

—*Library Journal* (starred review)

"Uncommonly frank. . . . A rarity in presidential histories these days: an argument for public service."

—*Chicago Tribune*

"Powerful. . . . A fascinating backstage pass. . . . No matter your political persuasion, *Grace* is a generous, lively and worthwhile read."

—*BookPage*

"Students of politics will gain an insider's perspective in presidential power and leadership in time of crisis."

—*Booklist*

"*Grace* is a refreshing departure from the flood of scandalous 'literary' flotsam that typically washes up in the wake of the transfer of power. . . . Like the president he served, Keenan tells his story with conviction, compassion—and amazing grace."

—*Washington Monthly*

"[*Grace*] is less a standard Washington memoir with a scorecard of political wins and losses and more a reflection on the painful process of forging change. It's a meditation on the craft of speech writing itself, and its place in a presidency that, more than most, was rooted in the power of rhetoric."

—CNN's Meanwhile in America

"There are plenty of romanticized depictions of the presidency on film, TV and written form. And then there is Cody Keenan's new book, *Grace*. . . . The heart of the book puts political realism to literature—a showcase about how the goal of a White House is often to fend off bad things, claw for incremental progress and, above all else, fight off cynicism."

—Politico

"A much-needed literary remedy. . . . A story that is gripping, nail-biting, and steeped in the best and worst of humanity."

—48 Hills

GRACE

President Obama and Ten Days in the Battle for America

Cody Keenan
Chief White House Speechwriter

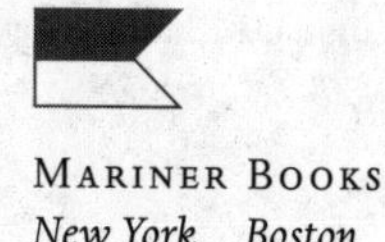

MARINER BOOKS
New York Boston

For Kristen

Grateful acknowledgment is made to the following for the use of the photographs that appear in the art insert: Unless otherwise specified, photographs courtesy of Pete Souza; courtesy of Kyle O'Connor (page 1, bottom); courtesy of the author (page 6, top and bottom; page 10, bottom); courtesy of Nick Ehrmann (page 7, bottom); courtesy of Chuck Kennedy (page 8, top; page 11, bottom left and bottom right; page 12, top and bottom); courtesy of Lawrence Jackson (page 10, top; page 11, top; page 13; page 14, top); and courtesy of Kristen Bartoloni (page 14, bottom).

A hardcover edition of this book was published in 2022 by Mariner Books.

FIRST MARINER BOOKS PAPERBACK EDITION PUBLISHED 2023.

Designed by Emily Snyder

Library of Congress Cataloging-in-Publication Data has been applied for.

ISBN 978-0-06-326933-0

23 24 25 26 27 LBC 5 4 3 2 1

And here we are, at the center of the arc, trapped in the gaudiest, most valuable, and most improbable water wheel the world has ever seen.

Everything now, we must assume, is in our hands; we have no right to assume otherwise.

—JAMES BALDWIN

Contents

Prologue

March 5, 2015

IT WAS SUPPOSED TO SNOW TWO DAYS BEFORE THE SPEECH. I stumbled out of bed and pulled aside the window shade, hoping the city would be covered in a fresh blanket of white.

Nothing. Damn it. I let the shade fall closed and grabbed my phone, swiping for that one email that would define the day, wondering how many other people across the city were doing the same—how many working parents were praying schools would stay open, how many young staffers were hoping offices would close.

I was in a strange hybrid position: I wanted to get the day off *and* to go to work.

I got my wish: The federal government had declared March 5, 2015, a "snow day." Not for a dome of polar chill that often pierced my lungs growing up in Chicago, not for the three-footers of heavy stuff I trudged through to grad school in Cambridge, not for the squalls of ice particles that sandblasted my face while canvassing for votes in Iowa. Just a solid four to seven late-winter inches on the way. Just enough for snow-phobic authorities to preemptively keep a couple hundred thousand employees off the District of Columbia's roads.

It offered the opening I was hoping for: unfettered access to the president of the United States.

I showered, dressed, and followed a lumbering salt truck down a quiet 14th Street to my office for the past six years: the White House.

Barack Obama stepped from the Colonnade into the West Wing, dusting a few of the day's first flakes from his single-breasted, two-button charcoal suit crafted by his favorite Chicago tailor. His white shirt bore vertical gray stripes; his tie was a British regimental pattern—stripes running from left shoulder to right waist—in alternating shades of black, white, and gray. All were neatly pressed. He gripped a white foam cup embossed with a gold presidential seal. He'd worn no overcoat for the short commute from the Residence; to walk the length of the Rose Garden took about fifteen seconds. More snowflakes snuck in past him, a few spoiling his freshly polished Johnston & Murphys, black with a modern toe. He'd shaved within the hour.

"Can you believe this shit?" His expression mirrored his tone. For someone who chided his speechwriters when he found a rhetorical question in his speeches, Barack Obama didn't hesitate to deploy them in private. "Chicago never shut down for a little snow!"

"That's because we're awesome, sir," I replied, affirming our shared Windy City bona fides from a red velvet armchair against the wall.

I'd been waiting with his two assistants, who were already at their desks in what we called the outer Oval Office, a small room tucked between the West Wing hallway and the Oval Office that functioned as a control tower of sorts, where, with the president's complete trust, they managed his meetings and his arrivals and departures to and from every event on his schedule.

Brian Mosteller, the director of Oval Office operations, was a man equally as fastidious as his boss in his professional appearance, and even more so in his professional demeanor; if he was at his station, he was a touch taciturn, even if he liked you. His passion was the work behind the work—how an event was staged, how a president knew where to go and when, how a speech got from words on a screen to printed pages on a lectern. From his desk, he could see the president at his. Brian was the only person who could boast that, even though he never would.

Ferial Govashiri, born in Tehran, raised in Orange County, California, and barely past thirty years old, acted as the president's private switchboard and managed the intersection of his personal and professional lives. She sat closer to the door of the Oval Office and balanced out Brian's reticence with her perpetual cheer and perfectly timed eye rolls.

Obama handed some files to Brian and strode past me. "Come on, Cody."

I stood up and frowned at my own shoes, the same dull, scarred, brown leather monk straps I wore every day, making a mental note to buy a replacement pair now that a squishy sock betrayed a brand-new hole in the right sole. Sneaking a glance in the gold-framed mirror hung over a console topped with fresh flowers and the morning's arrangement of newspapers, I scanned my shapeless navy suit, rumpled blue shirt, and fraying black tie. It was my favorite outfit.

I smiled at Ferial, who gave me a wink as I trailed the president of the United States into the Oval Office.

The first time you walk into the Oval, your mouth goes dry. It happens to everybody. You think you'll be ready for it; after all, it's the one room in the West Wing that movies and television dramas take pains to get right. But you're not ready for it. The gravitas of it squeezes the air from your lungs like pressure at the sea floor. The quality of the light is different, sharper somehow, like you just walked onto live television, everyone's watching you, and everything that's about to happen carries more weight than it would anywhere else. If your self-importance swells while ascending the White House driveway for a meeting with the president, the Oval Office punctures it right away.

It's the best home-court advantage in the world, and Obama pressed that advantage. He kept the temperature a little too warm—

pleasant for someone who had spent his first eighteen years between the 22nd Parallels, maybe, but enough to make everyone else fidget. He chose furniture that forced guests to sit awkwardly: If he beckoned you to the antique chair by the Resolute Desk, you'd sit two inches too low and at an angle that made you crane your neck to face him, like a dancer frozen midleap; if he motioned you to the caramel couches, plush and deep and maligned by critics as reminiscent of basement hand-me-downs, you could either perch on the edge, back straight, like the class goody two-shoes, or slouch like a child who didn't want to be called on.

By my seventh year in the Obama White House, though—and my third year as his chief speechwriter—the Oval Office and I had an understanding. I'd set my laptop on the infinity-edged mica coffee table—called out by the *New York Times* as "extremely contemporary"—and grab a Honeycrisp apple from the one-of-a-kind, hand-turned wooden bowl, then wait to see where he wanted to sit. If he stayed behind his desk, I'd walk over and remain standing in front of him, ignoring the short, rigid chair. If he walked toward his high-backed chair by the fireplace, I'd fluff two of the couch's overstuffed throw pillows and stack them behind me so that I could sit comfortably, like a normal human. Being in the room didn't intimidate me anymore.

I couldn't, however, say the same about my job. To be a speechwriter for Barack Obama is fucking terrifying.

"Okay, show me what you've got," the president said as he settled behind the thirteen-hundred-pound, oak-timbered Resolute Desk. He took a sip of his Lipton with honey and lemon and let out an exaggerated "*Ahhhhhhh*." He raised his eyebrows and offered an ironic smile. "Apparently I've got a lot of time today."

I smiled back—not at him, but to myself. His cleared schedule was why I had come to work rather than climb back into bed. The snow day was my scheme to heist as much of his time on the front end of a big speech as I could, and maybe even coax a little more collaboration from him than usual. I'd take all the help I could get to avoid faceplanting on a big speech—especially one that would tread the thorny subject of race in America.

On March 7, 1965, a group of protesters—mostly young, mostly Black—set out to march from Selma, Alabama, to the state capital of Montgomery with a simple demand: the right to vote.

They were led by Hosea Williams, a close advisor to Dr. Martin Luther King Jr.; and John Lewis, just twenty-five years old but by that point an old hand in the civil rights movement. Just two years earlier, Lewis had been the youngest, most incendiary speaker at the March on Washington. He was also one of the most fearless practitioners of nonviolence in the movement, someone who had bet his life again and again on Freedom Rides and voter-registration drives across the South.

The murder of Jimmie Lee Jackson, a twenty-six-year-old who'd been shot by police after a peaceful march a couple of weeks earlier while trying to protect his mother from a state trooper's billy club, imbued the protesters with additional resolve. But the march was rigged from the start: Alabama governor George Wallace had tarred the protesters as illegitimate, calling them socialists and outside agitators, even if, like Lewis, they were children of Alabama; he warned that their very presence would incite violence, even as he ordered his troopers to *be* violent.

Lewis knew the game and had schooled his unarmed, neatly dressed flock in the tactics of nonviolence before leading them out of Brown Chapel AME Church for the fifty-mile march. They didn't make it one mile before state police met them on the Edmund Pettus Bridge out of Selma, choking them with tear gas, breaking their bones with batons, and cracking Lewis's skull so badly he feared he might die.

The governor and the troopers thought they'd won, confident they'd scared the young Americans not only back over the bridge but away from the political process entirely. They were wrong. The photographs of bloodied, unconscious young men and women, Black and white alike, victims of state-sponsored violence in their own land, bounced across news services and ricocheted around the world. They shocked the conscience of the country, and more

Americans began to realize such cruelty wasn't a one-time event but a daily reality for Black Americans who'd been disenfranchised, denied their civil rights, and otherwise subjugated over a century of Jim Crow.

John Lewis, with his head still bandaged, returned to the chapel and told the press that more Americans would join the marchers. He was right: They did, including Dr. King himself. The troopers parted. The marchers reached Montgomery. Their sacrifice shifted public opinion. And their words reached President Lyndon Johnson, who sampled them just weeks later in an address to a joint session of Congress, pledging "We shall overcome" and soon afterward delivering the Voting Rights Act of 1965, building on the Civil Rights Act of 1964—two laws that pulled America closer to fulfilling its founding ideals.

Fifty years later, any president of the United States would travel to Selma to commemorate what had happened there. This president of the United States happened to be Black. As John Lewis, by 2015 a U.S. representative of nearly thirty years, would say, "If someone had told me when we were crossing this bridge that one day, I would be back here introducing the first African American president, I would have said you're crazy. You're out of your mind."

One might think, then, that a speechwriter's task would be easy: Let the symbolism do the talking. But to be a speechwriter for Barack Obama was never easy. He never let a captive audience go to waste. I knew he'd demand something more than words just praising Selma as a consequential moment in America's history. To meet his expectations demanded using Selma as a lens to examine and explain that history.

I'd thought about what the clash on the Edmund Pettus Bridge represented. It was something more than protesters and police. It was something more than one moment in a larger movement.

On one side of that bridge, led by a twenty-five-year-old whose parents had picked somebody else's cotton, gathered an unlikely crew of Americans. They were young and old, mostly Black, mostly disenfranchised, mostly poor and powerless students, maids, porters, and busboys, burning with the conviction that even though their country had betrayed them again and again, they could change it; together, they could, against all odds, remake America from what it was into what it was supposed to be.

On the other side of that bridge stood the status quo, the power of the state, white men who, even if they weren't individually powerful or privileged, belonged to a class protected by people who were—a ruling elite who warned them that "giving" equal rights to others would mean ceding their traditional station in society.

It was a simple encapsulation of a clash of ideas that stretched through the full story of Black America but also rang true for every American who, like Dr. King, was "tired of marching for something that should've been mine at birth." The story of justice moved forward thanks to women, farmworkers, laborers, Americans with disabilities, Americans of different sexual orientations, immigrants, the poor and the uninsured, and more. It moved forward through any group of people who had to organize and protest and march and push harder than anybody else—not for special rights, but for the *equal* rights, basic justice, and fundamental humanity our country had promised from the beginning.

Each of those struggles—each one of those clamorous challenges claiming that the American project is unique on this Earth because it doesn't require a certain bloodline or that you look, pray, or love a certain way—had riled the established order. And scheduled to speak in just over forty-eight hours at that sacred battleground in Selma was a president of the United States who represented something primal to each side of the conflict—someone who represented change, like it or not.

Behind Obama, snow was beginning to dust the South Lawn. He set his tea on the Resolute Desk's leather blotter and stretched his arm toward me, reaching for his remarks.

"How do you feel about them?"

I'd learned over the years to keep any reservations about a first draft to myself, or he'd dispatch me back to my office to keep working. Without any feedback from him on what I'd already spent days agonizing over, that just meant a few more hours of torturing myself.

"They're good, sir," I told him. Besides, if that wasn't true, he'd let me know.

"Okay," he said, flipping through the pages without reading them. "I'll let you know."

I turned around and padded out of the Oval and through a quiet West Wing, past the Cabinet Room, past the press secretary's office, and down the stairs to my quarters, tucked roughly underneath the Oval Office.

I did think the draft was good. But I knew it wasn't great. Not yet. It was faithful to his take on the American story. What those leaders and foot soldiers of the civil rights movement did to bend America's trajectory upward was a feat that had fascinated Obama growing up. The idea that ordinary people, without power or privilege, could come together to change their own destiny was a proof point that infused his organizing career with purpose, underpinned his politics, and breathed life into so much of his rhetoric.

Obama wasn't a perfect heir to that movement; he'd surfed its wake, raised half a world away in Hawaii and Indonesia by the white half of his family. His wasn't the dominant Black American story—when running for office, he could be dismissed as "too Black" and "not Black enough" at the same time—but his skin color being what it is, I didn't imagine life cared about the caveats. When he was a kid, his own parents' marriage would have been illegal in much of the country; when he was in high school, he endured racial epithets; when he was in college, he was profiled by the police. Through all those indignities, he ended up the first Black president of the *Harvard Law Review* and, well, the first Black president.

If you looked through his eyes, how could the broader trajectory of this country not inspire?

Out of this, I'd cobbled together an argument for the speech:

What could be more American than what happened in this place?

What could more profoundly vindicate the *idea* of America than plain and humble people—the unsung, the downtrodden, the dreamers not of high station, not born to wealth or privilege, not of one religious tradition but many—coming together to shape their country's course?

Selma is not some outlier in the American experience. It is the manifestation of the creed written into our founding documents: "We the People . . . in order to form a more perfect union."

Not everyone would agree, of course, that protest was the highest form of patriotism. Part of what made a speech like the one in Selma challenging was the presidential high-wire act of finding the right rhetorical path between competing audiences.

A new generation was taking to the streets, marching and impatient for racial justice after a series of high-profile police killings of Black men, joined by allies also hungry for action on economic justice that crossed racial lines, action in the face of a rapidly changing climate, action on a whole host of intersecting issues they felt with all of Dr. King's "fierce urgency of now."

There were Americans who disdained the protests, of course; there were also those who expressed sympathy with the young activists and signaled support for their causes but recoiled when that meant changing the status quo—the moderates King dismissed as preferring the absence of tension to the presence of justice.

If Obama went too far in either direction, he'd alienate one of those audiences. But if he walked a tightrope in the middle, he wouldn't satisfy any.

To consider such trade-offs was part of his job, and therefore part of mine, but it could make me feel like a sellout or, worse, like one of those well-meaning moderates who stood in the way without realizing it.

The longer I stared at a screen, consumed by that worry, the more my thoughts would shrink from the big picture to the pixels on a page. I'd spend too much time rearranging words in sentences and sentences in paragraphs as if the right combination would unlock the one codex to hush the babel of competing audiences and unite them around a simple sentiment: "Wow, what a speech; Obama did it again."

In my zeal to rise to the moment, all the different audiences a speech had to address blurred into an audience of one: him. Impressing him. Giving him a draft that he'd love. His opinion was the only one that mattered. I'd push myself past my limits to get a first draft right. Giving it to him was like a trip to the guillotine.

Barely half an hour had passed before Ferial called and asked me to come back upstairs.

Obama was standing at his desk in shirtsleeves, hands on his hips, about an inch of fresh snow resting on the South Lawn behind him. The swirling flakes erased the Washington Monument.

"Look," he said, holding a marked-up draft in one hand. "This is well written. I could probably deliver it as is." He said that a lot. He never meant it. He was setting up for a "but."

"But we have two days, so let's make it better." He started walking toward the couches.

When I'd first started writing for Obama eight years earlier, as an intern for the campaign speechwriting team, it could be crushing to see his edits across the page, his neat penmanship squeezed between paragraphs and along margins, thin lines surgically connecting his additions to the precise places he wanted them sewn in, each one a scalpel to my own self-confidence.

Over time, though, I realized that he worked so intimately with each draft because he was, perhaps more than any president before him, a writer. He was also our editor. His edits meant he liked a draft enough to engage with it, to help push it in the right direction. What he wanted from us, as his team of speechwriters, was a creative partnership, a collaboration where we could make each other better. Where we could take each other to places we couldn't reach alone.

Before I could ask for guidance, he walked over, sat down next to me, and offered it in a way he hadn't before.

"You took a half swing on this," he said. "Take a full swing."

He was generous to leave open the possibility that I might step back into the batter's box and connect with the ball. But it stung all the same, mostly because he was right. I had taken a half swing. I'd wrapped myself in fear of what different audiences would think of the final speech and, worse, the fear of what *he'd* think of the first draft, and that had cornered me into writing what I thought I should, not what I wanted to, something pretty but too safe and sterile to be beautiful.

"What greater form of patriotism is there," he continued, looking at me, "than the belief that America is unfinished? The notion that we're strong enough to be self-critical, to look upon our imperfections, and to say that we can do better? Right?"

"Mmm," I nodded, leaving his question unanswered. I always wished I could come up with what he did.

He stood up and walked toward the three floor-to-ceiling windows behind his desk. "What are we marching for today? What's the great unfinished business of this generation?" he asked. "Who's at the other end of that bridge?"

He'd left the edits he'd made in the thirty minutes between my visits to the Oval on the coffee table, and I leaned forward to peek.

He'd added two short paragraphs to the first page, the first consecrating Selma as a battlefield just as important to the American idea as any other:

> There are places, moments, in America where the nation's destiny is decided. Many are sites of war—Concord and Lexington, Appomattox and Gettysburg. Selma is such a place.

Then he elevated the battle fought there as critical to America's destiny:

> It was not a clash of armies, but a clash of wills; a contest to determine the meaning of America.

There are places, moments, in America where the nation's destiny is decided. Many sites of war — Concord and Lexington, Appomattox
~~This is a place where destiny was decided~~. In one afternoon, all our turbulent history – the stain of slavery and anguish of war; the sore of segregation and tyranny of Jim Crow; the nightmare of four little girls in Birmingham and the dream of a King; our past and our future – met on this bridge. It was not a clash of armies, but a clash of wills; a contest to determine the ~~idea~~ meaning of America. And ~~the ideas~~

I sat back into the couch. Damn. That was it, right there—the whole thesis of the speech:

> It was not a clash of armies, but a clash of wills; a contest to determine the meaning of America.

Hell, in just twenty words, he'd described everything at the root of our political life. The speech clicked for me in a way it hadn't before. I'd had days. He'd needed thirty minutes.

Obama hadn't seen me looking; still speaking, he was staring out the windows at the accumulating snow that made the Oval Office glow even more brightly than usual.

"We are still engaged in that fundamental contest between what America is and what it should be," he said. "Selma is about each of us asking ourselves what we can do to make America better. That's the American story. Not just scratching for what was or settling for what is—but imagining what might be. *Insisting* we live up to our highest ideals. So let's translate Selma for this generation. Let's give today's young people their marching orders."

He turned back toward me, and I took the signal to stand up. "There's always been a tension between those high ideals of our founding and how short we fall of them," he said. "We're at our best when we mind that tension. When we work to close that gap. Because we believe we can. *That's* what makes America exceptional."

He grinned at me and pointed to the draft on the table. "Go write that up."

1
Day One

Wednesday, June 17, 2015

1

AFTER NEARLY A WEEK OF NINETY-DEGREE TEMPERATURES, THE suffocating humidity had finally broken. The six o'clock air felt fresh and clean, cut by the occasional whiff of barbecue smoke. Staff dashed around the verdant South Lawn putting the finishing touches in place. Red, white, and blue balloon columns, tablecloths, everything down to the cups, plates, and utensils blared patriotic merriment. Just as the first guests finished the mile-and-a-half trek up Pennsylvania Avenue from the Capitol steps to the White House gates, the United States Marine Band, nicknamed "The President's Own," took the stage in short sleeves—it was still too warm for full dress uniforms—and began to play some family-friendly classic rock.

The annual congressional picnic would be the final event on President Obama's daily schedule. In the morning, he'd spoken at a jubilant ceremony in a downtown theater to bid farewell to America's first Black attorney general, Eric Holder, and to welcome its second, Loretta Lynch. Justice Sonia Sotomayor, one of the judges Obama had nominated to the Supreme Court and its first Latina, was on hand to swear Lynch into her new job. The president returned to the White House to meet with award-winning science, math, and engineering teachers, and called Steve Kerr, the coach of the Golden State Warriors, to congratulate him and the team on winning the NBA championship the night before. In perhaps the day's most dramatic moment, Lincoln, a red-tailed hawk often seen on the White House grounds, uncoiled its talons and snatched a duckling. Uniformed Secret Service agents fanned out to protect the others, narrowly preventing the North Lawn from becoming a killing field.

The president was safely ensconced in the Oval Office at the time, poring over briefings.

The only remaining obstacle between Obama and a quiet evening at home was an hour of forced schmoozing with Democrats, who'd just torpedoed trade legislation that he wanted, and Republicans, who'd tried and failed to torpedo his new attorney general before pivoting back to their usual agenda of winking at their voters' fevered belief that the president was an illegal sleeper agent hell-bent on destroying America.

For one night, though, they'd eat his hot dogs and beg him to pose for photos with their kids.

As exasperating as the picnic could be, ending the tradition would be a bigger headache. There was a stubborn belief among self-proclaimed "Washington insiders" that if a president threw back just enough cocktails with members of Congress, they'd do whatever he wanted—even though Republicans had long since decided that it was in their political best interest to block whatever he wanted. Regardless, many members of the press corps clung to this canard, summoning an image of LBJ, all six-foot-four of him, glowering at some poor five-foot-ten representative and asking why Obama wouldn't do the same—conveniently forgetting that for LBJ's entire presidency, Democrats held a majority in the House and a filibuster-proof supermajority in the Senate. The same reporters clamored for access to the Congressional Picnic anyway, eager to see their dreams of backslapping, bipartisan bonhomie come true.

The Obama administration may not have ushered in a new Era of Good Feelings, but by the fourth quarter of the presidency, those of us who'd been part of the mission from the beginning had a pretty good story to tell. If the first six years after the 2008 financial crisis felt like constant triage to plug the holes in the economic dike with one hand while using the other to fight off Republican nihilists willing to sabotage the arduous recovery if it might help them win votes, the seventh year felt like we were playing well and finally had a solid lead.

Obama had fought through unprecedented obstruction to check off most of the campaign promises he'd made and deliver on several he hadn't, like reversing the worst recession in eighty years and rescuing the auto industry. Jobs and wages were on the rise. The health care system, while still a patchwork mess, was on its way to insuring another 20 million Americans. Obama had done more to combat climate change than any other president and was close to convincing the entire world to sign on to a climate treaty. Over 90 percent of our troops had come home from Iraq and Afghanistan. And in one of my favorite bits of sloganeering, the American auto industry was alive, and Osama bin Laden was dead.

I also liked to point out that Obama's was the first administration in decades in which nobody had been indicted. It was a low bar, sure, but it was one that only he cleared.

There was a confidence to Obama in 2015 that hadn't always been there, one bestowed not by winning reelection in 2012 but earned by surviving adversity and trial. It was a liberated fearlessness that came from making and surviving mistakes. He'd sometimes liken himself to an aging athlete, one who was a little slower and couldn't jump as high, but who'd played enough seasons to know what he was doing and could hit the shot when it mattered most—which was usually in the fourth quarter.

With Republicans now in charge of both houses of Congress, significant legislation was off the table for the rest of the presidency. We had to find ways for Obama to get things done without them, and the remaining avenues for progress were to wield executive powers, leverage international diplomacy, and change people's thinking about America and its possibilities through judicious use of the presidential "bully pulpit"—which, as a speechwriter, happened to be my job.

We were far enough into the second term that another presidential election was underway, with candidates from Hillary Clinton to Ted Cruz already out campaigning to take Obama's place. So Denis McDonough, the scrupulous chief of staff—tall and angular, whose silver hair and striking resemblance to Sam the Eagle from *The Muppet Show* belied his mere forty-five years, and whose mischievous smile suggested he kept a permanent secret—had made the rounds early in 2015, telling White House staff that if we were thinking of leaving for a campaign or any other endeavor, do it *now*. Otherwise, stay and run through the tape.

"You'll never have another chance like this to make a difference," he'd say.

When people asked my plans, I joked that I wasn't going anywhere until the Chicago Cubs won the World Series and got their White House visit. But the truth was, when we won the 2008 campaign and Obama's first chief speechwriter, Jon Favreau, told me I'd be going to the White House with him, I promised I'd turn off the lights at the end. I intended to keep that promise.

Despite the grueling nature of the job, it wasn't a hard promise to keep. That interminable twenty-two-month campaign had forged a collection of strangers into a family, and our White House reflected that. There was little room or patience for ego or personal ambition; it was a place of purpose, commitment, friendship, and collegiality from start to finish. The number of staff who planned on remaining to serve out both terms far exceeded the record for previous administrations.

That evening, Denis canceled the nightly wrap-up meeting in his office for the president's innermost circle of staff, encouraging us to join the forced fun on the South Lawn and to press some flesh with the arriving senators and representatives. I doubted it was beneficence. In my mind's eye, I could picture the president saying, "If *I* have to do this, *you* have to do this."

I decided against such masochism, but I did slip out the French doors at the east end of the Colonnade, slink past the Rose Garden in full early summer bloom, and infiltrate the picnic, hoping to save a few bucks by snagging something from the White House grillmasters.

From the far end of the Rose Garden, I could see President Obama stalling at his desk in the Oval Office, his back to the picnickers straining to catch a glimpse. At least I enjoyed red meat. Obama, zealously committed to wholesome eating and someone who almost exclusively judged a meal on its nutritional statistics alone, was doomed to consume only bullshit for the next hour.

2

WITH AN EARLY DINNER OF TWO CHICAGO DOGS PILFERED FROM the party, I headed back into the West Wing, down the stairs to the ground floor, and into a mazelike chamber of three windowless offices. To reach my desk, I had to carve through an office staffed by two young assistants, then hang a left through the door to the right. Once inside my office, I could hang another left at my desk into a third, electronically secured room where my deputy, a friendly-faced father of two named Terry Szuplat, who was also the team's foreign policy and national security speechwriter, would greet me with a jolly "Hey, man" while pecking away at his keyboard, oblivious to the sun's position in the sky.

Our offices were nothing like the ornate, high-ceilinged, sunlit suites of the Eisenhower Executive Office Building that loomed across the driveway, where most White House staff worked. In the West Wing, you paid for your proximity to the president with drab rooms, low ceilings, and, in my case, no daylight—though the White House doctors did supply us with a steady stream of vitamin D pills. Unlike the Oval Office, where the quality of light was purposefully heightened and often improved by the sky's moods, ours was permanently neglected—a jaundiced fluorescence that never varied a wavelength.

No windows meant lots of beige wall space, so I stocked the office with political and Chicago sports memorabilia, family photos, an American flag, my grandfather's World War II medals, and an eighteenth-century writing desk that one of the White House curators agreed to let me keep with a scowl that said, "Don't make me regret this." A television hung over my desk, which I almost always kept muted while tuned to MSNBC during the day and ESPN at night.

I loved my office. I called it "the Speechcave."

With everyone else on the South Lawn, I turned to the array of speeches that my team would have to write in the days ahead. Most were somewhat rote at this point—an address to the U.S. Conference of Mayors, a couple of fundraisers in California, remarks at a reception for Pride month and for an Iftar dinner, and two economic speeches. Nothing we hadn't written before.

The following week, though, would be anything but rote. It was what we called "SCOTUS week," when the Supreme Court would issue decisions on a slew of cases, then adjourn for its summer vacation. We knew what cases were on the docket but not what the decisions would be or when they might come. The Supreme Court justices are the sphinx of the three branches of government—you know what they're looking at but not what they're thinking about.

The myopic lens of Washington politics tended to frame Supreme Court decisions as a "win" or a "loss" for the president. But we were waiting for two impending decisions that would intimately and immediately shape the daily lives of millions of Americans. And whatever the outcomes, it was my team's job to have speeches ready.

The first case was *King v. Burwell,* the second major challenge in just three years to Obama's signature legislation: the Patient Protection and Affordable Care Act, otherwise known as the ACA or "Obamacare."

For nearly a hundred years, ever since Teddy Roosevelt first called for it, universal health insurance had been progressives' North Star. Several presidents had tried and failed to enact some version. Medicare, Medicaid, and the Children's Health Insurance Program had filled some of the gaps, covering America's oldest, youngest, and poorest citizens.

But by 2009, some 46 million Americans remained uninsured. They were disproportionately Black and Latino, but also young and healthy individuals who didn't want to spend money on insurance they were less likely to use. Millions more were middle-class full-time workers, Democrats and Republicans and neither, who simply couldn't afford to pay premiums that climbed year after year.

If President Obama were starting from scratch and enjoyed absolute power, he would have enacted some form of a single-payer system, like Medicare for All. It would have been the best option. It would also have been by far the most disruptive, throwing at least 100 million Americans off their existing health insurance plan onto a new one. It would have made the year-long battle over the ACA look like a child's birthday party. And it would have been impossible. To overcome a Republican filibuster, Democrats needed sixty votes in the Senate, not fifty—and Connecticut Democrat Joe Lieberman, the Iraq War's biggest fan and the sixtieth vote, refused to budge. He wouldn't even vote for a scaled-down "public option," a federal insurance plan that would lower costs by competing with private insurers.

But after spending two weeks and a marathon weekend in March of 2010 working Democrats over the phones—*very* LBJ—Obama eked out just enough votes to get the Affordable Care Act through Congress.

The law wasn't anybody's first choice; it was a compromise, an unsatisfying mélange of rules and regulations, and President Obama acknowledged as much on a regular basis. But it was also, without question, one of the most progressive laws ever enacted by a president, on par with Social Security and Medicare, and despite far more hostile opposition.

For the first time, the federal government had assumed the responsibility to make insurance available to almost every American and offered help to pay for it. The Affordable Care Act expanded Medicaid and created a new, federally operated insurance exchange where Americans could pool their purchasing power and private insurers had to compete for their business. In return for those new customers, every insurer was required to adhere for the first time to rules on coverage and cost—a Patient's Bill of Rights that Democrats had tried to enact for years. To pay for all of it, the law raised taxes on the wealthiest Americans. And despite an embarrassing glitch-filled launch of the website designed to make it easier to buy insurance, more than 10 million people gained the economic security of health insurance in just the first year.

Where FDR, Truman, Nixon, Carter, and Clinton had all failed, Obama was on track to succeed.

After a year of legislative sausage-making to pass the law, one 2012 Supreme Court decision to uphold the law, a presidential campaign waged over preserving or dismantling the law, a Republican shutdown of the federal government aimed at defunding the law, more than fifty Republican-led attempts in Congress to repeal or weaken the law, and an endless torrent of disinformation campaigns from the right—the law still stood. But outside groups funded by conservative donors had been able to finagle another challenge before the Court. This time, unlike in 2012, the question at issue wasn't whether the entire law was legal. This case, ostensibly about the legality of the law's tax credits, was a breed of Trojan horse, one more Republican attempt to unravel the law on a technicality.

As the Supreme Court deliberated through the spring of 2015, more than 16 million uninsured Americans—nearly one in three—had gained coverage. In just five years, the uninsured rate for Americans in their early twenties had been cut in half, from one in three to one in six—and for the population as a whole, it was the lowest on record. Everybody else with insurance, however they received it, gained all kinds of benefits and protections they didn't have before, including a wildly popular ban on insurers dropping their care or jacking up their premiums based on a preexisting condition. If the Court went the other way this time, millions of Americans would be plunged back into an existence of daily dread that one illness or accident could mean financial ruin—including millions of Americans who loathed both the law and the president who signed it.

While *King v. Burwell* was going to determine whether America guaranteed the fundamental economic right to health care to its poor and its middle class, the other major case before the Court, *Obergefell v. Hodges,* was going to determine whether the Constitution guaranteed the fundamental equal right to marriage and dignity for LGBTQ Americans—or relegated them to second-class citizenship.

In 2003, Massachusetts became the first state to legalize marriage equality when its highest court ruled that the commonwealth's prior ban was unconstitutional. In 2004, Republicans weaponized that decision, promising to amend the U.S. Constitution to outlaw same-sex marriage. It was a cynical ploy to turn out more socially conservative and evangelical voters in a presidential election year. After a federal ban fizzled, a handful of states, most notably California, would enact their own bans. But the rest of the ensuing decade was a cascade of progress. By 2015, same-sex marriage was legal in thirty-six states and D.C.

A 1996 law, the Defense of Marriage Act (DOMA), stood in the way of extending that right nationwide. DOMA defined marriage as the union of one man and one woman, thereby denying federal benefits to same-sex couples: Social Security, veterans' benefits, pensions, tax breaks, student loans, copyrights, farm subsidies—more than a thousand federal benefits in all. The law also empowered states to refuse to recognize same-sex marriages performed in other states.

Every Republican in Congress, save for one openly gay congressman, voted for DOMA, codifying LGBTQ Americans as a separate class. So did two thirds of Democrats.

By then, a New York woman named Edith "Edie" Windsor had been with her partner, Thea Spyer, for more than thirty years. The two women had gotten engaged in 1967, even though same-sex marriage wasn't yet legal anywhere, but they kept their sexuality a secret at first to protect their careers. Ten years later, Thea fell ill and Edie ultimately became her full-time caregiver. In 2007, doctors told Thea she had less than a year to live, and, after a four-decade engagement, they married each other in Canada—a marriage that lasted almost two years before Thea died.

If Thea had been a man, Edie wouldn't have had to pay any taxes on the estate Thea left her. But thanks to DOMA, she owed more than $360,000. So Edie sued the federal government. On June 26, 2013, *United States v. Windsor* found the section of DOMA that defined marriage as a union between one man and one woman to be unconstitutional—a decision that guaranteed couples in the states that recognized same-sex marriage the same federal benefits as everybody else.

But the decision didn't answer the question as to whether same-sex marriages had to be recognized across state lines. That's when Jim Obergefell proposed to his partner, John Arthur. They had been together for more than twenty years but lived in Ohio, a state in which same-sex marriage was illegal. Suffering from ALS, John couldn't travel to apply for a marriage license. So Jim flew to Maryland, the only state that didn't require both applicants to appear in person for a marriage license, and got one. After that, family and friends raised funds to cover a medical flight on a specially equipped jet. Jim and John flew to Maryland, took their vows, and flew home a married couple.

That could have been the end of it. But a local civil rights attorney told them that because Ohio didn't recognize out-of-state same-sex marriages, John's eventual death certificate would list him as single, with no surviving spouse. Their lawful marriage would be erased. So they sued Ohio's governor and attorney general in a case that ultimately reached the Supreme Court.

The organized LGBTQ rights movement was younger than the campaign for universal health care. But after several decades of persistent struggle, there was a strong wind in its sails. The Supreme Court's decision in *Obergefell,* coming any day next week, would either be a landmark, putting an exclamation point on that progress toward justice and equality—or would throw it all into question.

For our generation, it was a no-brainer, a visceral civil rights issue, a question of fundamental equality. Of course we and our friends should be able to marry whomever we wanted. There was no way the Supreme Court would rule otherwise.

But what if it did?

What if, in just days, the Supreme Court set the movements for universal health care and LGBTQ equality back years? What would those decisions tell the world about who we were? What would those decisions tell *America* about who we were?

What would I write if that happened?

To craft victory remarks in either case would be a happy task. But to say something reassuring to millions of Americans who were suddenly terrified that they might lose the only way they had to pay for a sick child's treatment—that would be hard. To say something meaningful to millions more, including friends and colleagues, who'd just been told that their dreams of love and happiness were somehow worth less than everybody else's—that would be cruel.

There were ancillary stakes for so many of us who had gotten into politics not to create a legacy for Barack Obama but to bend, even just a little, the trajectory of this country. I thought about what losing would mean for Americans who'd been marching and organizing for decades, and what it might mean for a new generation that had voted for the first time, much of it for the first president who looked like them, a generation that, even if it hadn't fully developed a faith in democracy, had at least come to hope that, together, maybe we could change things for the better.

For an ensemble of ancient judges to extinguish that hope would be a dagger made of pure cynicism.

It would tell them "No, You Can't."

"Well, that's dark," I said to my empty office. I stood up, dropped the red-and-white checked paper basket from the picnic in the trash, and grabbed my keys. I could figure out what to write tomorrow. Walking out onto West Executive Avenue, the summer sky still light at eight o'clock, I could hear live music and laughter coming from the South Lawn. I tossed my backpack into the backseat of my car, drove through the hulking White House gates, and headed for home.

At the same hour, 550 miles to the south, a man parked his car, checked his gun, and entered a church.

3

SOMETIME AFTER TEN O'CLOCK, I WAS PLANTED ON THE COUCH watching the eighth inning of the Chicago Cubs game when I heard keys jangle in the door to the apartment I shared with Kristen Bartoloni.

"Hi!"

Kristen had a unique trademark on the word "Hi!" The first time I'd heard it was four Junes prior—June 27, 2011, to be exact. There was a knock on the door to the office I shared with three other speechwriters in the Eisenhower Executive Office Building. I opened it to find the then-director of White House research, Ben Holzer, with a woman I'd never seen before. She was tall and lean, with long chestnut hair; she wore a khaki skirt suit and cerulean blue T-shirt that matched her eyes. Her smile wasn't forced but real; the way she said "hi" wasn't with the clipped professionalism of someone who was already looking for angles to exploit or ladders to climb but bursting with the guileless warmth of someone delighted to be part of a new team.

Barely twenty-five, she'd already helped elect a woman to the senate in New Hampshire by flipping a seat that had been held by Republican men for thirty years, worked at an organization devoted to electing more women up and down the ballot, and wrote for a progressive thinktank.

It was Kristen Bartoloni's first day of work at the White House, and it changed my life forever. I can't remember anything that was said. I just knew everything would be different from then on.

Four years later, I still couldn't get over the way she smiled when she came through a door, craned her neck to look for me before putting her bag down, and aimed a "Hi!" like she'd crafted it for me alone. I always returned it, but I could never quite master the same sound.

I could make her a mean dinner, though, and I motioned to the plate of fresh pasta and glass of white wine on the counter and patted the space next to me on the couch. The Cubs were beating the Cleveland Indians 17-0, so I handed Kristen the remote. The windows were open, and the sound of laughter and clinking glasses floated up from the restaurant below. As she twirled bucatini around her fork, I took a swig of Pacifico, and we talked about our days.

By 2015, Kristen had been promoted to deputy director of the nine-person White House research team, which, like speechwriting, was part of the press and communications operation.

"Research" was not a good way to describe what they did. They were fireproofers.

They knew everything there was to know about Barack Obama—his past statements and positions, his voting record, his place of birth (classified).

They would vet every person he met with and every venue he visited to make sure there were no political landmines underfoot—criminal records, racist posts on social media, tax liens, poor labor practices.

They would fact-check his remarks meticulously—and for a speechwriter, overzealously and quite annoyingly—to make sure that whatever he said was both accurate and consistent with what he'd said before.

They were, in effect, pre-crisis consultants. They relentlessly rescued us from inadvertently creating an "optics" problem by having the president say or do something he shouldn't, with someone he shouldn't, at a place he shouldn't have been.

Imagine living with someone whose *job* it was to tell you that you were wrong all the time. That's how much I loved Kristen. And it's why we almost never fought at home. When she was fact-checking one of my speeches, we got it out of our system with a million little battles at work.

In our years together at the White House, I clashed with her and leaned on her more than anybody else.

Mouth full of pasta, Kristen put her head on my shoulder and asked if I'd heard about the Secret Service protecting the ducklings. We talked about the Supreme Court remarks I was working on, and I feigned persecution at the stridency of her fact-checks to an economic riff I'd written the day before. She feigned exasperation and opened her laptop to show me why she was right and I was wrong. More laughter drifted up from the street.

Then she froze. "Cody." There was something scared in her voice. I looked over her shoulder to see an email from Kelsey Coates, one of her colleagues.

Subject: Tweets—Shooting in Charleston

When breaking news happened after hours, it usually fell to someone on Kristen's team to blast the news to everyone on the president's staff for awareness. In the first few minutes, that news would come from tweets, ideally reputable ones, updated every few minutes with more tweets, then clips pulled from cable news, then longer write-ups from national news sources.

BREAKING: Mass shooting at Black church in South Carolina

Through eleven o'clock, rumors flew across Twitter in a race to be first and most retweeted rather than most accurate: There were several victims, a suspect was in custody, a suspect *wasn't* in custody, a killer was still at large, a bomb threat was made, the bomb threat was a hoax.

By midnight, the cable networks were broadcasting live. A contingent of political reporters were at the scene; they happened to be in Charleston because Hillary Clinton had campaigned for president there that day and Jeb Bush was scheduled to be there the next; he canceled his event. South Carolina governor Nikki Haley offered "love and prayers."

Shortly before one o'clock, even as police cruised the streets of Charleston searching for the killer, the mayor and the police chief briefed reporters, confirming that nine people were dead. News sources had identified one of them as the church's pastor, a state senator named Clementa Pinckney. The suspect was a white male. Mayor Joe Riley, standing with local Black leaders, labeled the shootings a hate crime in calm and direct language, lamented the easy access to guns, and offered some thoughts on the victims.

Politics may often seem remote, separate, disconnected from people's daily lives, but people look to their leaders in a crisis—and that's when the good ones shine.

I hadn't noticed that Kristen was clutching my hand. My brain had already switched tracks into speechwriting mode, a cold habit that often made me an awful dinner companion. I was thinking through what the president would have to say and what arguments and counterarguments he'd have to make, gathering facts and information and grace notes, wondering if Obama had been to that church and met its pastor, pecking out thoughts on my phone and emailing them to myself.

It was something I grappled with after six and a half years in the White House. When you analyze every angle and take apart every opposing argument, when you write about everything—you can start to feel nothing. I worried that speechwriting, in many ways, was making me more dispassionate, harder, and more cynical than I used to be.

But I did feel something now: I felt angry. I was angry that some asshole who shouldn't have had a gun had murdered a bunch of people who were in a place where they were supposed to be safe. I was torn up that another collection of parents and spouses and kids in an American city were wailing in anguish at the worst news of their lives. I was furious that a white man murdering nine Black people in a Black church would be celebrated in some of America's more rotten cavities, and that ringleaders would use the aftermath as a crowbar to crack open the country's racial fissures. I was preemptively pissed that everybody was going to fight about it the next day—a predictable and tiresome pattern of quarreling about guns and race and who's to blame, even as the makeup of Congress virtually guaranteed that the pattern would repeat before long.

Either I or another one of Obama's speechwriters had written about mass murder more than a dozen times before. Each time took an emotional toll. Each time was a mocking reminder of how hard it was to change things.

More laughter wafted up from the sidewalk. Kristen wiped a tear from her cheek. We hugged each other tighter than usual, then climbed into bed to do the same.

But not before I rolled my alarm clock backward an hour to 5:00 A.M.

Day Two

Thursday, June 18, 2015

1

TIME MOVED DIFFERENTLY IN THE WEST WING.

To lift a parenting adage, the days felt like years, and the years just days.

But there was a fluidity to the hours too.

The mornings began around six thirty, when the "media monitor"—usually the youngest communications aide, right out of college—roused White House inboxes with a spatter of stories from the major newspapers that soon coalesced into a steady stream of news that didn't slow for twelve hours.

At 7:45 sharp, twenty or so of the president's top aides, the heads of each council and department in the White House—the national security advisor, the national economic advisor, the press secretary, the communications director, the White House counsel, and so on—took our seats around two shiny, ten-foot wooden tables pushed together end-to-end in the chief of staff's office for the senior advisors meeting, just as Denis McDonough barked, "Good morning, everybody, let's go."

The rest of the day was a rush of meetings, a race to stay on top of emails, each deadline met and replaced by the next. The minutes moved faster the closer you got to midday, like the point in a river where the water squeezes between stones. A press aide wanted your eye on a release; a policy advisor wanted your ear for an idea; a speechwriter at a cabinet agency wanted to rub shoulders; the president wanted to walk you through the meticulous edits he'd made on a draft speech overnight.

Obama departed the Oval for dinner with his family at 6:30 sharp. That was sacrosanct. As his daughters grew older, he wanted to make the most of every moment he had with them, and it wasn't wise to be the final person in his way. Once the president stepped out onto the Colonnade for his brief commute home, senior advisors would return to Denis's office for our nightly wrap-up meeting—a review of that day and a run-through of the next. By the time the final meeting finished, twelve hours after the first, most staffers were heading home and the daily torrent of emails had slowed to a trickle.

Not many of those twelve hours were generally conducive to deep thinking, let alone writing. Any minute spent in a meeting was a minute I wasn't cracking the code on a speech.

I preferred the edges of the day, the banks where the flow was slower.

If a speech draft wasn't as tight as I wanted it, I might go to work early, arriving at the West Wing Mess takeout window just as the culinary experts of the United States Navy hoisted it open at 0600 hours to hand me a cup of fresh coffee. Or I might stay late, ordering dinner from the same window just before it closed at 8:00 P.M. and carrying it back to my office, fourteen hours after I arrived, the waters finally still, to write free of interruption.

And then there were mornings like that Thursday, when we woke up to a river already at flood stage.

Jen Psaki, the whip-smart, flame-haired communications director, emailed at 5:48 A.M. to ask if I was drafting a statement. From a stoplight on 14th Street, I replied that I was. Minutes later, I walked into the West Wing with the mid-June sunrise, grabbed my coffee with one hand, juggled my keys with the other, and unlocked the door to the speechwriting labyrinth.

"Bro." I looked behind me to see Lisa Monaco, the homeland security and counterterrorism advisor standing square in my doorway. I hadn't even taken the lid off my coffee yet. Lisa always called me "bro." I liked it. She had twelve years on me and exuded a big-sister vibe. She was short, funny, feisty, and good at ribbing colleagues with her Boston accent—all qualities that might obscure her intellect to someone who didn't know her. She'd already had a prestigious career at the Department of Justice and as an assistant U.S. attorney, taking down terrorists and white-collar criminals alike. By 2015, she'd become one of the president's three highest-ranking national security aides, along with Susan Rice, his national security advisor, and Avril Haines, the former deputy director of the CIA who'd returned to the Obama White House to serve as deputy director of the National Security Council.

We called the three women the "Furies," after the Greek goddesses of vengeance.

For Lisa to barrel into my office wasn't unusual; she worked across the hall and sometimes came by late at night looking for a finger or two of the bourbon I kept in the antique writing desk that the White House curators let me keep. For her to appear at 6:01 in the morning, though, signaled something less pleasant.

"This is not public yet," she said, unsmiling, approaching my desk. "The suspect entered the church basement a little after eight P.M. and asked to join a Bible study in progress. After about an hour, he said he was there because, quote, 'You rape our women, you're taking over our country, you have to go,' unquote, and opened fire. Nine people are dead. The suspect is still at large, but the FBI has him and his license plate from the church's surveillance footage."

"How do we know all this?"

"He left someone alive on purpose. He told her it was to tell people what happened."

I leaned back in my chair. "Jesus." The anguish and helplessness at some faraway slaughter felt familiar to all of us by now. We'd been through mass shootings many times. Immigrants in Binghamton. Soldiers at Fort Hood. A congresswoman and her constituents in

Tucson. Schoolkids in Newtown. Moviegoers in Aurora. Sikh worshippers in Oak Creek. Christmas shoppers in Clackamas. Other Americans in other towns with ordinary names that had become shorthand for tragedy.

In 2015 alone, there would be more than three hundred mass shootings in America, defined as four or more people shot in one event, not including the shooter. The country had become so numb to the bloodshed that only the most horrifying ones seemed uncommon.

They were usually over in minutes. Sometimes the killer was dead. It was irreversible. For all the power of the presidency, there was little a statement could do but show some moral clarity and give a frightened and grieving community some reassurance that the world would keep spinning.

2

TWO AND A HALF YEARS EARLIER, ON A FRIDAY MORNING JUST before Christmas 2012, a man with a semiautomatic rifle and three hundred rounds of ammunition murdered six adults and twenty students at an elementary school in Newtown, Connecticut.

The students were all around six years old. They were children.

A quiet, profound horror took hold of everybody in the White House that day. It afflicted parents, I noticed, more deeply than those of us who didn't have kids. The president's personal assistant at the time, a hypercompetent young woman with a blond bob named Anita Decker Breckenridge, who'd worked for Obama longer than anybody else, did something that someone at her desk did only once in all eight years of the Obama presidency: She called First Lady Michelle Obama and asked her if she'd come to the Oval Office to be with her husband.

In those days, I shared an office—a sunny one, with windows—with Jon Favreau, my predecessor as chief speechwriter. Favs and I drafted a statement on the shooting together. Trying to find words amidst the trauma was a numbing exercise, a feeble attempt at quantifying incalculable grief. Once Mrs. Obama was gone, we walked into the Oval in silence and handed the president a single page. He was standing behind his desk and didn't sit as he read it over.

Picking up a pen, he bent over and struck one paragraph. It was something I'd added about how his first reaction had been to think of his own daughters in their classrooms, to imagine what it would be like if he'd gotten that call, what it would be like if he, like the parents in Newtown, had rushed to the school only to be kept from his children by yellow police tape, praying that they would come out.

"Too raw," he said. "I wouldn't be able to get through that."

He returned the piece of paper to me. "You know, kids that age, they trust you. They trust everybody. For someone to violate that trust . . ." He capped his pen without finishing the sentence.

An hour or so later, in a packed White House Briefing Room, even with that paragraph removed, he couldn't get through the statement. "The majority of those who died today were children. Beautiful little kids between the ages of five and ten years old." For twelve seconds, he stared at the page, trying to compose himself, wiping away a tear. Once he continued, his voice caught on more than one word. "They had their entire lives ahead of them. Birthdays. Graduations. Weddings. Kids of their own."

His emotion, more than any words from me or Jon, was what struck a chord with people. The video of Obama's statement would become the second-most-watched video on the White House YouTube channel—just behind his remarks the night of the bin Laden raid—and remain there for years.

Later, Obama would tell me that day was the first time he cried in the Oval Office.

He did it again the next day, as we talked about what to say in a eulogy for twenty little kids.

I tried to give Obama prompts in sessions like these, something that might spark a stream of consciousness from him while I tried to type fast enough to capture it. That Saturday afternoon in the Oval

Office, with the eulogy scheduled for the next day—just forty-eight hours after the unimaginable—I had little to offer.

He was searching for something too.

"The question that every religion seeks to answer is, Why are we here? What gives our life meaning? What gives our life purpose?"

He spoke slowly from one of the high-backed chairs flanking the fireplace in the Oval Office while I pecked away from the couch.

"We are born and then we die. During the years we have on this Earth, there are going to be fleeting moments of pleasure and pain. And at the end of those days, we have to ask ourselves, What did this all mean? What was God's purpose here? What was *our* purpose here? Were we true to that purpose? Each of us grips through the darkness and confusion and we understand how limited we are, and that bad things happen, and we ask ourselves why."

He seemed to be grasping through the darkness himself, seeking something familiar to hold on to.

"And the only anchor we have—the only things we are *sure* about—is the love that we feel for our children. The cling of their hugs at night before we tuck them into bed. The warmth of their breath on our necks. Seeing their joy. That's what matters. That's all we've got. That's the only thing we're sure of. So we gotta make that count."

His eyes welled up as he spoke. When a tear finally broke free and ran down his cheek, it brought him back to the room and his gaze back to mine.

"And somehow, I gotta deliver that. And I gotta stop crying. All right? So go write that up."

I did the first thing I could think of: I called my mother and asked her how on Earth to eulogize twenty little kids and the six educators who died trying to protect them. Her response was similar to Obama's—that our kids are the only thing that matter. And if we don't do everything we can to protect them, then why are we here?

I worked through the night, sending Obama a two-page draft the next morning. Air Force One was scheduled to carry us to

Connecticut that afternoon, but first, a smaller version of his motorcade ferried Obama through a quiet winter Sunday in Northwest Washington to Sasha's school so that he could watch his daughter practice for an upcoming dance recital. He sat to the side of the auditorium, occasionally looking down to write new sections of the eulogy longhand while his daughter and a gaggle of eleven-year-olds twirled onstage.

Early that evening, after the full-size presidential motorcade wound through the dark, wooded lanes of Newtown, I climbed out of a van into the frigid air and approached Obama's limo. He handed me two yellow legal pages filled with his handwriting. I added them to the eulogy as he spent nearly three hours going from classroom to classroom in the town's high school to console each family in turn, hugging parents still in shock and playing with little siblings who tugged at their tiny suits and dresses, too young to understand where their brother or sister had been for the past two days. It was, he'd later tell me, the only time he saw Secret Service agents cry. Then he gathered himself in a bathroom and took the stage in the school auditorium to address the nation again.

After a mass shooting, Republicans and the gun manufacturers' lobby reliably rally around the Second Amendment, shielding it better than they shield our own kids. They immediately gaslight the country, churning up bullshit like an octopus trying to blind a predator with sand. Everything is to blame but guns. After Newtown, the head of the National Rifle Association skipped over the killer's semiautomatic rifle and two handguns and assigned liability to video games.

In the decade before Newtown, America had spent more than a trillion dollars and devoted entire federal agencies to preventing terrorist attacks on our soil. But Republicans had explicitly blocked federal agencies from even collecting data on how we might reduce tens of thousands of gun deaths *every year,* trying to eliminate a baseline of facts from which serious solutions could sprout, so that after every mass shooting their collective response—after mustering "thoughts and prayers"—could be a shrugged "What can you do?"

One option would be a universal background-check system. The idea had the support of 90 percent of Americans. Most Americans already thought it *was* the law. But in April 2013, four months after Newtown—after Obama had eulogized twenty little kids and six educators who died trying to protect them, after he used his State of the Union Address and the honeymoon days of his second term to push for gun reforms, after he held impassioned rallies with the parents of Newtown victims—Republicans used the sixty-vote filibuster to block bipartisan universal background-check legislation, with those same parents watching aghast from the Senate gallery.

An hour and a half later, surrounded by the families of Newtown, Obama spoke in the Rose Garden. It was rare that he didn't make any edits to the draft of a speech. This time it was because I'd written the remarks angry, and that suited him. He'd even warned me, just before walking out, that he was going to extemporize a bit.

"I've heard folks say that having the families of victims lobby for this legislation was somehow misplaced." His voice dripped with disdain. "'A prop,' somebody called them. 'Emotional blackmail,' some outlet said. Are they serious? Do we really think that thousands of families whose lives have been shattered by gun violence don't have a right to weigh in on this issue? Do we think their emotions, their loss, is not relevant to this debate?

"So all in all, this was a pretty shameful day for Washington."

He hugged the families and stepped back through the door from the Rose Garden into the Oval Office. I was in the outer Oval, where I'd been watching him on television. He saw me through the open doorway and walked over.

"The next time this happens, I don't want to speak." His words could have cracked the planet in half. "What am I supposed to do? What am I supposed to say? 'Well, we tried; we're just not going to *do* anything about this anymore?'"

In my time at the White House, I would only witness him angry two other times—once previously, when a right-wing heckler had posed as a journalist and shouted at him in the middle of a speech in the Rose Garden, and later, when a staffer sheepishly confessed that a new website designed to help people buy health insurance didn't work as he'd assured Obama it would.

This was worse.

3

OBAMA DIDN'T GET HIS WISH. IN THE THIRTY MONTHS BETWEEN Newtown and Charleston, he'd issue another handful of statements after mass shootings and deliver two eulogies: one after a gunman killed twelve and wounded eight at the Washington Navy Yard, and another after a soldier killed three and wounded fourteen at Fort Hood in Texas. It was the second time in five years that Obama had delivered a eulogy after a mass shooting at the same Army base.

Each statement and eulogy became a tick angrier than the last, each one closer to a jeremiad.

"It should be clear that the change we need will not come from Washington, even when tragedy strikes Washington," he said at the Navy Yard. "The question is, Do we care enough? . . . Our tears are not enough. Our words and our prayers are not enough. If we really want to honor these twelve men and women, if we really want to be a country where we can go to work, and go to school, and walk our streets free from senseless violence, without so many lives being stolen by a bullet from a gun, then we're going to have to change. We're going to have to change."

The day after the Charleston slaughter would be the fourteenth time President Obama addressed the nation after a mass shooting. The fourteenth time I'd have to find a new way for him to offer some reassurance that the world would keep spinning, even when it was full of holes.

There had been no debate as to whether or not the commander in chief would speak after two mass shootings on military bases. But today, I wondered if he'd hold the line he drew that day in 2013.

The circumstances of the massacre decided that for us. Early reports from the scene suggested a racial motivation—a white man murdering nine Black people in a Black church; you didn't need to be Batman to piece that together. But it had become official when Lisa Monaco marched into my office to relay what the killer had told his victims.

Reading the news that morning, I'd learned that Emanuel African Methodist Episcopal Church was the oldest AME church in the South. Slaves seeking liberty had helped to found "Mother Emanuel" nearly two hundred years earlier. The church was later burned to the ground for seeking slavery's end. When South Carolina outlawed all-Black services, its parishioners conducted them in secret. Some of the brightest leaders of the civil rights movement spoke and led marches from Emanuel's steps.

"It's not just a church," a South Carolina historian told the *Washington Post*. "It's also a symbol . . . of Black freedom."

An attack on a place of Black dignity, community, and safety conjured up some of America's oldest and ugliest demons and echoed the violence visited on Black Americans like Emmett Till, Medgar Evers, four little girls in Birmingham, and untold, unnamed others through centuries of slavery and Jim Crow—violence meant to "keep people in their place," to instill fear in Americans who posed a "threat" to the established order.

Such violence wasn't relegated to history. In the 1990s, a string of Black churches across the South were firebombed or burned. Another in Massachusetts was set ablaze the day President Obama was elected. Every few months, a video of police killing an unarmed Black man would rocket around the internet, and the protests were getting louder and more immediate.

From the television above my desk, I heard a mourner talking to a reporter: "If we're not safe in the church, God, you tell us where we are safe."

I stood up and walked across the hall to Lisa Monaco's office, a low-ceilinged bunker like mine.

"Can we call this terrorism?" It sure looked like an act intended to strike fear into a particular community.

"DOJ and the FBI have opened a hate crimes investigation."

"Can we call it terrorism."

"We shouldn't," she said. "We don't know enough yet. We don't even have a suspect in custody. And that word has a whole federal legal definition-slash-thornbush stuck to it. I'll tell you any time I learn something new. Okay?"

I thought of any one of a dozen other statements I'd drafted after other mass shootings in which lawyers like Lisa insisted I add the word "alleged" before "murderer" or "killer."

"That's absurd," I'd protest each time, especially when a killer was already in custody. "Normal humans don't talk like that."

"Normal humans don't have to worry that their words will be responsible for getting a federal case thrown out because they influenced a jury," the lawyers would reply. "The president of the United States does." As someone who not only valued the rule of law but taught the constitutional flavor of it in law school, the president agreed with them.

It was frustrating. The fact that it was terrorism was obvious, plain as day. The killer practically admitted as much. But I knew Lisa was right, as I conceded to her before retreating to my office. We didn't really know much yet, and this was something too important to be wrong about straight out of the gate. Obama's responsibilities as president constrained indulgences like passion. If things were going to get tense in America, it would fall to him to lower the temperature.

His political opponents didn't constrain themselves in such ways. Lindsey Graham was one of South Carolina's two senators and one of America's foremost political opportunists. After the Boston Marathon bombing in 2013, he implied that the bomber, a Kyrgyz American, was part of a larger Muslim problem and, despite his American citizenship, "should be designated as a potential enemy combatant and we should be allowed to question him for intelligence gathering purposes to find out about future attacks and terrorist organizations that may exist." On his way to Charleston this very morning, presumably to the scene of the massacre at Mother Emanuel, Senator Graham didn't suggest a larger homegrown extremism problem. Instead, he dismissed the Charleston killer as "one of these whacked-out kids. I don't think it's anything broader than that."

Just as I was putting on my jacket to head upstairs for the 7:45 A.M. meeting in Denis's office, he marched into mine. I'd always liked Denis. He was a Midwesterner like me, even if his noble features made him seem a more patrician version. But there was nothing patrician about his Irish Catholic upbringing outside Minneapolis. He had ten brothers and sisters, two of whom became Catholic priests. I could have seen Denis taking the same path—he spent time as a young man teaching in Latin America—but I suspected he loved cuss words and his wife, Kari, too much to ever wear the cloth.

Instead, he took a vow of service. Denis didn't bounce in and out of the private sector; he was a career staffer, someone who preferred to work behind the scenes, like I did. Every Wednesday, he'd walk across the driveway to the Eisenhower Executive Office Building for Taco Wednesday (why it wasn't Taco Tuesday, I never knew), and waited in line at the taco bar, hands in pockets, chatting in an avuncular manner with young staffers, many fresh out of college. He saw himself as someone on our level, even if the youths saw him as someone way above theirs.

"Hey, Buster. You doing okay?" One of my favorite things about Denis was that when he asked how you were, it wasn't cursory. He really was checking on you. This was somebody who took the time to send handwritten notes of congratulations or thanks to someone in the building every day. I'd been the lucky recipient after a speech or two. He knew that writing and rewriting these statements took a toll.

"I'm pissed and sad."

"Me too," he said, as we walked up to his office together. "Hey, I think the president should call this domestic terrorism."

I laughed for the first time that day.

I also liked the twenty or so senior advisors who gathered around his table each morning. (Technically, only three aides held the official title "senior advisor," even though the meeting was called the "senior advisors morning meeting," or "senior advisors" for short. Nobody cared.) It was a solid team made up of good people who'd served in all levels of government and considered it a high calling. We were all casual with each other, but as the youngest, thirty-four years old at the time, I maintained a sense of collegial deference. After two and a half years as chief speechwriter, they took me seriously and seemed to respect, even admire, what I could do.

But there were also times when being the youngest got me treated that way. For the next forty-five minutes, in the first meeting since the shooting, two dozen advisors told me how to do my job. They were tense about this statement to the country in a way they hadn't been for others. If they didn't have an opinion on what the president should say, they made sure to tell me that it was a very important statement. If they did have an opinion, they argued with each other.

He should call it "senseless violence." No, it wasn't "senseless," it was "targeted."

He should call it a "hate crime." No, that suggests that the crime was done to one group, when it's an assault on the very idea of a multiracial democracy.

He should call it "terrorism" to evoke a strength of feeling that we're all under attack here. No, that has a specific legal meaning that we don't yet know the alleged killer will meet.

Well, whatever we call it, he should say, "This is a tragedy that has no place in America." Bad news, pal—this type of tragedy pretty much *only* takes place in America.

I was already anxious enough about writing something that met the moment, and an unfocused barrage of opinions wasn't reassuring. My face was in my hands, which I then let fall hard on the table. It was my turn.

"Look. After Republicans blocked background checks, the president said that he didn't want to say anything after these shootings anymore. Everybody always expects him to because it's reassuring. It ends the cycle. But it's absolution without penance. It lets the country off the hook. And nothing's ever going to change."

Halfway through my rant, I regretted it. But as a speechwriter, I felt I had to finish the argument.

"I understand *why* we have to do it this time. But every minute we debate how I should write a statement I've written a dozen times is another minute I'm not writing anything at all. How about I just go do my job and run it by him to see if it's what he wants?"

Nobody said anything, and I felt worse. Nobody was trying to tell me how to do my job. Everybody felt as pissed and sad as I did, and they just wanted to do something to help. I wanted to hide—not because I was angry at them, but because I was ashamed of myself.

Denis broke the silence. "Okay, let's do it. Cody, you're up—and let us know if we can help."

After the meeting, Josh Earnest, the president's press secretary, pulled me aside in the hallway outside the Oval Office. Josh had grown up in Kansas City and, despite nearly two decades in politics, still had an air of the Heartland about him, with an unguarded smile and a very un-Washington willingness to reveal boyish wonder at a new discovery.

"That was not a helpful meeting," Josh said with a laugh. "And I understand why you feel this way. But I think people need to hear from Obama after this one. At a minimum, he should say something before he disappears to California for three days."

The president would be departing for California that afternoon with a light West Coast schedule—one speech, a couple of fundraisers, and some golf with friends.

"We can't let him do that without saying something," Josh added. "You know that. This is a tough one, but if there's anybody who can nail it, it's you."

For Josh to feel like he had to intervene made me feel doubly chagrined. Nobody in politics had a last name that more perfectly described their demeanor than Josh Earnest. (Maybe Anthony Weiner.) Josh had a way of offering suggestions, criticism, and even edits to speeches in a way that made you feel better about yourself—and even a little fired up.

It was exactly what I needed just then. Obama had to give a statement later in the morning that I hadn't started yet—and the clock was ticking.

4

WITH THE ANGER AND SELF-PITY FLUSHED FROM MY SYSTEM, IT was time to write. I looked at my watch as I walked toward my office. It was eight thirty. The first item on Obama's daily schedule was always his national security briefing. That would end around ten thirty. Worst case, I had two hours to get him a draft. I'd done more with less.

My eager-to-please assistant, Susannah Jacob, was already at her desk. She stopped typing and looked up at me with big, sad eyes that said, "This is awful, and I want to help."

Any other day, she couldn't stop smiling over the fact that she got to work in the White House. The night I promoted her from intern to assistant, she crossed Pennsylvania Avenue to sit in Lafayette Park just to look at the White House for a while before treating herself to a drink at a nearby bar, where she got carded. Her innocent bearing belied a toughness that won her a campuswide election at the University of Texas to become editor in chief of the *Daily Texan*. Still, just twenty-three years old, she practically burst with a hopefulness to the point where you wanted to protect her from the world breaking her heart.

The television above her head was tuned to MSNBC, with a chyron on the screen that read DOJ INVESTIGATING AS HATE CRIME and archival footage of Loretta Lynch, the brand-new attorney general immediately saddled with the grim investigation.

"I don't know what would be most helpful," Susannah said, "but I've been compiling some stories about the victims and the church, and I've been reading some old Martin Luther King speeches to see if there's anything relevant there."

I thanked her and asked her to pull anything the slain pastor had said about his church.

Valerie Jarrett, the president's close advisor and one of his oldest friends from Chicago, had told me earlier that morning that Obama had met Pinckney once on the campaign trail. From the press coverage I'd seen so far, I got the sense that he was one of those people who impressed you instantly. He was preaching by age thirteen, a pastor by age eighteen, and elected to the state legislature by age twenty-three, where he represented a sprawling swath of South Carolina's Lowcountry—one of the most neglected parts of America. It was an area that needed so much—especially, it seemed, someone like Clem Pinckney.

I was immediately struck by the way one of his friends described him: "When he entered a room, it was like the future arrived." What an extraordinary thing to say about someone. What a terrible thing to lose.

Susannah sent a speech Pinckney had delivered in 2013 about the freedom that Mother Emanuel represented—a freedom that one of its founders, a man named Denmark Vesey, never fully saw realized.

Vesey was born into slavery. As an adult, he purchased his way out—but he couldn't do the same for his wife and children. In 1818, he helped found the African Methodist Episcopal Church in Charleston at a time when the city was home to more Blacks than whites. Within three years, white authorities ordered it closed upon rumors that the church was teaching slaves to read. Meanwhile, Vesey had been organizing something that made the authorities even more fearful—a slave rebellion. His plot was discovered, he was tried by what would be a kangaroo court if it didn't have the official backing of the city, he was hung in public, and his church was burned to the ground. One of his sons rebuilt it.

In his speech, Pinckney had said, "Could we not argue that America is about freedom whether we live it out or not? But it really is about freedom, equality, and the pursuit of happiness. And that is what church is all about: freedom to worship and freedom from sin, freedom to be full of what God intends us to be, and to have equality in the sight of God. And sometimes you got to make noise to do that. Sometimes you may have to die like Denmark Vesey to do that. Sometimes you have to march, struggle, and be unpopular to do that."

I wished I'd heard of Pinckney before he died.

But "sometimes you got to make noise" was as good a writing prompt as any. I got to work, trying to thread all the usual needles for a statement like this.

To empathize with the suffering:

> Another American community is grieving today. Michelle and I know several of the parishioners at Emanuel AME Church. It's one of the oldest Black churches in America. We knew their reverend, Clementa Pinckney, who was murdered last night along with eight others, after prayer and worship—in the kind of act that conjures up a dark history of violence against Black churches.

To dismiss "thoughts and prayers" as lazy writing and empty gestures:

> And to say our thoughts and prayers are with them and with their community doesn't say enough to convey the sadness and heartache and anger we feel.

To mock the way the Lindsey Grahams of the world worked harder to excuse hatred than to extinguish it:

> I've had to express these emotions too many times. And I've got more to say once there's more we know. But to describe it as just another act of senseless violence, or the work of a troubled mind—that's too soft. That's too easy. We've done that too often.

To reassure everyone that someone was in charge and the world would keep spinning:

> The FBI is on the scene with local police, and more of the Bureau's best are on their way to join them.

To tweak the lawyers:

> As the investigation proceeds, federal law might ultimately classify what happened last night as a crime of hate, or an act of domestic terrorism, or something else, and I'll let the best of law enforcement do its work.

And just to vent, adding something I knew would be too theatrical for Obama:

> But we don't have to wait for the results of an investigation to know that their killer is a coward who will meet justice in this world and the next.

"Bro." Lisa reappeared in my office.

"I'm sending everyone a draft now. I hadn't shared it yet because everyone was annoying me."

"Welcome to my world," she said. "Cops found out who the shooter is. It's a twenty-one-year-old named Dylann Roof. His father identified him from the surveillance video."

"Harsh."

"He's got some priors on drugs and trespassing, but that's it. The FBI is going through databases for you right now to see if there's any terrorist link."

"Wait, what? For me?"

"I was kidding. That's their job."

Once the killer's name was made public, reporters raced for his social media profiles. Within minutes, they had found a photo of him scowling in a swamp, wearing the symbols of failed apartheid states. He was telling people who he was.

Within an hour, police took him into custody in Shelby, North Carolina. Almost immediately, about twenty people forwarded the news alert to me and Ben Rhodes.

Ben, Obama's closest national security advisor and one of my best friends, sat in the office next door. With close-cropped hair that was shedding as quickly as Obama's was going gray, and a stern face that belied his quick, explosive laugh, he was a bit of a ringer for the actor Rob Corddry if Corddry ran three miles every morning.

By the tenth email, he walked into my office laughing. "Hey, did you get the news?"

I swiveled to face him. "It's a real speechwriting-by-committee day around here. Speaking of which, give this statement a quick read so I can send it around, will you?"

Ben leaned over my shoulder and gave the statement a scan. "Looks good," he said, pounding my fist. "Fuck terrorists."

On my way to the Oval Office five minutes later, draft in hand, I ran into Jen Psaki tottering down the stairs, one arm on the railing for support. She was about nine months pregnant. "I just read the statement," she said. "The ending made me a little emotional. Then again, so does a good sandwich right now."

I mustered a smile. "When in doubt, Dr. King."

I walked into the outer Oval. A meeting had just broken, and several senior aides were still standing around, waiting for me. I ignored them and raised my eyebrows at Ferial, our code meaning, "Can I go in?"

She pointed at the door to the Oval. Obama was leaning against it, scrolling through something on his BlackBerry. "Hey, brother."

"I'm sorry." I meant it on a lot of levels. "I understand you knew the pastor."

"We met him once." He put his phone in his pocket and stood straight. "He was an impressive young man. But you shouldn't say we were friends or anything. That the statement?" I nodded. He motioned to Ferial's chair. "Sit down."

When time was running short and Obama was ready to speak, he didn't uncap a pen. Instead, he unseated poor Ferial so that he could stand over my shoulder and dictate his edits to me on the fly. (For security reasons, White House printers weren't wireless, so finishing a speech on her computer, rather than on my laptop, was the fastest option.)

If that wasn't stressful enough, this was the first time I could remember that staff stayed to watch us work. I sat there, staring at the screen while Obama read the draft, burning white hot while everyone else gawked at us.

He was going paragraph by paragraph. "That's fine . . . that's fine . . ." It was rare to get a "good."

He paused when he got to this paragraph:

> As president, my words have to be more restrained than I'd sometimes like, especially when an investigation is underway. I've had to make statements like these too many times. We have had to endure this too many times. And to describe this as just another act of senseless violence, or the work of a troubled mind—that's too soft. That's too easy. We've done that too often.

After reworking it in his head for ten seconds or so, he started writing aloud.

"Here's what I'd say: Until the investigation is complete, I'm necessarily constrained in terms of talking about the details of the case. But I don't need to be constrained about the emotions that tragedies like this raise. I've had to make statements like this too many times. Communities like this have had to endure tragedies like this too many times. We don't have all the facts, but we do know that, once again, innocent people were killed in part because someone who wanted to inflict harm had no trouble getting their hands on a gun.

"Now is the time for mourning and for healing. But let's be clear: At some point, we as a country will have to reckon with the fact that this type of mass violence does not happen in other advanced countries. It doesn't happen in other places with this kind of frequency. And it is in our power to do something about it. I say that recognizing the politics in this town forecloses a lot of those avenues right now. But it would be wrong for us not to acknowledge it. And at some point, it's going to be important for the American people to come to grips with it, and for us to be able to shift how we think about the issue of gun violence collectively."

My fingers flew across the keyboard, trying to keep up. As cynical as I'd become about our political capacity to do something about gun violence, I was surprised to find myself relieved that he offered a pathway anyway, however narrow.

I wondered what, if anything, he'd say on race. I hadn't drafted much—I didn't want to without the chance to talk with him first.

"The fact that this took place in a Black church obviously also raises questions about a dark part of our history. This is not the first time that Black churches have been attacked. And we know that hatred across races and faiths pose a particular threat to our democracy and our ideals."

These sentences took longer for him to get out than the ones on guns. He was thinking it through as he was speaking. I appreciated the democracy point. It was hard for one to thrive when some Americans didn't believe that others should exist, let alone be treated as full and equal citizens.

To me, at least, he seemed a little grim. But if Obama was true to one thing, it was offering people a shred of hope. "The good news is," he continued, "I am confident that the outpouring of unity and strength and fellowship and love across Charleston today, from all races, from all faiths, from all places of worship, indicates the degree to which those old vestiges of hatred can be overcome."

He laid the printed draft on the desk and walked back into the Oval to put on his jacket, adding a thought over his shoulder: "And then the King thing is good."

Susannah had pulled remarks that Dr. King had delivered in 1963 after four little girls were killed in a bombing in a Black church in Birmingham, Alabama. And that's how Obama ended his televised remarks in the Briefing Room a few minutes later. "'They say to each of us,' Dr. King said, 'Black and white alike, that we must substitute courage for caution. They say to us that we must be concerned not merely about who murdered them, but about the system, the way of life, the philosophy which produced the murderers. Their death says to us that we must work passionately and unrelentingly for the realization of the American Dream.'"

Obama didn't hide his disappointment and frustration. Not at the fact that he had to do this again. But at the fact that he had to do this again because America wasn't doing enough to stop it.

Underscoring the point, flags across South Carolina, three states to the south, had all been lowered to half-staff. Except for one: The Confederate flag on the state capitol grounds still flew high. State law prohibited taking it down.

Day Three

Friday, June 19, 2015

1

"HELLO, WORDSMITHS," I BELLOWED AS PRESIDENT OBAMA'S TEAM of speechwriters filed into my office on Friday morning. I hoped an attempt at normalcy would buck everybody's spirits.

The greeting was a holdover from my first two years in the White House, when David Axelrod, the mustachioed Chicago strategist who steered Obama from the Illinois state senate to the White House, used it to welcome the speechwriting team into his Oval-adjacent office each morning while dabbing a fresh stain out of his tie.

This 9:00 A.M. meeting was still my favorite of the day, a bolt of ideas and energy. Some of our speechwriters had more than a decade of experience, having climbed the long ladder from congratulatory messages to big speeches, and I trusted them to draft almost anything. Some were closer to those first rungs and still needed some mentoring. But all of them had heart. All of them were idealists who saw being a White House speechwriter not as the pinnacle of a career but as a platform to help make a positive difference in people's lives.

That was especially true of Ben Rhodes stretching back even before our earliest days on the campaign, when we'd stay out too late at the Houlihan's on the Chicago River, complain about politics as usual, and make plans to change the world over cheap beer, chicken wings, and cigarettes. He'd grown up in Manhattan, dreaming of becoming a novelist, until the sight of the towers falling on 9/11 radicalized him into politics and ultimately a job as Obama's national security speechwriter. By now, our seventh year in the White House, his job as deputy national security advisor for strategic communications meant more strategy sessions and less writing than in the first term, and as Obama's point person on ending the embargo against Cuba, he would disappear abroad for days at a time on covert diplomatic missions. But he occasionally crashed our meetings because he knew that his general stature and seen-it-all demeanor intimidated the younger scribes.

Sarah Hurwitz, Michelle Obama's chief speechwriter, had also joined the Obamas during the first campaign. Despite their shared Harvard Law pedigree, she may have had even less in common with her boss than I did with mine. Sarah was a petite, overcaffeinated lawyer from Wayland, Massachusetts, who, after developing a distaste for corporate practice, made the jump to speechwriting and became the chief speechwriter on Hillary Clinton's 2008 presidential campaign. She had a penchant for barging into my office with a three-point torrent of opinions before I could say "Hi." Like the First Lady, though, she was compassionate, self-effacing, and suffered no bullshit. Nobody captured Michelle Obama's voice better.

Sarah's deputy, Tyler Lechtenberg, came close. He'd grown up on a farm in Iowa before packing up his pickup and heading west with dreams of becoming a sportswriter. Once Obama announced his candidacy, Tyler took a U-turn, quitting his new career, driving home to organize an entire county, and ending up at the White House working in the First Lady's correspondence office. That's where, in a remarkable feat of talent scouting, Sarah noticed his work and pulled him into speechwriting. The blond, milk-white farm kid from Strawberry Point became so good at capturing the voice of a Black woman from the South Side that, before meeting him, President Obama assumed Tyler was Black too.

I was trying to poach Tyler into writing for the president, but it would have to be a delicate and elaborate heist. The First Lady loved Sarah and Tyler, and the three of them had a rapport that would be extremely difficult to counterfeit with a new speechwriter. Where the president liked staying up late to edit the first draft of a speech the night before he delivered it, Mrs. Obama preferred receiving a draft almost two weeks early, talking through it with her speechwriters over several days, and casually but carefully editing a number of versions. On what we called "gameday," she could outperform her husband, delivering quotidian remarks with a welcoming warmth and consequential speeches with a mesmerizing passion that rode the razor's edge of tears.

Terry Szuplat, the deputy director of speechwriting and affable old man of the group at forty-two, sat in the windowless office even closer to the underworld than mine. With a thick shock of hickory hair parted on the left and lids that drooped over the outer edges of his blue eyes until they met the creases that betrayed years of laughter, he could have been mistaken for a Kennedy if not for his preference to work behind the scenes. Other than Kristen, and with Ben trapped in the Situation Room half the day, Terry served as my most important advisor and sounding board. Over two terms in the White House, he probably drafted more remarks on foreign policy and national security than any other presidential speechwriter in history—even though, like Obama, he was out the door every evening at 6:30 sharp to have dinner with his wife and two children at their home in Virginia before reopening his laptop to work later at night.

(One drawback to his office's position was that National Security Council staffers had to walk through mine while couriering classified documents to Terry. It felt like whenever I tried to steal a catnap on the couch after a late night of writing, someone I'd never seen before would interrupt my sleep to ask, "Is Terry in there?")

I'd known Sarada Peri the longest, over a friendship stretching back to graduate school. She boasted a broad smile and easygoing demeanor, sincere qualities that served a secondary purpose: When she showed you why you were wrong, you listened. As a feminist and an Indian American and the only speechwriter of color on our team, she rightly chafed that so many white people wrote for the Obamas. It's one reason I hired her. In our final interview, she also told me that we were clumsy at writing for female audiences. That's another reason I hired her. For all her fearlessness, though, and a writing style as incisive as she was, she and I shared a tendency to undersell our speech drafts to others as a form of self-preservation—a habit we pushed each other to break.

Megan Rooney had practically swapped roles with Sarah Hurwitz—she'd written for Mrs. Obama on the campaign, then for Hillary Clinton while she was Obama's secretary of state. Like Kristen, Megan hailed from Staten Island, the conservative outpost of New York City with neighborhoods known for the kind of parochial resentment that Republicans lived to exploit—which also made it the source of her reservoir of empathy for folks outside the chattering class. She was unfailingly cheerful and unabashedly optimistic, two traits I admired and wished I had.

David Litt was the youngest member of the speechwriting team, still in his twenties, but the lingering whiff of preppy Yale on him sometimes gave him the boyishly old look of an English member of Parliament. He was the team's workhorse and joke writer, eager to take on any assignment, no matter how minor, and serious about doing a good job. More than the others, he asked for feedback and sought to improve, which I respected.

It was a phenomenal team of writers with an easy camaraderie, and I was lucky to work with them. I made sure each of them got to sit with the president in the Oval Office to download his stream of consciousness before each speech, and I carried over a tradition Favs initiated to have them travel with the president on Air Force One for any speeches that were out of town. Your speech, your trip.

Sometimes, one of us would bring doughnuts to our daily team gatherings; almost always we began with gossip and small talk before turning to the speeches each writer was working on. The first writers in the room would claim the two side chairs; the rest would squeeze shoulder to shoulder on the small couch along one wall. All would look at me expectantly, thinking more of me than I did of myself. There's not a thing I wouldn't have done for any of them.

There was no small talk today. "Is he going to go to Charleston?" Sarada asked.

Whether Obama would deliver another eulogy was all anybody seemed to want to know that day. I knew that some of the president's advisors upstairs were pushing for it already.

"Not yet," I replied.

"I'm with him if he doesn't want to. It's not on him alone to fix this every time," she said. "Or you," she added. "But it's hard, though. This time is different. This one is way too fucked."

That wouldn't make it any easier to find the right words for a speech that I'd already started worrying about, a speech that would have to be more than a eulogy, but a balm, a sermon, a way forward. I didn't know what those words were yet. Maybe someone smarter did. Maybe someone else should have my job. Neither thought was new to me.

In the meantime, I *did* have the job, and the team was waiting for edits, assignments, and guidance.

Megan asked if Obama had made any edits to the speech he would deliver in San Francisco that day to a convention of America's mayors. She and I had rewritten sections of the draft the afternoon before to include new language on Charleston and gun violence, racing to finish it before he landed in California. For a speechwriter, Air Force One inching closer to its destination on a map is no different than a clock's second hand approaching zero.

"Just one," I replied, handing Megan two lines he'd added overnight. It wasn't much.

> The nature of this attack—in a place of worship—adds to the pain; the apparent motivations of the shooter remind us that racism remains a blight that we have to combat together. But as much as we grieve this particular tragedy, we need to step back and recognize these tragedies have become far too commonplace.

"It's wild that he's going to end up giving a speech on guns in San Francisco," Terry said.

I didn't follow. "Why's that?"

"Isn't that where he got in trouble on the campaign for saying that people cling to guns and religion?"

I cringed. It was. At a fundraiser on the campaign trail in 2008, Obama had made the mistake of trying to diagnose the electoral psyche of economically suffering, blue-collar, mostly white voters, arguing that politicians had disappointed for decades on promises of economic change.

The full quote—unscripted, I'd add—was: "And it's not surprising then they get bitter, they cling to guns or religion or antipathy to people who aren't like them or anti-immigrant sentiment or anti-trade sentiment as a way to explain their frustrations."

It was indelicate and violated a tenet he'd always tried to instill in his speechwriters: Don't assign motives to people. The quote dogged him for weeks, exacerbating a grueling stretch in the campaign.

"Well"—I sighed—"maybe he was right about the guns and antipathy part."

Tyler had just finished crafting remarks for the First Lady, who was on a trip through Italy, for her to deliver to American troops stationed in Vicenza. Terry was handling a speech about reforms to the federal government's hostage policy. I assigned Sarada remarks for a Pride month reception the following Wednesday, and David and Megan two economic speeches slated for the following Thursday and Friday. And I asked Susannah, still new at speechwriting—as green as I'd been in the early days of the 2007 campaign—to try her hand at a short video script linking climate change to public health. She brightened at the opportunity in a way I missed in myself.

That left the remarks for the Supreme Court decisions that loomed over us the following week.

I reserved the remarks on the Affordable Care Act decision for myself. With some of our first-term speechwriters gone, I'd absorbed the ACA as one of my spheres of expertise—and as my penance for the fact that we were still defending it at every turn. By 2015, I'd written most of Obama's speeches on the ACA, and I felt a duty to see it through to the end.

I'd been assigned the president's remarks for the Sunday night in March 2010 that the ACA passed the House of Representatives and headed to his desk to become law. I sent a draft to him early that afternoon and, with a little time to kill, went to a nearby bar to watch some of the NCAA basketball tournament with two colleagues, including his first personal assistant in the White House, Katie Johnson. As the hours passed, I grew increasingly impatient, refreshing the inbox on my BlackBerry for some sign that Obama had looked at his remarks.

Around five o'clock, Katie started laughing. "Obama's emailing me that he wants to have a party tonight for the staff who worked on the ACA."

I stared at her with my mouth open. "Wait, what?"

"Yeah, he wants me to put together a list of people and he wants to know what we should serve at the party." She laughed again. "He wants to know if we have any taquitos!"

I threw my hands up. "No, I mean, I've been waiting for him to look at his address to the nation on finally winning health reform, and he's fucking party planning?" I ordered another beer.

Ultimately, Obama didn't make any edits to the remarks. We watched the House vote from the Roosevelt Room in the West Wing, then trekked over to the East Room in the Residence, where I watched him say, "This is what change looks like." And that night, on the Truman Balcony—at the party he'd planned—Obama raised a martini glass to his staffers to finish the thought.

"In some ways, this is more gratifying than election night. That was just the chance to deliver change. Today, you all saw it through. This is why we do what we do."

There was plenty of champagne—but no taquitos to be found.

Five years later, with the law before the Supreme Court for a second time, I now had to prepare two more sets of remarks—one for winning, one for losing. Because Kristen and I were leaving town that afternoon for a weekend wedding in Massachusetts, I'd already scratched out a rough draft of each, but I'd been playing the defeat version close to the vest, sharing it only with a small group of policy wonks because it was more complicated. They'd have to triage some in-case-of-emergency-break-glass policies to protect people who'd lose their health insurance.

I hadn't shared the victory version with anyone. I wasn't superstitious—but if jinxes *were* real, I didn't want to be wrong.

I'd thought hard about the remarks for the Supreme Court decision on marriage equality and, at the end of the meeting, asked Sarada to take the pen on those. She was our only speechwriter who knew what it was like to live outside the traditionally protected classes in America. That was an unfair position in which to put her and a reminder that my team, like everything else in society, needed a more diverse set of backgrounds and perspectives. But in the moment, I had hers.

"Happy to," she said. "Win and lose?"

"Win and lose. I haven't heard anyone speculate that we might lose. That doesn't mean we won't, of course. So crush the victory speech and just do a draft of the defeat speech."

"What should he say?"

"Go out and trumpet it as a massive victory for equality," I said. "Progress that people have marched for over the course of decades. Another step toward living up to our founding ideals. But also subtly make the point that Obama has helped speed change along, from ending Don't Ask, Don't Tell, to securing hospital visitation rights, stuff like that. And you can take a little technical credit for the ruling with his decision not to enforce DOMA."

"Okay. I can't promise they'll be any good."

I knew she'd clear the bar she set for herself by a country mile. "Yes, they will." Then I pretended to scowl at her. "The dignity and happiness of millions of Americans depend on it."

As the team filed out to put words on pages, Terry lingered.

"Hey man. Why don't you let one of us handle the ACA remarks?

You know that you and Obama are going to end up doing this eulogy. Don't kill yourself over something we can do."

I loved Terry. Speechwriting was never easy, but Terry made it seem more effortless than most. He'd been writing speeches since the nineties, when he was a young scribe at the Pentagon before becoming the secretary of defense's chief wordsmith at the ripe old age of twenty-five.

And he wasn't being hyperbolic about my killing myself with work. In April 2013, when I was one month into being chief speechwriter and desperate to prove I was worthy of the post, even through another particularly grueling week of events—the final rallies before the background checks vote, the Rose Garden rebuke after it failed, a eulogy after a factory explosion in Texas, the Boston Marathon bombing and manhunt and its assorted statements and eulogy (which Terry, a native Bostonian, infused with a local pathos that made grown men watching in Roslindale pubs cry), and a long fiscal policy speech that only Obama thought was a good idea—I worked my way right into Walter Reed Hospital with an irregular heartbeat that was diagnosed as a bout of hypertension. When I returned to the office the next day, Terry was the one who told me that I had to start trusting the team I'd already written with for years, or this would never work.

"I appreciate it," I told Terry now. "But I already wrote the ACA ones."

I halfway lied: I'd halfway written them. And if anything was tugging at my blood pressure again, it was the thought of writing a eulogy for Charleston.

2

AFTER THE KILLER'S CAPTURE, THE DETAILS BEGAN TO BACK UP Sarada's assessment: This was indeed way too fucked.

Dylann Roof wasn't some "whacked-out kid." He'd become a white supremacist without leaving his bedroom. Deluded into believing that the media was hiding an epidemic of Black-on-white crime, he self-radicalized on the internet. He waved the Confederate banner and adopted the totems of white supremacy. He crisscrossed the state with his new "Confederate States of America" license plate, visiting the Confederacy's sacred places—the island where slaves were bought and sold, the plantations where they toiled, the graveyard where its soldiers were buried.

He immersed himself in white power websites, consuming enough poison to metamorphose from a run-of-the-mill teenager into someone who felt special, filled with a purpose. He penned a white supremacist manifesto and posted it online, complaining that while Blacks were taking over the world, whites were being relegated to second-class citizenship and nobody was doing anything about it—so he'd have to take it upon himself.

His justification—the nonsense that Black-on-white rape and violence were widespread scourges from which nobody was protecting whites—was the same kind of toxic victimhood the guilty use to absolve themselves after countless racial terror campaigns, a sick blend of the Blacks-as-unstoppable-savages trope and "replacement theory," the white supremacist notion that an elitist cabal is behind schemes for Jews, immigrants, or Black Americans to replace whites. Simply put, they were lies to stoke fear about some looming threat; lies that offered a permission structure to eliminate that threat; lies that, after the fact, were used as a rationalization for preemptive violence.

Lies, as Obama added to his statement from the White House on Thursday morning, that posed a unique threat to the idea of a democracy.

The killer had started buying the accessories for the AR-15 he'd get whenever he had the money—magazines that held more rounds, a forearm that made it easier to grip when the barrel got hot. Police once questioned him about the budding arsenal when they searched his car, but in South Carolina, none of it was illegal. His parents gave him some cash for his twenty-first birthday, but it wasn't enough for the rifle he wanted, so he bought a semiautomatic pistol and eight magazines filled with hollow-point bullets that expanded on impact, mushrooming inside the body in a way that pointed bullets didn't. Bullets designed to kill better.

Surveillance footage showed the twenty-one-year-old pull into the church parking lot at 8:16 P.M. He didn't idle in the car thinking things over. He climbed the one step between the blacktop and the wooden door, hiking his pants up his slim frame midstride, pulling his gray shirt with the Border Patrol logo down, and patting the bag around his waist one last time to make sure the gun was still there. Then he opened the door and went inside.

From photos, it could have been any church basement in America: a drop ceiling with tiles the same off-white as the linoleum floor, faux wood-paneled walls and columns supporting the pews above, announcement boards, folding tables with thirty-cup coffee urns. Rows of black and white folding chairs were still set up for the dozens of worshippers in a larger meeting that had wrapped up twenty minutes before he arrived.

The eight o'clock session was more intimate, a group of twelve Black parishioners arranged around a table in the back of the room. The stranger was the only white person there. Reverend Pinckney, who'd spent the day in meetings at the statehouse in Columbia before casting a vote and returning to Charleston, offered him a seat with a smile.

The worshippers were studying the Parable of the Sower—an allegory for why some live the word of God and others reject it. The stranger listened for about forty-five minutes, his gun resting in the bag on his lap. As the study group ended around nine o'clock, the parishioners rose for their traditional benediction: "The Lord watch between me and thee when we are absent from another."

That's when the killer pulled out his gun and shot Reverend Pinckney.

Jennifer Pinckney, the reverend's wife, was in the pastor's office with their younger daughter, Malana, when they heard the shots. She didn't know what was happening, but she locked the door and called 911.

Then the killer aimed his gun at an eighty-seven-year-old woman named Susie Jackson.

Her nephew, a young man named Tywanza Sanders, said, "You don't have to do this. We mean you no harm."

"I have to do it," he shouted. "You rape our women and you're taking over our country. And you have to go."

Sanders jumped in front of his aunt to protect her and was shot at least five times. His mother, Felicia Sanders, dove to the floor with her eleven-year-old granddaughter, rubbed herself in her own son's blood to make it look as if she'd been shot, and whispered to the child to lie still.

She watched the son she had brought into this world leave it.

All told, the killer fired seventy-seven bullets. At least sixty of them—the hollow points designed to kill better—tore into the worshippers.

Cynthia Hurd, Susie Jackson, Ethel Lance, DePayne Middleton-Doctor, Reverend Clementa Pinckney, Tywanza Sanders, Sharonda Coleman-Singleton, and Myra Thompson died in their church. Daniel L. Simmons Sr. would later die in the hospital.

Sixty-nine-year-old Polly Sheppard survived. She was hiding under a table, praying, when the killer's boots approached. He bent down to look at her and told her to shut up.

"Did I shoot you yet?"

"No," she replied.

"I'm not going to. I'm going to leave you to tell the story."

He spit racial epithets over the bodies as he walked out, then peeked out the church door. When he saw nobody there, he walked to the car, turned on the headlights, backed out, and drove away.

The next morning, police in Shelby, North Carolina, almost 250 miles north, pulled him over after another driver recognized him and called 911. Police dashcam video later showed several officers approach his car, two with their hands on their weapons. He was searched, handcuffed, and walked to a squad car. He was interviewed at a local police station, where he told the FBI that he chose the church on purpose and wanted to start a race war.

He also said he was hungry. The police officers bought him a meal from Burger King.

3

THREE MONTHS EARLIER, JUST DAYS BEFORE OBAMA WAS SCHEDuled to speak in Selma, Rudy Giuliani buffed his veneers and took the stage at a Midtown Manhattan event for conservative movers and shakers.

When I first entered politics back in 2002, in the wake of 9/11, Giuliani had cultivated a reputation as "America's Mayor," at one point the favorite to succeed President Bush after his second term. But after he flamed out of the 2008 Republican presidential primary, he retreated into the right-wing information bubble, a safe space where making millions by grifting off 9/11 and bathing yourself in the sludge of conspiracy theories were seen not as tacky but as signs of strength.

Each angrier and more paranoid strain of the Republican base had a new name—the Tea Party, the Birthers—each variant hiding behind a half-baked justification for loathing a Black president. They'd uncovered that Obama was actually a double-secret Muslim with terror sprinkles and a fake birth certificate, hell-bent on destroying America. They shared tropes on social media that, when called out as racist, became "just a joke"—even as traffic to white supremacist websites soared (the leading white nationalist website crashed the night Obama was elected). They led the party now; they were doing the work—and they demanded to be fed, to know that you were on their side.

Some politicians who thought they led the base, even as they were being led by it, were clumsier at the game than others.

"I know this is a terrible thing to say," Giuliani sputtered in a preamble that might inspire most rational people to second-guess their next words. In conservative circles, though, it served as an airhorn to make sure an audience knew that the speaker too despised "political correctness" and was about to stick it to some coastal elite.

Giuliani, a lifelong coastal elite, speaking to coastal elites, continued: "But I do not believe that the president loves America. He doesn't love you. And he doesn't love me. He wasn't brought up the way you were brought up and I was brought up through love of this country."

You could practically see him sweating, hoping he'd done enough to tar Obama as illegitimate without attracting any penalty flags for overt racism from the media elites whose approval he still craved. Hoping he'd fed the beast while keeping it confined to its cage.

He probably tried to high-five an event organizer afterward, asking, "Did I do it right?"

Such bile was often shrugged off by the larger political media as nothing but a dopamine fix for those in on the joke, but each little dose of poison led to a larger cirrhosis: The only president since Eisenhower to win more than 51 percent of the vote twice was deemed by a good chunk of the country to be illegitimate at best and a legitimate threat at worst.

I worried about the viewers who weren't in on the joke—whose belief that some Americans were enemies who had to be stopped would only solidify. And I hated it.

Giuliani's asinine comments rematerialized in my mind two days before the Selma speech, on that wintry March morning in Washington.

By early afternoon, the snow was falling hard enough that the world outside the Oval Office had disappeared. Obama and I were alone, trapped inside the world's most secure snow globe. Ironically enough, the president accused of failing to adequately love America was busy rhapsodizing on its brilliance.

Obama was standing behind his desk, joyously recounting the events of Selma, remarking on all those young people whose country treated them as second-class citizens, relegating them to separate water fountains and segregated schools, infringing upon their basic voting rights with poll taxes and literacy tests and absurdities like guessing the number of jellybeans in a jar or bubbles on a bar of soap.

But they didn't despair or grow cynical, he said, they persevered, still believing in this country enough to fight for its promise and push it into becoming a full democracy. No matter the obstacles in their way, they organized, and marched, and did the most patriotic thing imaginable—they risked their lives in a way we could all be proud of, so that someday, even fifty years later, America would be better in a way from which all of us would prosper.

I wished we could livestream him sometimes.

Still, I knew that pressing Obama's buttons over the political idiocy du jour, especially when it involved him in some way, often shook loose a good rant. Sitting on the arm of one of the couches, I asked him if he'd heard about Giuliani calling him insufficiently American.

Obama had a lower core temperature than I did. He just laughed and said, "Who gives a fuck what Rudy Giuliani has to say?"

It made me feel better about him and worse about myself.

Then he fiddled with the bait. "But it does offer an idea worth taking on."

He walked around the side of his desk. "Who gets to decide what it means to be an American? Who gets to be the arbiter of which Americans are worthy and which aren't, who belongs and who doesn't, whose views are valid and whose aren't?"

He sat against the front edge and crossed his arms. "Enough with the 'Real America' shit," Obama said. "Bald eagles and Sarah Palin and who can wear the most flags. That's *part* of America. But you know what? There's a lot more to America than that. I'd argue that getting your head cracked in because you're trying to make this country better is pretty patriotic. There are a multitude of other Americas out there, and our claims are just as valid. Even more so. And I'm betting that, over time, the people who see America like you and I do are only going to grow."

He extended his arms like he was going to bear hug an old friend. "What's more American than Selma?"

He was comfortable with our complexity; he'd developed a way of talking about America as a big, bustling, inclusive democracy that could make anybody feel good about it. A place with purpose.

It began with his 2004 speech in Boston, where he said that in no other country on Earth could his story even be possible. It was the start of a thread that wound through all of his biggest speeches, a story of progressive change rooted in American history and our founding documents.

It incorporated the idea that "We the People, in order to form a *more* perfect union," explicitly argued that America was an *imperfect* endeavor, and gave each new generation the directive to close, not widen, the gap between the lofty ideals of our founding and the realities of our time.

It made the argument that looking upon our historic mistakes and striving to do better isn't a condemnation of America but a confirmation of what it means to *be* American—that looking upon our flaws and changing ourselves for the better is not a repudiation of our darker history but an extension of our better history in line with the values for which generations of Americans fought and died.

It was patriotism. It was a story that was more honest about America's flaws than most politicians ever had been, because it was a story about a country that's great because it continually perfects itself. In Obama's mind, we were all products of the sins of our past, but we weren't bound by them; we were free to rise above them if we chose to. When praising the marchers of the civil rights movement, for example, he added a line to one of the Selma drafts:

> Their endeavors gave the entire South the chance to rise again—not by reasserting the past but by transcending the past.

He had wrapped his candidacies in a pro-American story that represented racial and political redemption. You didn't have to reject our past to recognize that America evolves. That's the genius of it. That approach gave moderates, even conservatives, the space to be proud of our American identity while casting progressive change as a part of what made us American. It assuaged voters that he wouldn't ignore the realities of race in America but, regardless of what Fox News might have you believe, he wasn't out to overthrow white America, either.

He applied a wide-angle lens to America, showing us how far we've come *and* how far we have to travel. He'd often tell young audiences who believed that change hadn't come fast enough that America isn't static, that we have reason not to be cynical about racial progress. Go ask a Black man who lived through the fifties or sixties if nothing's changed, he'd say. He'll set you straight. It's indisputable that things have gotten better. That doesn't mean institutional racism doesn't exist; it does. To remind us how far we've come doesn't ignore how far we have to go. But it should show you that progress is possible. You should take hope from it, protect it, and go win some more. And if we made as much progress over the next ten years as we did over the last fifty, things would get better still.

At his best, he'd cast progressive change as part of the vital work of *being* American. I was always particular to a formulation that Favs and Obama had concocted for his nomination speech at the 2012 Democratic National Convention in Charlotte, North Carolina.

> We don't think government can solve all our problems. But we don't think that government is the source of all our problems—any more than are welfare recipients, or corporations, or unions, or immigrants, or gays, or any other group we're told to blame for our troubles.
>
> Because we understand that this democracy is ours.
>
> We the People recognize that we have responsibilities as well as rights; that our destinies are bound together; that a freedom which only asks what's in it for me, a freedom without a commitment to others, a freedom without love or charity or duty or patriotism, is unworthy of our founding ideals, and those who died in their defense.

> As citizens, we understand that America is not about what can be done for us. It's about what can be done by us, together, through the hard and frustrating but necessary work of self-government.

The story needed an update for the Selma speech, something true to the marchers on that bridge and all who waged similar battles for the equal rights promised at our founding.

It struck me that many of the obstacles in their way were endorsed, even enforced, by most of the men who sat in the Oval Office that Obama was now pacing.

I quipped to Obama on that wintry March day that most political speeches about American history covered the founding fathers, beating the Nazis, going to the moon, and that's about it.

"Okay," he said, the snow now a jazz brush on the Oval Office windows, "if we're making Selma the manifestation of our American creed, then let's celebrate it with all the characters who really made this country what it is."

He talked about Black music—the way that spirituals, the blues, and R&B could absorb centuries of hardship and sorrow and turn out something beautiful and full of hope; the way Ray Charles's version of "America the Beautiful" possessed the same lyrics as everybody else's but was infused with a deeper and more vital patriotism; the way time stopped when Aretha Franklin sang.

He asked if I knew Walt Whitman's "Song of Myself." My grandmother had given me a copy of *Leaves of Grass*, I told him, but I confessed I hadn't read it since high school. He cut me off and called it the most American poem. The narrator shares everything he sees of everything we are, with all our noise and contradiction—strapping young farmers and runaway slaves, teachers and machinists, Yankee girls and pioneers and newly arrived immigrants. Through Whitman, he said, you see a bustling diversity of energy that sets this country apart.

He suggested I gather Rhodes and the rest of the speechwriting team and update that list of characters for our time. "Who are people we can see a bit of ourselves in? Who really made America what it is?"

I emailed my team, snug in their apartments, and we fleshed out the speech with that kind of fullness in mind, with what became a rollicking roll call that told a truer tale of our history, a list with no "them," only "us," Obama's canonization of a new class of American saints.

Together—Obama, my speechwriters, and I—came up with a new twist on the story, with a new cast of characters:

> Fellow marchers, so much has changed in fifty years. We've endured war, and fashioned peace. We've seen technological wonders that touch every aspect of our lives and take for granted conveniences our parents might scarcely imagine. But what has *not* changed is the imperative of citizenship—that willingness of a twenty-six-year-old deacon, a Unitarian minister, or a young mother of five to decide they loved this country so much that they'd risk *everything* to realize its promise.
>
> That's what it means to love America. That's what it means to believe in America. That's what it means when we say America is exceptional.
>
> For we were born of change. We broke the old aristocracies, declaring ourselves entitled not by bloodline, but *endowed* by our Creator with certain unalienable rights. We secure our rights and responsibilities through a system of self-government, of and by and for the people. That's why we argue and fight with so much passion and conviction. That's why, for such a young nation, we are so big and bold and diverse and full of contradictions, because we know our efforts matter. We know America is what we make of it.
>
> We are Lewis and Clark and Sacajawea, pioneers who braved the unfamiliar, followed by a stampede of farmers and miners, and entrepreneurs and hucksters. That's our spirit. That's who we are.

We are Sojourner Truth and Fannie Lou Hamer, women who could do as much as any man and then some. And we're Susan B. Anthony, who shook the system until the law reflected that truth. That is our character.

We're the immigrants who stowed away on ships to reach these shores, the huddled masses yearning to breathe free—Holocaust survivors, Soviet defectors, the Lost Boys of Sudan. We're the hopeful strivers who cross the Rio Grande because we want our kids to know a better life. That's how we came to be.

We're the slaves who built the White House and the economy of the South. We're the ranch hands and cowboys who opened up the West, and countless laborers who laid rails, and raised skyscrapers, and organized for workers' rights.

We're the fresh-faced GIs who fought to liberate a continent. And we're the Tuskegee airmen, and the Navajo code-talkers, and the Japanese Americans who fought for this country even as their own liberty had been denied.

We're the firefighters who rushed into those buildings on 9/11 and the volunteers who signed up to fight in Afghanistan and Iraq. We're the gay Americans whose blood ran in the streets of San Francisco and New York, just as blood ran down this bridge.

We are storytellers, writers, poets, artists who abhor unfairness, and despise hypocrisy, and give voice to the voiceless, and tell truths that need to be told.

We're the inventors of gospel and jazz and blues, bluegrass and country, and hip-hop and rock and roll, and our very own sound with all the sweet sorrow and reckless joy of freedom.

We are Jackie Robinson, enduring scorn and spiked cleats and stealing home plate in the World Series anyway.

We are the people Langston Hughes wrote of, who "build our temples for tomorrow, strong as we know how."

We are the people Emerson wrote of, "who for truth and honor's sake stand fast and suffer long"; who are "never too tired, so long as we can see far enough."

> *That's* what America is. Not stock photos or feeble attempts to define some as more American as others. We respect the past, but we don't pine for it. We don't fear the future; we grab for it. America is not some fragile thing; we are *large,* in the words of Whitman, containing multitudes. We are boisterous and full of energy, perpetually young in spirit. That's why someone like John Lewis at the ripe age of twenty-five could lead a mighty march.

There was also a riff I'd been playing with in my head for almost a year, something stashed away in my ideas folder, just waiting for the right moment to use it. Selma felt like the right place.

> The single most powerful word in our democracy is the word "We." We the People. We Shall Overcome. Yes We Can. That word is owned by no one. It belongs to everyone.

It wasn't particularly profound, but it was the type of line that audiences like, even if it flirted with the kind of sugary rhetoric that Obama didn't. It survived until the penultimate draft, when he struck "Yes We Can."

Because Selma shows us that America is not the project of any one person. Oh,

Because the single most powerful word in our democracy is the word "We." We The People. We Shall Overcome. ~~Yes We Can~~. It is owned by no one. It belongs to everyone. What a glorious task we are given, to continually try to improve this great nation of ours.

I knew he'd always thought "Yes We Can" a little corny, and in this case, I feared he'd think it too self-referential. (The phrase, a refrain from Obama's first campaign, had taken on a long life.) But what pithier way to sum up the American project, let alone his idea of it, than "Yes We Can?"

What's more, I wanted to use the words to create a continuum, to remind today's young activists that they weren't alone, that they had examples to look to; that they were the updated version of the "We the People" generation of founders who got this thing started, the heirs to the "We Shall Overcome" generation of civil rights leaders who put our democracy on a sturdier course.

"Mr. President," I pled my case, "if you're worried 'Yes We Can' is too self-referential, it's not. Yes, it's something people chanted at your rallies. But it doesn't belong to you. It belongs to the young people you want to inspire. They made it their own. And besides, it wasn't yours to begin with—you stole it from César Chávez."

(Unfortunately, Kristen was not present to tell me I was wrong; it was Dolores Huerta who came up with the chant during one of Chávez's hunger strikes in the 1970s before it became the slogan of the United Farm Workers.)

Obama chuckled. "Okay. Give me a clean draft and let me look one more time."

When he returned the final draft, I immediately flipped to the last page.

Yes we can.

Because Selma shows us that America is not the project of any one person.

Because the single most powerful word in our democracy is the word "We." We The People. We Shall Overcome. It is owned by no one. It belongs to everyone. Oh, what a glorious task we are given, to continually try to improve this great nation of ours.

"Yesssss," I gloated. I didn't get to do that often.

Over the course of that snowy afternoon and the following day, I'd shuttle five drafts up and down the stairs from my office to Obama's, each improving on the last, each making the other better. It was the purest collaboration we'd had up to that point in our partnership.

4

THERE WOULD ALWAYS BE AMERICANS THAT OBAMA'S STORY wouldn't reach.

Republicans were both cultivating and consumed by a base that had co-opted the banner on the far side of that bridge in Selma, their core beliefs shrunken to the conviction that not only was a Democratic president somehow illegitimate, but that half the country was too, a horde of ungrateful agitators out to destroy the established order. There's a patriotic "us" and an unworthy "them," the argument went, and if we don't keep "them" in their place, we're going to lose America. Democrats and a multicultural America were not people with whom to compromise but people to conquer. And a Black president was a potent avatar of that perceived threat.

But the right underestimated Obama by reducing him to a boogeyman. Republicans who knew that their demographics were shrinking correctly understood that Obama was doing something very dangerous for their political prospects: constructing a patriotic identity in which the "real Americans," the ones true to our better history, are the Americans from any background who recognize our shortcomings and work to overcome them.

Obama bet that there were enough Americans open to the story of a country that's great enough to change, who didn't see our democracy as a zero-sum game but as a place where our fates are bound up in each other. He offered a story that didn't exclude anyone but gave everyone a role, with all the rights and responsibilities of citizenship.

And "Obama's America"—a multiracial, multiethnic democracy as the core of American identity—was, as Republicans feared, only growing demographically.

Barack Obama could tell that story in a way no other politician did because he'd lived a life no other politician had—a life that made the White House unlikely from the start.

It's important to remember that he didn't win the presidency by pointing out that he'd be the first Black president. People were able to figure that out on their own. Part of the genius of the campaign's "CHANGE" slogan was that you could project anything you wanted onto it, including a Black guy photobombing the lily-white composite of forty-three former presidents.

Obama didn't hide from his Blackness, either. He was versed in the language of Black communities, able to connect with them in a way that never seemed like code-switching. Even so, for most of 2007, most Black voters supported Hillary Clinton, not Obama. Before the January 2008 South Carolina primary, 40 percent of Black voters told pollsters they didn't think America was ready to elect a Black president. More somberly, many others told campaign volunteers on the ground that they weren't ready to mourn one.

But Obama never made his skin the issue. He didn't have to. This is America, after all, where Black skin means you're Black and society treats you that way. When Obama was born, his own parents' marriage was illegal in most of the country. His upbringing in Hawaii largely, but not always, insulated him from experiencing much of what it was like to be a young Black man on the mainland. Once he enrolled in college in L.A. and then New York City, he'd deal with more of the daily indignities of race in America. And once he started community organizing, he experienced the full brunt of how a long legacy of racism and failed policies conspired to deny most Black Americans a true shot at equal opportunity.

In his mind, though, he didn't have to choose between the white or Black worlds—he was a part of both. He met his Kenyan father only twice, but he was raised by a white mother and white grandparents who loved him and made sure he had every chance in life.

That's why, when he campaigned for the U.S. Senate in downstate Illinois in 2004, and shook hands with farmers, and ate pancakes in union halls, he didn't seem like he was code-switching there either. They were his grandparents. They shared his values.

Those values didn't change, even after two successful campaigns for the White House and all the trappings of the presidency. After a May 2015 speech in South Dakota, the two of us riding in his armored limousine surrounded by little but farmland and the horizon, Obama told me that, while talking with the governor and the mayor, he'd learned that they were both married to their high school sweethearts. "Coastal elites discount things like that," he said with complete sincerity. "But it's important."

In May 2011, I traveled with him to Ireland. The Keenans are easy to trace back to the Emerald Isle, but nobody had thought to trace Obama's full lineage until he ran for president. As it turned out, an ancestor named Fulmouth Kearney had emigrated from the tiny hamlet of Moneygall—in Ireland's center, a smudge on the map with barely three hundred residents—and settled in the American Midwest. At first, people thought the presidential visit to Ireland was good for a laugh—Barack O'Bama, he's one of us! But I was there as he toured his great-great-great-grandfather's home, still intact, marveling at walking the same floorboards as his forebears had. It moved him, a family connection made no less real by his Black skin.

He fully inhabited both worlds, Black and white, and it infused his speeches.

I did not inhabit two worlds; I inhabited one. That's why writing about race always felt so daunting, like taking college-level science when you're still in high school. Most of what I knew about it came from Barack Obama. So I would often try to put myself in *his* shoes, fit the words to the audiences *he* had to reach, give in to the restraint *he* had to exercise. That was the job.

He wasn't entirely a walking yin and yang. There was a political calculation too. He knew he was a Black man named Barack Hussein Obama. He'd run for president less than six years after 9/11, and in order to win, he would need enough of the white vote to get over 50 percent. He couldn't just speak to white people's hopes—he needed to disarm their fears that he'd be a further threat to their way of life.

Being Black meant he had to be twice as good. (Having the middle name Hussein meant he had to be three times as good.) Only Black politicians, for example, were expected to lecture people who looked like them to embrace "responsibility," to turn off the television and read to their kids. Where were the politicians telling white parents to do the same—or, at minimum, to stop giving their children birthday money to buy a gun?

The need to be three times as good pushed him, and his staff, to demonstrate his broad appeal and mainstream values at every opportunity. We banked on the ideas that physical attributes like race and gender aren't determinative, and that winning depends on how you present yourself, the policies you promote, and the words you choose.

That political calculation coincided with what he believed. He knew from experience, personal and professional, that the long tentacles of racism infused almost every one of society's structures. But he didn't lecture audiences about what they were doing wrong, or what they were saying wrong, or that their whole life was built on a historical sin. He didn't shame people for not holding the most politically correct viewpoint on any given issue. He gave Americans the permission to get there on our own, which was a more sustainable path.

Throughout the campaign, and then later in the White House, he felt the presence of activists on his left, revanchists on his right, and the weight of legacy lifting him up or weighing him down. But by staying true to himself and disciplined to the message, he believed he could not only inspire new voters to join him but bring in enough voters who occupied the middle too.

Over time, a conventional wisdom solidified that Obama had won his elections thanks only to the demographics of a nascent America made up of younger, more diverse, more educated voters. And they were vital to those victories. But a full third of Obama's coalition was made up of whites without a college degree. He performed better with the white working class than any other modern Democrat. (It helped that, in 2012, he kept a relentless focus on the economy, which was the number-one issue for every demographic group of Americans.)

He won a landslide victory in 2008 not because he represented racial and political recrimination—but because he represented racial and political *redemption*. Because he believed that it was less important to lay out all the fundamental truths about racism, or win ideological fights, than it was to win the power to *do* something that would make things better.

As young speechwriters, we wanted to shout right and wrong from the campaign trail and the roof of the White House with a searing moral clarity. But you can be a purist, or you can be the first Democratic presidential candidate to win North Carolina in thirty-two years, the first to win Indiana in forty-four. You can't be both.

Only once do I remember Obama getting the credit he deserved for negotiating the tightrope he did: when the writer Ta-Nehisi Coates described him as someone who "walked on ice and never fell."

But we did hear the ice crack once or twice. And when he slipped—when he even slightly deviated from the brand—it got him in trouble.

The first time was halfway through Obama's first year in office, when he answered a question about a Black Harvard professor being arrested in his own home by saying that the police had "acted stupidly." His answer was inartful, and probably colored by Obama's own experience on his own college campus of being asked for his ID when he hadn't done anything wrong and having to answer the question, "What are you doing here?"

Days later, once it had been spun into the biggest story in politics, Obama apologized, regretting the clumsiness of his answer to the reporter's question if not the reasoning. He even invited the officer to the White House for a beer. But the damage was done. It was a moment tailor-made for conservative media—an elitist liberal Black president siding with an elitist liberal Black professor to humiliate a white, working-class cop just trying to do his job. The fracas caused the single biggest drop in Obama's support among white voters, and that support never fully recovered—while many of Obama's Black supporters were disappointed that he apologized at all.

Three years later, in an Orlando suburb, a self-appointed neighborhood watchman approached a Black teenager half his size with nothing on him but a pack of Skittles and a bottle of iced tea, and asked him, "What are you doing here?" He called 911 and, against the advice of police, followed, shot, and killed Trayvon Martin.

It wasn't national news at first. Local officials stonewalled any investigation. But Trayvon Martin's parents persisted until they won access to the 911 tapes, only to hear their own son cry for help before being murdered. Soon, an online petition demanding a federal prosecution gained a million signatures. The Department of Justice opened a civil rights investigation. White supremacist websites fanned fears that a Black militia would invade the town seeking vengeance.

Pressure mounted for Obama to say something. But with an active Department of Justice probe, he had to be careful with his words. And with the murder occurring in a pivotal county in a pivotal state in a reelection year, he had to be perfect.

As it turned out, though, we never had the chance to prepare remarks. After one of the most boring speeches possible—a speech nominating the next head of the World Bank—a reporter shouted a question about the Trayvon Martin case.

"My main message is to the parents of Trayvon Martin," Obama replied. "If I had a son, he'd look like Trayvon. I think they are right to expect that all of us, as Americans, are going to take this with the seriousness it deserves and are going to get to the bottom of exactly what happened."

It was a direct connection to Black parents, aunts, uncles, siblings, anyone who'd been forced to have "The Conversation" with their kids: Don't run. Don't put your hands in your pockets. Don't talk back to a cop. It was a fear I'd never know, a conversation I'd never have to have. I thought Obama's response eloquent. But it enraged conservatives, who accused Obama of playing the race card.

A year later, in July 2013, a jury found the killer not guilty. There were no Black jurors.

In the first 7:45 A.M. senior advisors meeting after the acquittal, someone mentioned that Ahmir "Questlove" Thompson, the drummer for the Roots and bandleader on *Late Night with Jimmy Fallon,* had penned a viral, emotional essay about the reality of being a Black man in America titled "Trayvon Martin and I Ain't Shit."

The idea was raised for Obama to pen an open letter in response. I scoffed. It was three months after Obama had said he didn't want to speak after another mass shooting, but this wasn't that. With mass protests on the sweltering summer streets, and a lectern and a press corps at Obama's disposal, an open letter somehow felt feebler than saying nothing at all.

Danielle Gray was a friend of mine going back to the early days of the Obama campaign and one of the Black senior advisors in the meeting. She'd first worked for Obama on his 2004 Senate run and, like him, had been on the *Harvard Law Review*. She was a brilliant lawyer who'd clerked on the Supreme Court, became one of the highest-ranking Black women in the West Wing, and had been described in print as "the most powerful White House staffer you've never heard of."

As a Black woman, she knew that Americans who were angry and hurting would want to hear from Obama that the verdict was wrong and to see him finally give in to being the "angry Black man" furious about what was going on in the country. As the liaison between Obama and his cabinet, and as someone voted "most likely to be a Supreme Court justice" by her classmates at Harvard Law, Danielle knew that he couldn't do either.

While the rest of the table debated writing a letter to Questlove, Danielle slipped out, walked upstairs to her desk on the second floor of the West Wing, and scribbled down five concrete things Obama could do to improve the odds for young Black men in America.

At the top, she wrote the words "My Brother's Keeper"—a pull from Scripture, and a callback to a line from the 2004 convention speech that made Obama famous.

Danielle shared the document with me and Valerie Jarrett, and Valerie suggested we take it to Obama in the Oval Office. It was an uncomfortable conversation, one of those times when it felt like Obama was mad at us, even when we knew he was really upset at the situation.

"What the hell am I supposed to do?" It was more of a shout than a question. "What do people *want* me to do? Do they want me to go out and say that the verdict was wrong, and that I'm pissed, and that things are fucked up, and then just not be president anymore?"

Danielle told him that he *should* be angry about it, but that he should also remind Americans that they were not without agency. She handed him the list, and I opened my mouth to tell Obama what I'd been playing with for a statement.

"I'm going to write this one myself," he interrupted.

If I hadn't already been aware that I was the only white person in the room, I would have been after that. But it stung for a different reason: I'd only been chief speechwriter for four months at that point, and it felt like he didn't trust me to do the job.

But I also knew he was right. This was a job for him. He jotted down some notes by hand, outlined in his usual logical structure. He memorized as much as he could. Then he went to the podium in the Briefing Room to address a hastily organized press corps and the cameras behind them.

"When Trayvon Martin was first shot, I said that this could have been my son. Another way of saying that is Trayvon Martin could have been me thirty-five years ago. And when you think about why, in the African American community at least, there's a lot of pain around what happened here, I think it's important to recognize that the African American community is looking at this issue through a set of experiences and a history that doesn't go away."

He spoke slowly, glancing at his notes only to remember his next idea, using them as handholds on the cliff he was climbing without ropes. He talked about being followed while shopping, hearing doors lock when you walk by, living while laws treat you differently. He pointed out the vulnerability of young African American men disproportionately involved in the criminal justice system, and the lingering inequality and dysfunction born from a violent history at the root of that disparity. He acknowledged the growing protest movements and then gave life to Danielle's sketch—concrete policies that would make a real difference, from policing reform to laws to thinking creatively about how to lift up Black boys.

He waved away requests for a convened conversation on race as staged and unproductive but once again offered people the possibility to transcend. "In families and churches and workplaces, there's the possibility that people are a little bit more honest, and at least you ask yourself your own questions about, Am I wringing as much bias out of myself as I can? Am I judging people as much as I can, based on not the color of their skin but the content of their character? That would, I think, be an appropriate exercise in the wake of this tragedy."

In the three years between Trayvon's murder and the Charleston massacre, the murders of more Black boys and men had roiled the country. Some of the killings were captured on video that rocketed across social media, constant and uncomfortable reminders of the daily abasements still visited on much of Black America. Several of the victims were killed by police officers.

With every killing, more and more young people took to the streets, not so eager to concede that the longer arc of America was actually one of progress. After Trayvon's killer was acquitted, the hashtag #BlackLivesMatter took root on social networks. After an eighteen-year-old Michael Brown was killed in 2014, reportedly with his hands up, Black Lives Matter became manifest on the streets, and "Hands up, don't shoot!" became a rallying cry. It was inspiring, even as many of the protesters were as frustrated with Obama as they were with the status quo. It did feel like more Americans were awakening to systemic racism we'd never noticed because so many of us had never endured it. It felt like the possibility Obama left open, that people were getting a bit more honest, just might be starting to happen. I hoped it were true.

But hatred has a long tail. The very white nationalist propaganda ginned up around Trayvon Martin's murder is what ensnared and radicalized Dylann Roof, who used it as justification to take a gun into his own hands and murder nine Black Americans. Who knew how many more of them were out there, if this was the end of something or just the beginning, or just another stain on the longer tapestry of history?

On top of that, my mind was increasingly gripped now by the knowledge that any eulogy in Charleston would be its own stressful, frustrating, and frightening highwire act.

5

IT WAS ONLY TEN MINUTES FROM THE WHITE HOUSE TO THE BRIGHT, high-ceilinged, and airy terminal of Washington National Airport, but after the past two days, leaving town for a wedding in Massachusetts felt like traveling to a different world.

Even with Obama on the West Coast, I felt guilty about abandoning my desk. With time before our flight, and with Kristen fielding reporters' fact-check questions about guns, I called to check in with Anita Decker Breckenridge, Obama's all-business, no-nonsense, longest-serving aide who knew him better than almost anyone.

She began working for him in 2003 when she was just twenty-five and he was still an anonymous state senator. When he ran for the U.S. Senate, she spent countless hours driving him from campaign event to campaign event in southern Illinois as he made phone calls and smoked cigarettes out her passenger window. She then ran his downstate offices once he won.

After a two-year stint as chief of staff at the National Endowment for the Arts, she returned to Obama's side as his personal assistant in the outer Oval Office in 2011. I can't remember which marked-up speech draft she handed me when we met, but I know we became friends immediately, bonding over our love for the Chicago Cubs and shared experiences growing up less than a mile from each other just north of the city. We lived in different school districts and were two years apart, so our paths never crossed—but there was a high likelihood that we'd both spent a summer Saturday just feet from each other eating ice cream at Homer's, an old-fashioned parlor in town.

In 2014, Obama appointed Anita White House deputy chief of staff. Two days after the Charleston shootings, she was traveling with him in California.

"How's it going out there?"

"Eh. The usual," she said. "Nicer than being in Washington. How's it going *there*?"

"Everyone here is starting to do their usual shtick where they push for Obama to go give a big speech while they offer no ideas whatsoever," I told her. "Just claim your seat on Air Force One while one of us stays up for seventy-two straight hours killing ourselves on a eulogy, and the press beats him up for being an ineffectual wimp who can't somehow get a bunch of NRA-funded Republicans to vote for gun reforms."

It did feel better to vent to a friend.

"Wow. You're dark," she said. "Is the wedding bar not open yet?"

"I wish. I'm at the airport. Sorry. I just don't know if I can do this again. I don't know if I'm capable of it."

Anita was not someone who indulged self-pity. She was someone who cared about getting the task at hand done right—or eliminated entirely. "Well, you're in luck. You didn't hear it from me, but he does *not* want to go. He said, 'What would I do?' So you can tell everybody else to gas up their cars and head that way if they want to go to Charleston so badly."

I exhaled, relieved.

Because the thought of writing this eulogy had been scaring the shit out of me.

Day Four

Saturday, June 20, 2015

1

I WOKE UP ON SATURDAY IN A ROADSIDE MOTEL NESTLED INTO THE Berkshire Mountains a few miles south of the Vermont border, nursing a mild hangover from the wedding's welcome party at an old New England tavern.

As quietly as I could, I made some sad hotel coffee from the single-serving machine next to the old television, the kind of coffee that boasts "robust" on the generic packaging but tastes like tree bark steeped in hot water. Paper cup in hand, I carefully turned the doorknob and pulled the door open, but sunlight rushed past me, leaping onto the bed like a child ready to play.

Kristen grumbled a protest and rolled over while I whisper-shouted "sorry" over my shoulder, slipping barefoot out the door and into the morning so that she could sleep in. The skies were a deep blue, traveled by an armada of big, fluffy clouds; the air was crisp, about twenty degrees cooler than a once-again swampy Washington. It felt like autumn, but the trees were at their fullest and most green. I loved it. Plastic Adirondack-style chairs were scattered across a grassy patch between the parking lot and a burbling brook that hugged the country road like a third lane. I cursed my way across the gritty tarmac, wishing I'd worn shoes after all, until I reached the safety of the grass. I plopped down in one of the chairs, downed two Advil from the wedding's "welcome bag," and sighed.

It was Father's Day weekend, and with the First Lady and daughters still on their official visit to Italy, Obama was golfing in Palm Springs with his best friends from high school.

Whenever he traveled, he took the White House with him—the flying fortress of Air Force One and armored convoy, a military-run communications system, and staff who carried everything from the nuclear codes to nutritious cuisine.

When I or any other staff traveled on our own, we didn't have those luxuries. Instead, we remained electronically tethered to the White House by a secure "work phone" we were expected to keep handy. By mid-2015, we'd finally moved beyond BlackBerries, so I identified my two iPhones with different cases—black for business, blue for fun.

No case, however, could transform two phones into tasteful accessories for whatever beautiful dress Kristen chose for such escapes from Washington. Whenever we'd find our place settings at a wedding, we'd ruin them by stacking our four phones in front of us like poker chips. Elegance, along with extravagances like children and hobbies, were put on hold for us during our White House years.

There was no true escape. Not for weddings. Not on weekends. (Obama once called while I was at a Sunday night Cubs game in Chicago and convinced that a 5:30 A.M. return flight to Washington would keep my cover. No such luck: Wrigley Field's iconic pipe organ betrayed me. Obama, a White Sox fan, groaned and directed me to get him a fresh draft of the speech we were working on first thing in the morning.) And forget about a proper vacation. Over all my years in the political world, it was understood that you'd get two weeks off: one in August, when Congress recesses for the month and the humidity settles in at its most suffocating; and one at Christmastime, regardless of religious affiliation. To take time off outside those two weeks in those two months was seen as selfish and unserious.

Events, though, didn't care about your rare out-of-office message. August 2009 saw the Tea Party's birth spasm and Ted Kennedy's death from brain cancer, which ultimately cost Democrats a Senate seat and nearly killed the Affordable Care Act. In August 2010, the Gulf Coast was still feeling the effects of a months-long oil spill and Obama moved his vacation there to show that its beaches were safe; in August 2011, Republican brinksmanship led to America's first-ever credit downgrade, which tanked the stock market; in August 2012, we were in the heat of a reelection campaign and preparing for the party conventions. August 2014 delivered a trifecta: the Ebola epidemic in Africa, a spike in the number of unaccompanied children showing up at the southern border after harrowing journeys, and the terrorist organization ISIS beheading journalists on YouTube. Each of these events was tragic on its own. None of them directly threatened Americans at home. All of them were demagogued by Republicans to maximum effect in the run-up to that year's midterm elections.

Even the one place I couldn't be reached—an airplane—rarely provided relief. The afternoon before, as Kristen and I barreled down the runway on our way to the wedding, I ducked the flight attendant's watchful gaze to send Megan Rooney, the team's Staten Island speechwriter back at the White House, some edits to the remarks Obama would shortly deliver in San Francisco to the annual gathering of the U.S. Conference of Mayors. I tapped SEND just as the plane slipped from cellular reach and spent the next hour worried that my email was stuck in limbo, madly refreshing my inbox on descent until the signal grabbed me again and Megan confirmed that she'd made the edits.

Onstage in a cavernous Hilton ballroom packed with mayors from all over the country, Obama took the opportunity in his Friday speech to clap back at the pundits who said he'd waved the white flag in his statement about the Charleston shooting on Thursday morning.

Using the Senate's 2013 failure to approve universal background checks as a launchpad, he said first,

> We don't know if it would have prevented what happened in Charleston. No reform can guarantee the elimination of violence. But we might still have some more Americans with us. We might have stopped one shooter. Some families might still be whole. You [mayors] might have to attend fewer funerals.

Then, taking aim,

> And we should be strong enough to acknowledge this . . . I know today's politics makes it less likely that we see any sort of serious gun-safety legislation. I remarked that it was very unlikely that this Congress would act. And some reporters, I think, took this as resignation. I want to be clear: I am not resigned. I have faith we will eventually do the right thing . . . at some point, as a country, we have to reckon with what happens. It is not good enough simply to show sympathy.

He called out the gun lobby and its allies who tried to muddy the waters every time a shooter killed innocent people, the Ted Cruzes of the world who were already bellowing that Democrats were using Charleston "as an excuse not to go after" criminals but to somehow confiscate 300 million guns from good, law-abiding, God-fearing Real Americans, as Republicans defined them. It was perennial bullshit designed to do nothing more than scare people who already owned guns into adding to their arsenals, lining the pockets of gun manufacturers, who then tossed their pieces of silver into Republican campaign chests.

Obama drove the point home:

> You don't see murder on this kind of scale, with this kind of frequency, in any other advanced nation on Earth. Every country has violent, hateful, or mentally unstable people. What's different is not every country is awash with easily accessible guns. And so I refuse to act as if this is the new normal, or to pretend that it's simply sufficient to grieve, and that any mention of us doing

> something to stop it is somehow politicizing the problem . . . Ultimately, Congress acts when the public insists on action. And we've seen how public opinion can change. We've seen it change on gay marriage. We've seen it begin to change on climate. We've got to shift how we think about this issue. We have the capacity to change, but we have to feel a sense of urgency about it. We, as a people, have got to change.

A Friday afternoon speech occasionally rewarded us with a weekend free of news. I doubted this weekend would be one of those. I took a sip of my coffee, less savoring it than enduring it, and swiped through the news to see if there was anything I'd missed while traveling to the wedding and catching up with friends in town, determined to ignore every email that wasn't from the president.

And what I'd missed might have been the pivotal event that changed everything.

2

ON FRIDAY AFTERNOON, TWO DAYS AFTER HIS MASSACRE IN Charleston, Dylann Roof had appeared in court, via a video feed, for his bond hearing. He was charged with nine counts of murder, which in South Carolina made him eligible for the death penalty—a punishment that Governor Nikki Haley had already called for. He wore a striped prison jumpsuit. Two armored guards stood behind him. All three were impassive, expressionless. He looked even paler on the video feed than he did in photos; his voice as he answered the judge's questions was quiet, younger-sounding than I'd expected. Somehow it made me angrier. He didn't deserve the pity that might elicit.

Roof wasn't looking into the camera, and therefore not into the eyes of the family members of the victims who'd gathered in the courtroom. He was looking down, almost as if ashamed, until I realized he was likely looking at a monitor. He *was* looking at the family members, after all.

In a cringe-worthy moment, the judge urged viewers to remember that the killer's family were victims as well. Logically, I could accept that was on some level true, but it was a revolting thing to say. The killer had made the people in that courtroom widowers and motherless. He'd stolen their elders, their children, their grandchildren. The comment was tone deaf at best; at worst, it was a callous reminder from a position of authority that suffering was subject to a racial hierarchy too.

But then something remarkable happened. The first family member of the worshippers already known as the Charleston Nine approached a microphone to address their murderer. I thought about what I might say, what vitriol I might spew, what sick burn I might leave to rattle around in that scumbag's brain as he rotted in prison until he died.

Then I heard her voice. "I just want everybody to know, to you, I forgive you."

Wait, what?

The text on the video identified the woman as Nadine Collier, the daughter of seventy-year-old Ethel Lance, a sexton who took care of the church. "You took something very precious away from me. I will never talk to her ever again. I will never be able to hold her again. But I forgive you and have mercy on your soul. You hurt me. You hurt a lot of people. But God forgives you. And I forgive you."

She wailed the words, but she was fully in control of them, a lamentation that froze the air and made the hair on my neck stand up. One by one, others followed her, all of them with voices louder and stronger and surer than the murderer on the screen. They didn't scream. They didn't swear. They'd reached some other plane of human emotion.

The words of Felicia Sanders, who'd watched her twenty-six-year-old son die while she was covered in his blood, burst forward like an advancing army. "We welcomed you Wednesday night in our Bible study with open arms. You have killed some of the most beautifulest people that I know. Every fiber in my body hurts. And I'll never be the same. Tywanza Sanders was my son. But Tywanza was my hero. Tywanza was my hero. But as we say in the Bible study, we enjoyed you. But may God have mercy on you."

The hand that wasn't holding my phone was pressed against my mouth. I didn't remember putting it there. It was moral whiplash, from massacre to mercy in a matter of minutes.

Each short speech, punctuated by sobs from the gallery, followed the same theme.

From a man whose grandmother was murdered: "I forgive you and my family forgives you."

From a woman whose sister was murdered: "We have no room for hating, so we have to forgive. I pray God on your soul."

From a woman whose grandfather was murdered: "This is proof; everyone's plea for your soul is proof that they lived in love and their legacies will live in love. So hate won't win."

I felt the rare and genuine surprise that comes from bearing witness to something that isn't supposed to happen. And then something I hadn't felt in years: an ache behind my eyes that I quickly closed off; a choke rising in my throat that I quickly pushed down. This didn't feel like something I was allowed to be emotional about. I turned around in my chair, looking to see if anyone was watching. Confident I was alone, I let my phone fall into the grass and just stared for a while at the trees swaying in the breeze, their leaves rustling in a sustained hush.

How did those people do that?

I'd just read excerpts from a killer's white supremacist rantings that didn't surprise me and then watched an act of mercy that did. *How fucked up is that?* I thought. *How fucked up am I,* that a racist murderer's repugnant ramblings and nonsensical motivations somehow felt more normal, more like the natural way of things in America, than an act of forgiveness and grace?

I wasn't a religious person. I had been baptized, raised, and confirmed in the Episcopal Church. I'd read the Bible cover to cover in high school, which I wouldn't recommend (for "the greatest story ever told," it's not told very well). But I liked the community I found at church and felt comfortable in its practices: We welcomed everybody to Communion, we even had a gay bishop, and we took summers off! My priest remained a friend and thoughtful advisor once I went to college, but, away from home, I never found a new church. Once I graduated, the rise of the evangelical right in politics, with all its cruelty disguised as compassion, pushed me even further away.

Still, I'd spent enough time in the pews that the contemporary liturgy of the Holy Eucharist was always at hand, every word seared beneath layers of memory, much like the lyrics to an old favorite song you haven't heard in years.

And after I entered the White House, Obama and his pastor, a Black man named Joshua DuBois, taught me a little about Black theology.

Joshua was a year younger than I was, with a baby face that made him look ten years younger than he was. He'd grown up in the AME Church; his father pastored at Bishops' Memorial Church in Columbia, South Carolina, where the Confederate flag still flew at the state capitol building, and knew Reverend Pinckney well. Joshua never attended seminary, but he served as an associate pastor in Cambridge, Massachusetts, while an undergrad at Boston University, and then as a lay pastor in Washington, D.C., where he became determined to work for Obama after seeing his speech at the 2004 Democratic National Convention.

In 2005, Joshua became a junior aide in Obama's U.S. Senate office. Sometime that year, Obama asked if anyone could help him write a chapter focused on faith in his second book, *The Audacity of Hope*. As Joshua looked around the room, nobody raised their hand. So he did. Once that chapter was complete, Joshua mailed it to pastors around the country, and in 2007, he asked Obama to let him help build a faith-based operation for his presidential campaign.

Obama asked him to lead the operation. Joshua was just twenty-five years old.

During that first campaign, when Obama was going through a tough stretch, Joshua came up with the idea to send him a devotional. He asked Obama's bodyman and "little brother," Reggie Love, a six-four forward on Duke's 2001 National Championship team, for Obama's personal email address.

"I'll give it to you, man," Reggie said, "but it's a terrible idea and you're gonna get fired."

Joshua rolled the dice and sent the candidate a devotional anyway—a reflection on Psalm 23 and a poem by Wendell Berry titled "The Peace of Wild Things."

Joshua didn't hear back for ten minutes, suddenly panicked that Reggie was right and it would be the final email he'd send as part of Obama for America.

But then Obama wrote back, asking Joshua if he'd do it every day. He did, and even as he ran the Office of Faith-Based and Neighborhood Partnerships in the White House, he'd spend his Sundays lugging his Bible and quotation books to a little park on the Potomac River, where he'd draft Obama's morning devotionals for the week. He never once called himself Obama's pastor. We did, though—the title stuck after a *Time* magazine story calling him "Obama's Pastor in Chief."

"Obama's pastor" became my lifeline for eulogies, prayer breakfasts, and any speech where the president wanted to talk about his faith. Joshua had taught me that in the AME Church, forgiveness and grace were inviolable tenets. Even the most casual churchgoer knew the weekly bargain: Forgive us our trespasses, as we forgive those who trespass against us. But in the AME Church, to welcome the stranger and forgive the trespasser were not half of a negotiation—they were a conviction.

Even so, I still couldn't comprehend what I'd just seen on the video from that courtroom. These people were betrayed. The people they loved most had welcomed the stranger, and it had brought them nothing but horror and death. For the families to forgive that trespass, rather than demand Old Testament justice, was a commitment to faith that I doubted I would be able to summon in my own life.

The one thing I knew is that I knew nothing. If it didn't feel right to cry about the families' act of grace when I was alone, it sure didn't feel like something I was allowed to opine on—and it damn sure didn't feel like something I was allowed to write about. I was even more relieved that I wouldn't have to draft a eulogy.

Besides, they didn't need words from Obama after all! The killer said he wanted to start a race war, and his first victims had snuffed out the fuse. It was the opposite of his deranged intentions. What an incredible backfire. What a tone to set for the country to follow.

So far, Charleston appeared to be following it. Thousands had already gathered in churches across the city and for a multicultural, interfaith prayer vigil infused with lessons about slavery's thick roots there. One of the speakers was Charleston's mayor of four decades, Joe Riley, who'd stepped up with calm and powerful words the night of the shooting. He was a white man who'd once led an unsuccessful march to remove the Confederate flag from the state capitol building. "If that young man thought he was going to divide this community or divide this country with his racial hatred," he said, "we are here today and all across America to resoundingly say he measurably failed."

Maybe the country would make it through this episode unscathed after all, I hoped, maybe even better. But I'd also seen enough to know that vigils, words, or performative social media gestures alone weren't enough to spur change.

Still, just as I was about to heave myself out of my Adirondack chair to rouse Kristen from sleep, I was surprised and heartened to see Mitt Romney, the Republican nominee for president just three years before, become by far the most prominent member of his party to call for removal of the Confederate battle flag from the state capitol.

Take down the #ConfederateFlag at the SC Capitol. To many, it is a symbol of racial hatred. Remove it now to honor #Charleston victims.

He was right, of course. It felt sad that such an obvious position to hold was considered an act of courage for a Republican, and annoying that it was slobbered over by the press corps. But right is right. Maybe the tone the families had set was spreading.

Obama, en route to the golf course in Palm Springs, emailed a directive to retweet Romney's sentiment. While Obama did dictate or approve the content of his tweets, he didn't have the ability to tweet from his own phone. Only morons would allow a president to do that.

That power, to tweet words of healing or division to tens of millions, fell to two young staffers who followed an established protocol to circulate a draft of each tweet to a small group for editorial and legal approval. I was one of those people—a responsibility I didn't enjoy. Getting asked at all hours of the day to edit draft tweets was just as conducive to writing—or relaxing!—as someone throwing Nerf balls at my head.

Some on the approval team questioned whether Obama should retweet his former opponent at all, worried that backup from Obama might do Romney and his position more harm than good. "That's his problem with his party," I argued. "Romney said the right thing. So should we."

As hard as we'd campaigned against Mitt Romney in 2012, as pathetic a commentary on the Republican Party it was that he was the only leading voice calling on the South Carolina state capitol to take down the Confederate flag, the vast majority of the country that wasn't engaged in daily partisan warfare would hail Obama and Romney agreeing on something.

So we teed up a tweet for the president to send:

Good point, Mitt.

> **Mitt Romney** @MittRomney · Jun 20, 2015
> Take down the #ConfederateFlag at the SC Capitol. To many, it is a symbol of racial hatred. Remove it now to honor #Charleston victims.

Kristen was one of the team tasked with approving tweets too. She must have been scrolling through emails in bed, because I soon heard her soft cursing as she padded her way across the tarmac toward the lush safety of the grass.

"Hi. We leave town for one weekend, and we're talking about retweeting Mitt Romney?"

I laughed. "Good morning! How are you feeling?"

"I have a hangover and my phone just died." She had a bad habit of not plugging in her phones overnight. I knew that in addition to a headache, her anxiety was firing at the thought of missing something important.

I asked if she'd seen the news about what had happened in the Charleston courtroom. She hadn't. It was rare that two of us would miss a big news story, but a good sign for our well-being that we'd both ignored emails the night before and trusted our teams to pick up the slack if necessary.

While she stood barefoot in the grass, wearing a gray T-shirt and New York Knicks boxer shorts, her hair wild and fluttering in the breeze, I did my best to encapsulate the words and actions of the victims' families. As I spoke, Kristen's shoulders seemed to settle, and a serenity came over her face. The account soothed rather than surprised her. Of the two of us, she was the optimist whose first impulse was to look for the good in others. Of course their actions made sense to her.

"Wow," she said contemplatively.

I used the arms of the chair to stand up. "How are you doing?"

"I'm relieved you don't have to write a eulogy this weekend and that I don't have to fact-check it. And I'm cold," she added, rubbing her arms. "And I need a bacon, egg, and cheese. Come on, let's go get one." She waved at me to follow her, like I was a puppy. "Come on!"

I watched her tiptoe across the pavement until she disappeared inside the motel, wondering how I got so lucky.

3

FOUR JUNES PRIOR, AFTER THAT KNOCK ON MY OFFICE DOOR AND my first sight of the tall, chestnut-haired Kristen Bartoloni, I knew that I'd have to play a long game.

My parents met on my mom's first day of work at their company and went on their first date the same night. But that was 1974. Things were different in 2011. I didn't want to make Kristen feel uncomfortable in a new job or to feel she had to indulge someone's flirtations to avoid rocking the boat. I also didn't want to get fired.

By Kristen's second day on the job, she was already fact-checking draft speeches. I'd never so fully enjoyed being wrong. But I focused solely on being a pleasant and professional colleague, albeit one whose banter over email appeared more effortlessly charming than anyone else's.

That autumn, Kristen traveled as her team's representative on a presidential swing through Asia, a researcher embedded with the traveling White House in a time zone twelve hours ahead of Washington's. Ben Rhodes was on the same trip, as was Ferial Govashiri, who at that time was Ben's assistant before she was Obama's. When Ben and Ferial returned from the other side of the world, the two barreled into my office to say, "There's this new girl who's perfect for you."

I hadn't told anybody that, by then, I'd already mustered up the courage to ask Kristen to casual drinks. She'd said no.

I let two months pass before asking her again, as if that were some magical interlude of propriety and legality. She said no again.

I wasn't going to ask a third time, until a friend of hers suggested that I do. Kristen said no again!

Chastised, dispirited, and suddenly paranoid that her friend's suggestion had been a trap, I told myself, *Three strikes, you're out, and you're lucky that's all you are—get over it and be professional.*

But the next morning, a Saturday, Kristen sent me a note: "I changed my mind."

Three days later, we met at a tavern decked out with Christmas décor and crowded with young professionals playing pool and darts so that she wouldn't think I was trying too hard—and a stone's throw from the apartment that she shared with a friend so that she'd feel like she could go home whenever she wanted.

We hadn't told our colleagues we were going on a date. She was adamant about it; she didn't want anyone in the office to think she was dating somebody who'd just been promoted and moved into the West Wing so that she could advance her own situation at work. If she was self-conscious about the appearance of our date, she wasn't during the date itself—she ordered a grilled cheese and dug in, wondering if she should get some chicken fingers too. We talked for five hours. The conversation was full and fun, free of awkward silences. I tried extra hard to be interesting and, more important, to listen. Considering it took six months to get her to say yes to a first date, I figured that would be the best way to get her to say yes to a second.

At two in the morning, the bartender told us it was time to leave, a warning repeated on our second and third dates. We kept our budding relationship a secret in the office for as long as we could, but it's a smart crew at the White House—people noticed a stolen glance in meetings, too many afternoon coffee runs to be a coincidence, more visits by Kristen to the office Favs and I shared than a researcher needed to make.

She'd been working up the courage to tell her boss in research, and then his boss, Dan Pfeiffer, the White House communications director. Tall, in his midthirties, with a buzz cut and slight pug nose, Dan was deeply thoughtful, mildly sardonic, and well liked by the staff who reported to him. Kristen respected him and thought it important that we disclose our relationship.

"I know," he said. "Everybody knows." Kristen was mortified.

Secrecy on my end was never really an option, not when I lived with Tommy Vietor and Michael O'Neil, colleagues and friends from the 2008 campaign. Tommy was the president's sandy-haired national security spokesperson who maintained single-digit body fat, a love of Boston sports teams, and a relentless curiosity about all things. He was also about to leave the White House to start a political consulting business with Favs. Michael was the president's political fixer whose many hobbies included running marathons, drunk-buying absurd trinkets on eBay, and a bottomless knowledge of Ohio trivia. Tommy's blood pressure seemed always to run low; Michael perpetually ran a little fast, like a child's toy that had been wound two turns too many. Tommy was early to bed and early to rise; I'm not sure Michael slept at all. Indeed, after Kristen moved into our rented townhouse off 14th Street, I'd find her and Michael on the couch at three in the morning on a weeknight, eating popcorn and binge-watching *Friday Night Lights*. When Tommy's girlfriend Hanna and Michael's girlfriend Stephanie were there too, and friends flooded through the doors unannounced, it felt like I had a family beyond my own.

What an extraordinary gift to ride the highs and lows of the job with people as passionate about it as I was. It was a family that made the hard times bearable and the good times great. A family that knew you and what you were going through, sometimes even before you did. A family of people who made each other better.

Kristen epitomized those qualities. She became more than a colleague and a girlfriend, but a partner and best friend. We became tight with each other's friends and comfortable with each other's families. On May 16, 2015, I asked Kristen to marry me.

Somehow, she was surprised. This time she said yes on the first try.

By then, Tommy and Michael had left Washington, and Kristen and I rented a place of our own, a small one-bedroom apartment at the corner of 14th and U Streets in Northwest D.C. We hadn't sketched out any of our life together beyond the end of the second term, so a place with a quick commute to work, everything within walking distance, and each other was all we needed.

4

AFTER BACON-EGG-AND-CHEESE SANDWICHES AND AN AFTERNOON hike, Kristen and I prettied ourselves up, collected our four phones, and went to our first wedding as an engaged pair. The groom, Nik Steinberg, was an old friend from graduate school. As I'd entered the cushy environs of the White House, he'd gone undercover, doing years of dangerous and important fieldwork around the world for Human Rights Watch. When Obama chose Samantha Power—someone who'd done even more dangerous work in her twenties—as the U.S. ambassador to the United Nations, she asked me for a speechwriter. I put her and Nik together. They made a great team. (However challenging it could be to write for Obama, at least I wasn't writing for a Pulitzer Prize winner.)

Samantha had come to Nik's wedding. I'd known her for nearly a decade, first as her student in "Human Rights and American Foreign Policy" at the Kennedy School of Government, then as her colleague on the first Obama campaign. The ceremony was on a mountaintop with views for miles but not completely isolated—a neighbor of the hosts was running his riding mower as the procession was about to begin. In what must have been the strangest home visit he'd ever received, Ambassador Power's burly protective detail from the Diplomatic Security Service politely asked him to hold off for a while.

"Cody!" Samantha hugged me. "Obama's going to give an amazing eulogy in Charleston, right?"

I laughed, thinking she was messing with me.

"I'm serious. This is news around the world. The world is going to watch how he handles this."

I went to the bar.

Sarada and her husband, Naseem, were guests too. By day, Naseem was an easygoing negotiation expert with a vague resemblance to a pre-fame *Born to Run*–era Bruce Springsteen. By night, that likeness helped him exude an effortless cool as lead singer for Kingsley Flood, a rock band with a small but passionate following in Boston and D.C. Sarada sometimes joined him onstage to sing backup, and Nik had asked the two of them to perform the music for the ceremony.

The reception was outside under a billion stars dimmed only by swaying strings of old-time Edison bulbs. Over bourbons for me and Naseem, single-malt Scotch for Sarada, and white wine for Kristen, we talked about the past four days—the horror, the hatred, the forgiveness—and the days ahead, what might or might not happen with marriage equality, and what it all meant for America.

We danced too. We weren't joyless.

My astonishment at what had unfolded in that Charleston courtroom had congealed throughout the day into anger that it had to happen at all. I railed about the fundamental unfairness of Black Americans who endured trauma after trauma, yet being the ones expected to possess a bottomless reservoir of patience—to show grace, stand down, or deescalate the situation every time violence was visited upon them.

Sarada, never afraid to call me out when wrong, said, "That's *one* way of thinking about it."

"Shit. What am I missing here?" Like a lot of white men, even or especially as a white man who thought he was on the right side of things, I still had a lot to learn. The ground was shifting under our feet in inspiring and often uncomfortable ways that I saw the need for, but it wasn't easy.

"Well, look, I don't know," she said, probably just to throw me some cover. "But I don't think they're being submissive. Forgiveness isn't submission. It's power. They didn't play the victim card. You know who did? The killer."

Naseem snorted. "That's not a great defense strategy."

"But he probably believes it," Sarada replied. "He doesn't see himself as somehow privileged. He sees his way of life being overtaken by Black people, women, poor people, immigrants, gay people, whoever. He straight up admitted it!"

Kristen piped up: "I get what you mean. What's that saying? When you're used to privilege, equality feels like oppression?

"No one thinks they're privileged," Kristen continued. "That makes people think of, like, country clubs and the Kardashians. But if you had a shitty childhood and somebody comes along to tell you about your privilege, you're not thinking of how your life has been easier."

Sarada jumped in. "And when the far right leans into that, and gins it up in conservative media, and any maladjusted white supremacist can buy a gun . . ."

One of Obama's more famous speeches was tugging at the back of my brain, even if I couldn't summon the exact words at a wedding. In March 2008, during one of the most grueling stretches of the primary campaign, after videos emerged of his old pastor in Chicago expressing some incendiary racial opinions, Obama delivered a long, thoughtful, and honest speech exploring America's racial stalemate. The speech was seen as a turning point for the campaign.

Speaking from the National Constitution Center in Philadelphia, he'd detailed how so many of today's injustices could be traced directly to America's history of racial injustice—but then he'd added something unexpected.

> In fact, a similar anger exists within segments of the white community. Most working and middle-class white Americans don't feel that they have been particularly privileged by their race. Their experience is the immigrant experience—as far as they're concerned, no one handed them anything. They built it from scratch. They've worked hard all their lives, many times only to

> see their jobs shipped overseas or their pensions dumped after a lifetime of labor. They are anxious about their futures, and they feel their dreams slipping away. And in an era of stagnant wages and global competition, opportunity comes to be seen as a zero-sum game, in which your dreams come at my expense.
>
> So when they are told to bus their children to a school across town; when they hear an African American is getting an advantage in landing a good job or a spot in a good college because of an injustice that they themselves never committed; when they're told that their fears about crime in urban neighborhoods are somehow prejudiced—resentment builds over time.
>
> . . . To wish away the resentments of white Americans, to label them as misguided or even racist, without recognizing they are grounded in legitimate concerns—this too widens the racial divide and blocks the path to understanding.

I offered up a far less eloquent, two-bourboned version of that to the group, a nod that people who felt like they'd been screwed over their entire life while everybody else was getting an unfair advantage didn't tend to come around to a new point of view after being labeled racist.

"This is why I've never envied you guys," Naseem interjected, sipping his own whiskey. "Obama can't be honest about racism, or he pisses everybody off."

"But he *is* honest about racism," Sarada replied. "He just doesn't use it to drive people back into their corners. He asks us to acknowledge where we've been, where we are, and where we can go, ideally together."

She was right, and I was as inspired as I had been watching the Charleston families that morning.

"I still don't think it should be on the president to fix this mess with another big speech," Sarada said. "So I'm glad you're off the hook. People need to start being grown-ups and actually *want* to change things. Bad people exploit legitimate grievances. Good people need to do a better job of countering that."

I changed the subject. "How are the marriage equality speeches coming?"

"I can't bring myself to write the bad one yet."

"Yeah. Well, let's hope you don't need to."

"Cheers to that," Naseem said. "I'm gonna go tear up the dance floor."

Kristen leaped from her seat, reached out her hand for mine, and dragged me behind them.

Day Five

Sunday, June 21, 2015

1

IN FEBRUARY 2013, PRESIDENT OBAMA TRAVELED TO THE HYDE Park Academy public high school in Woodlawn, on the South Side of Chicago. It wasn't far from where he'd started his career as a community organizer, working to show people without wealth or power that if they banded their voices together, they could make a difference.

His visit came just three days after his State of the Union Address, and just two weeks after a fifteen-year-old girl named Hadiya Pendleton, a majorette who'd recently performed at his second inauguration, was shot and killed in a South Side park. The First Lady had attended her funeral, and Obama and I wove Hadiya into the emotional peroration of his State of the Union Address with her parents sitting in the gallery above, a moment that dared everybody in the chamber to stand and applaud for a vote on gun reforms.

On that chilly February afternoon at Hyde Park Academy, in a neighborhood still mourning Hadiya Pendleton, Obama delivered a speech presenting an array of policies aimed at inverting inequality in places like the South Side. He was also scheduled for a brief surprise "drop-by" at a discussion circle with a group of teenagers in Chicago's Becoming a Man program for at-risk youth—boys who showed potential but found themselves getting into trouble that could derail everything.

Obama pulled up a chair and talked with them for an hour, ignoring staffers' attempts to keep him on schedule. The teenagers gave voice to their lives and their struggles and how their world made it hard to do the right thing. He told them about growing up without a dad and the anger that came with it, about making bad choices and selling himself short, about being lucky enough to have people who gave him second chances and pushed him to make the most of himself.

The boy next to Obama asked him, "Wait, are you talking about *you*?"

A few months later, on Father's Day weekend 2013, he brought the same students to the White House for lunch and a second conversation. For almost all of them, it was the first experience on an airplane. Now they were in the Oval Office with the first Black president.

Before putting on their hand-me-down suits and ties, a few of the boys snuck out of their D.C. hotel and went to a convenience store. Once in the Oval, they gave Obama what they'd bought—a Father's Day card they'd all signed for him.

One of the boys looked at Obama and told him, "I never signed a Father's Day card before."

Obama, always aware of what his words meant, closed the card and looked back at the boy. "I've never signed a Father's Day card either."

2

THE MORNING AFTER THE WEDDING, I MADE A FRESH CUP OF THE Massachusetts motel's bark water, claimed an Adirondack chair, and called my dad to wish him a happy Father's Day. I always tried to remind him and my mom that I was grateful for the life they'd worked so hard to secure—the path they set me on, the time they invested in my younger sister and me, the emotional and financial support that gave us every chance to make the most of ourselves.

I'd signed plenty of Father's Day cards. It wasn't the only thing that made me as different as could be from Obama.

That was easy to see at first glance: His suits fit like a glove, and every movement was graceful. My suits had patches and I moved like a Mack truck. He was monkish in his habits. All of mine were bad. As someone with a nuclear arsenal at his disposal, he limited himself to two martinis a week—one on Friday, one on Saturday. My minimum was two bourbons a night. He called food "fuel" and his meals were always the same—one part lean protein, one part whole grain, one part steamed or raw vegetables. I could teach a course on the phylogeny of encased meat products. (When on the road around voters, though, Obama would consume whatever local delicacy was politically required: Skyline Chili in Cincinnati, Cuban sandwiches in Tampa, cheesesteaks in Philly, wings in Buffalo, tacos in East Los Angeles, fried everything at the Iowa State Fair. And pie. The man loved pie. But inevitably, some press outlet would snark that he was a hypocrite for not following the First Lady's healthy eating guidelines. He couldn't catch a break.)

Obama came to call Chicago his hometown—but that was the rare overlap in our biographies.

I was born and raised in Chicago—Wrigleyville, to be exact. My parents met in their early twenties at an advertising agency in New York City—my dad was a surfer jock from Southern California who earned an MBA, my mom a farm girl from central Indiana who taught high school English and got her master's degree in journalism at Northwestern University. After they moved to Chicago to start a family, they competed for business at rival agencies, but at home they were endlessly devoted to their kids, anchoring us in a neighborhood where we'd be exposed to people of all different backgrounds, all bound by good Midwestern sensibilities. Being able to walk to day games at the best ballpark in America was a bonus.

The Red Line connected the city's two baseball stadiums. But traveling from Wrigley Field to Comiskey Park and beyond, a north-south journey through one of the most segregated cities in America, could be like traveling to a different world. Being a kid on the North Side gave me better odds from the start. And by the time I turned six, we'd moved ten miles north—another world away—to Wilmette, a town where our parents let us walk and bike on our own to excellent public schools, well-funded public parks, and an extraordinary public library where I spent most of my summer days. Halfway through eighth grade, my dad's career took us to Ridgefield, Connecticut, a town with all the same amenities but even farther removed geographically from some of life's harder realities. My first jobs were running a hot-dog cart (fun!) on the town's idyllic Main Street and caddying for rich assholes (terrible!) at the local country club.

Both towns were comfortable and happy places in which to grow up, and I knew I was lucky.

Those who can't imagine why somebody would go into politics hoping to help people often ascribe guilt as a motive. But I never felt guilty about my childhood. I did feel some sheepishness that almost everything I knew of other people's hardships came from books I checked out of that library—*The Color Purple, The Sound and the Fury, I Know Why the Caged Bird Sings*. I was probably twelve when I first read *There Are No Children Here,* Alex Kotlowitz's searing account of the despair and deprivation in projects just five miles from my first neighborhood—projects the *New York Times* once described in an op-ed titled "What It's Like to Be in Hell." It haunted me to learn that kids who grew up so close to where I did had long since lost an innocence that I still enjoyed.

I missed the Midwest and chose to attend Northwestern University, where I studied the ways that America didn't do enough to make sure more kids had the same opportunities I did. And I came to understand that there were people in power dead set on keeping it that way.

After graduating from Northwestern in 2002, I moved to Washington with no connections beyond my friends Nick Ehrmann and

Chris Tracy, schoolteachers in some of the District's worst public schools, who let me move into a run-down Dupont Circle townhouse with them and three other young professionals. Nick slept on a futon in the dining room.

I sent a hundred résumés that never got answered; I went to a dozen interviews and never heard back. Then one desperate Friday afternoon, I cold-called the internship coordinator in Massachusetts senator Edward M. Kennedy's office, who asked if I could start on Monday.

My chest swelled. Somebody finally saw what I had to offer. Nick, Chris, and I celebrated all weekend.

I walked in on Monday morning to find that I was one of fifty summer interns. The internship coordinator had added me to the list because she'd just wanted to get off the phone.

I was assigned to a windowless mailroom, tasked with walking the senator's Portuguese water dogs, Sunny and Splash (a later addition, Cappy, would be part of the same litter as the Obamas' first dog, Bo); running letters and memos around Capitol Hill; giving tours to constituents; even cutting stories from the newspaper—literally, with scissors—arranging them on a page, and photocopying them for staff, a prehistoric version of a media monitor.

I was also tasked with opening, reading, and routing letters from Americans asking for help. The senator received hundreds of letters a day from constituents and from people all across the country who hoped the last Kennedy brother would hear their pleas for specific assistance with Social Security and veterans' benefits, a good education, and decent health care.

More often, though, they just wanted the senator to know about their lives. Some of the letters were deeply personal, tales from ordinary people who did what the country expected of them but couldn't seem to make life work out the way we're told it should.

Yet even when the ink was smudged where the writers had wiped a tear off the page, I still saw something hopeful in the act of writing—trust that the system still worked, that someone on the other end would read their story and care enough to try and help.

It was my best education. Kennedy was widely regarded even by Republican senators as one of the greatest legislators of all time, someone who fought for what he believed in, raging against injustice on the Senate floor like a category 5 hurricane (while an aide like me nervously tried to figure out which chart to hold up behind him as he went off script).

Publicly, he relished being a partisan lightning rod. But behind closed doors, he bridged the divide with genuine effort and success, even as bipartisanship appeared to be dying off. He was of the old breed who saw politics as a noble calling, an effort that kept differences of philosophy from becoming barriers to cooperation.

What made him unique was that his own suffering and his own failings made him more alive to the afflictions of others. Quietly, he called and wrote each one of the 177 families in Massachusetts who lost a loved one on 9/11, sometimes taking them sailing, not just in the days after but every year after.

More famously, he made universal health care the cause of his life. It wasn't something he found in a poll or something he used simply to fire up his base, it was a commitment drawn from sheer empathy. When his son Teddy Jr. slept off his cancer treatments in the hospital, the senator would wander the halls and talk with other parents keeping watch over their own kids, unsure what they'd do when the next bill came. The very best health care, provided by Congress, was a privilege that guaranteed his son's care but not his survival, putting the senior senator from Massachusetts in the same intimate circle of fear in the middle of the night with parents terrified they might lose their own children. They, not a policy, became his cause—making sure that every single American had good health care as a matter of right and not of privilege.

I was born a generation after JFK's New Frontier, long after the torch had been passed to a new generation of Americans, well after liberalism's once limitless possibilities had dimmed. But for three and a half years, I got to work for someone who still embodied a truly noble set of attitudes about civic life. I got to bask in the inspiration of that very Kennedy-esque idea that America is not the project of any one person; that anybody can make a difference, and everybody should try to.

Then I saw someone else who felt the same way and who updated that calling for a new time.

In 2004, the Democratic National Convention took place in Boston. Senator Kennedy was everywhere that week, thrilled to be hosting the convention in his hometown. Any of his staffers willing to take vacation days to go up from Washington to help received a reward: a floor pass for one night of the convention programming. I received one for the convention's second night, considered the lineup with the least star power—until a young state legislator from Illinois with a self-proclaimed funny name took the stage.

Wedged into a corner on the floor of the FleetCenter, craning my neck to see around people's signs and surrounded by strangers competing with one another to wear the most pieces of patriotic flair, I watched Barack Obama speak about politics the way I wanted it to be—as an imperfect but noble endeavor in which, even in a country with all sorts of different ideas and beliefs, some common purpose binds and compels us, together, to do great things that we can't do on our own. His rhetoric felt different, fresh, unburdened by overused platitudes that had been sanitized and sanded over by a platoon of consultants.

After the last of the week's balloons fell, and I dragged my memorabilia back to Washington, I must have talked about that speech a lot. Because it was right around then when my boss, a wiry, bespectacled policy strategist named Michael Myers, asked me if I knew how to write a speech and gave me my first chance to try.

It was a ten-minute "floor speech" that Senator Kennedy would deliver for the benefit of an empty chamber, a few reporters in the gallery, and the die-hard C-SPAN viewers at home. Set against the pantheon of political rhetoric, the speech I wrote was instantly forgettable. Nobody hung on every word except me (and my parents, whom I'd alerted). But to see someone else speak words I'd written sent electricity right up my spine and out my hair.

Democrats were wiped out in those November 2004 elections as President George W. Bush won a second term. The confetti and balloons did fall, though, for Senator-Elect Barack Obama. Sometime that month, as he was working to build a Senate staff of his own, his communications director Robert Gibbs told him he'd need a speechwriter. True to form, Obama rejected the suggestion at first, most likely reminding Gibbs that he had written the Boston speech himself—something he'd remind me a dozen times over the coming years. But once Gibbs explained how the Senate would eat away at his hours—the meetings, the fundraising, how being one hundredth in seniority meant spending more time sitting in a chair presiding over a nearly empty chamber than anybody else—Obama reluctantly asked whom he had in mind.

Gibbs suggested Jon Favreau, a thoughtful, buzz-cut, twenty-three-year-old junior speechwriter searching for a job after John Kerry's losing presidential campaign. Obama and Favs quickly hit it off, developing what would be described frequently as a "mind meld" once Obama announced his candidacy for president in 2007.

Soon after Obama jumped into the race, Stephanie Cutter, a disciplined and driven strategist who, as Kennedy's communications director had been a mentor to me and then, as Kerry's communications director, a mentor to Favs, introduced the two of us. We also hit it off immediately.

I was a student at the Kennedy School of Government by then, with plans to return to JFK's youngest brother's office with a sharper set of policy analysis skills. But I had a portfolio of speeches I'd written for Senator Kennedy, Favs was a constituent from Massachusetts and a Kennedy fan, and, most important, he was drowning in work and desperate for help on the growing presidential campaign however he could get it. Obama may have delivered two or three speeches a week while in the Senate, but the campaign trail demanded two or three a day.

Less than three years after watching Obama mesmerize a crowd in Boston, I threw a couple of duffels into my 1998 Dodge Durango and drove west to my hometown, excited to intern for the campaign speechwriting team. I was accompanied for the fifteen-hour drive by Obama reading his books *Dreams from My Father* and *The Audacity of Hope* on the sometimes-functioning CD player.

At first there were only two speechwriters: Favs, the chief speechwriter and mayor of the campaign's social scene (though his budding fame never overshadowed his fundamental kindness and empathy); and Adam Frankel, a bookish, bespectacled former assistant to JFK's speechwriter, Ted Sorensen. That summer, Ben Rhodes became the third. And after Obama beat Hillary Clinton in the primaries, Favs hired two more full-time speechwriters: Hillary's chief wordsmith, Sarah Hurwitz, and me.

Once Obama beat John McCain in the 2008 general election, Favs took the team he'd assembled to the White House, where he moved into the Speechcave and the rest of us packed into a large, boisterous, and jovial suite in the Eisenhower Executive Office Building with two more new hires: Jon Lovett, a math savant and former stand-up comic who had reported to Sarah Hurwitz on the Clinton campaign; and Kyle O'Connor, a twenty-three-year-old assistant who said "gee" without irony.

I was determined to make myself the workhorse of the team, writing more speeches than I could handle and loving every minute of it. For the first two years, few of them were of any significant consequence, memorable only to me (and to my parents), but I treated each one as if it was the most important thing I'd ever write, a blow against injustice and for a better America, making sure that anyone who came to see the president of the United States speak was going to leave satisfied.

Then on January 8, 2011, Favs called. It was a Saturday, but he was in the office working on the State of the Union Address. News had broken of a mass shooting in the parking lot of a supermarket near Tucson, Arizona. The local congresswoman, Gabby Giffords, was holding a question-and-answer session with constituents—

"Congress on your Corner," she called it—when the quintessentially American scene was shattered by a man with a semiautomatic pistol. He shot nineteen people, killing six and putting Giffords in critical condition with a bullet through her brain. The prognosis was so grave that CNN and NPR wrongly reported her dead before correcting themselves.

Favs asked me if I could come into the office right away to draft a statement for Obama. When I arrived, I was pulled into the Situation Room. It was my first time inside. The president was sitting at the head of the table, flanked by advisors several levels above me—Communications Director Dan Pfeiffer, Homeland Security Advisor John Brennan, National Security Advisor Tom Donilon, Legislative Affairs Director Phil Schiliro, Deputy Chief of Staff Jim Messina, and Bill Daley on his first day as Obama's chief of staff. Brennan was briefing everyone after sifting through intelligence to make sure that the attempted assassination of a member of Congress wasn't part of a larger plot.

Later that afternoon, Obama delivered a statement from the White House. By Sunday, we were told there would be a memorial service in Tucson seventy-two hours later, and that he would deliver the eulogy. "You wrote the statement, you do the eulogy," Favs said.

I was terrified. It would be my first prime-time, nationally televised speech. But I knew that, in the politically charged days after the shooting, the eulogy needed to stand as a surprising, hopeful, and even joyous celebration of the way the people who died had lived their lives and how they might inspire us to live ours. I stayed awake for two days to write it, sending a draft to Obama the night before the eulogy. He revised it on the computer—a rare phenomenon for someone who preferred to edit by hand—and sent it back after one o'clock in the morning.

In Tucson, Obama brought the crowd to its feet with the adlibbed revelation that Congresswoman Giffords had opened her eyes for the first time that afternoon, then brought it to tears with an ending that described what America could be, written through the lens of the youngest victim, Christina Taylor Green, who had been just nine years old.

Obama was praised almost universally, not only by Democrats, but by Republicans and even by several of his most avid critics, who called the eulogy "brilliant," "courageous," even "magnificent." The presidential speechwriter-turned-journalist James Fallows said it surpassed the best Reagan and Clinton had to offer. Major newspapers ran headlines like "With Obama's Tucson Speech, His Presidency Turns a Corner" and "Barack Obama's Tucson Speech Rose to the Moment and Transcended It."

Flying back to Washington on Air Force One, around midnight Eastern Standard Time, I was celebrating the reviews with no idea that, two cabins behind me, my cover was being blown. A reporter asked how the speech had come together, and Robert Gibbs, whom Obama had appointed press secretary upon entering the White House, took the unusual step of mentioning that Obama and I had worked on it together.

A reporter asked, "Would you spell Cody's name for us?"

"It's *C-O-D-Y K-E-E-N-A-N,*" Gibbs replied. "And I'll double-check that, but I'm almost positive that's it."

I didn't get home from Joint Base Andrews until three in the morning, so I slept in, still unaware of Gibbs's revelation. I woke up to an avalanche of email. Savannah Guthrie, NBC's White House correspondent, had emailed just after six o'clock to ask if I'd talk with her for the *Today* show, and it got weirder from there, with reporters phoning my parents and sister in search of interesting nuggets about my life.

I declined every request for an interview, feeling sheepish that it was happening to me and not the other writers on the team and guilty because speechwriters are supposed to be anonymous. Yes, I'd had the pen on the draft. But Favs had offered brilliant edits as usual. Kyle O'Connor's research uncovered the anecdote that made for a showstopper of an ending. My mother, whom I'd called in a panic for advice, provided some of the keenest insights. Obama had worked on the eulogy himself late into the night, taking parts of my draft to places I couldn't reach. I could craft a great line, bang out a riff that brought an audience to its feet, even tug on their heartstrings with an emotional moment that pulled them closer to the stage. But it was Obama's moral imagination that often led to the finest moments in his biggest speeches.

It was something that would haunt me for the rest of my career: the knowledge that whatever credit I received, whatever heights I'd reach, I hadn't earned them; they belonged to others.

Some nights, I was almost as good as people thought I was. But the one person who would always know the truth, the one person who would always know it more intimately than anyone else, was the one person I cared about impressing the most: Obama.

A few months after Tucson, Favs named me as his deputy director of speechwriting, and I hauled my laptop across the driveway to the West Wing, where the two of us upgraded to a sunny office just a twenty-second walk from the Oval. By the time the second inaugural came around in 2013, Favs had been with Obama for eight years and decided it was time to strike out on his own. He sat down with Obama and recommended that I succeed him as assistant to the president and director of speechwriting.

After two years of spending twelve hours a day with Jon Favreau, I wasn't surprised that Obama concurred. But I was worried that, for all of Jon's patient and generous mentoring, I didn't deserve the job of chief speechwriter, wasn't up to the task, and couldn't figure out why nobody else—especially Obama—felt the same way.

Favs and Obama had spent two years together in a small and intimate Senate office, merging worldviews, crafting the stories that would turn Obama into a global icon, coming up with the soaring stuff that ended up on posters and in pop songs. Favs had become famous in his own right as the Wunderkind of the White House who held a place near the top of every "under forty" list in politics, even showing up in paparazzi photos dating a movie star.

Jon and I were good friends who worked well together, hung out together on weekends, and texted most days after he departed the White House. He even offered to read and edit drafts of big speeches whenever I needed a thought partner, pointing out that he'd always needed one too. Despite all that, for the rest of my years in the White House, I would be engaged in an endless, one-sided rivalry with the ghost of Jon Favreau, constantly trying to prove that I could fill his shoes.

With little faith in my ability to appeal to an audience with the big, intellectual argument like Favs could, I focused on grabbing them by the guts, hoping a visceral connection would pass for wisdom. But even at the height of my powers, I was plagued by the idea that I was a talented mimic who'd stumbled upward into the top job.

Surely Obama had figured that out. It was just a matter of time until somebody else would.

He might have sensed my angst, even if he never called it out. At the halfway mark of 2013, Obama assembled his senior advisors for a Saturday meeting around the long table in the Roosevelt Room to take stock of how the year was going.

"I'm really happy with this team," he said, "especially the people who stepped up into new roles. Cody in particular—I think you've done a great job picking up where Favs left off."

The fear that I was a fraud would never go away—but in the moment, that one sentence helped.

The first time I met President Obama was our first week in the White House. Neither of us had any gray hair.

When I became chief speechwriter in the second term, I was as aware as ever that I stood on the shoulders of the Obama for America speechwriting team. Here we are the day before the 2008 election. *Front row, left to right*: Jon Favreau, Sarah Hurwitz, Ben Rhodes, and Adam Frankel. *Back row, left to right*: Me and Kyle O'Connor.

Preparing for a sight gag at the 2009 White House Correspondents' Dinner. Being the most junior member of the team required some grunt work.

On board Air Force One on our way to the memorial service after the January 8, 2011, mass shooting in Tucson, Arizona. Obama was often hands-on until we were wheels down.

The day of the Sandy Hook Elementary School shootings on December 14, 2012, was the hardest of Obama's presidency. Two days later, he worked on his remarks for the vigil while watching Sasha's dress rehearsal for *The Nutcracker;* he'd miss the performance to deliver the eulogy in Newtown, Connecticut, that night.

Obama dictating some final edits in Newtown High School before spending three hours with the families whose children were murdered, then delivering their eulogy.

The trio who taught me everything I know about speechwriting: (*left to right*) Ben, Favs, and the boss.

Obama didn't have a problem with nerves. He was a lot more relaxed the evening before a State of the Union Address than I was.

The muse hits: Obama writing longhand on a yellow legal pad.

As most of the first-term speechwriters departed, I gradually built my own team. Obama pulled us together for a photo after we gave him a gift for his fifty-fifth birthday: a list of every time he'd added some variant of "I reject that notion" to his speeches. *Flanking Obama, from left to right*: Steve Krupin, Tyler Lechtenberg, Susannah Jacob, Sarada Peri, me, Terry Szuplat, Sarah Hurwitz, and Ben Rhodes.

Meeting Kristen changed everything. Balancing work and our relationship was tricky, but, as this 2012 Fourth of July photo shows, we made each other happy.

I always felt extra fortunate when we got to travel the world together as part of our jobs, including this weeklong swing through Asia in 2014.

Obama and Kristen got along famously, probably because both were skeptical of anything I said.

I saved for a ring for more than a year, then proposed to Kristen atop Rockefeller Center. Obama advised me to bring an umbrella. He was right.

It could be a lonely job, especially when the clock was ticking on a speech.

Once in a while, Obama would stop by the Speechcave unannounced and play a game of mini-cornhole. That's Terry Szuplat on the left.

Our relationship progressed over the years, ultimately including Obama delivering lessons about Miles Davis and "finding the silences," as he is doing here in his private dining room off the Oval Office the week before the 2015 State of the Union Address.

Thanks to a snow day, the Selma speech became our purest collaboration. We had uninterrupted time to talk and pass drafts back and forth, each one better than the last.

Editing Obama's statement in the outer Oval Office the morning after the Charleston massacre. If we were pressed for time, I'd sit at Ferial Govashiri's computer. That's Ferial and Joe Paulsen on the left, with the Rose Garden as background.

Obama didn't edit the remarks I'd prepared in case the Supreme Court ruled against the Affordable Care Act. But he did leave some feedback. He's delivering the victory remarks in the far background, flanked by Vice President Joe Biden.

I rarely went to watch the president deliver remarks in the Rose Garden, but this week was different. Here, staff and I are watching him speak after the Supreme Court upheld Obamacare.

The next day, as a crowd waited outside the Oval Office to hear the president deliver his remarks on the Supreme Court marriage equality decision, Obama continued to work on the Charleston eulogy. In the foreground, Brian Mosteller is giving the politest it's-time-now ahem he could muster.

I knew Obama well enough to know he was genuinely moved while speaking about marriage equality. He tried to downplay it as just being tired from working on the eulogy.

With staff after the Supreme Court affirmed a constitutional right to marriage equality.

Five minutes after his remarks in the Rose Garden, Obama was already walking me through his newest additions to the Charleston eulogy just before he, Valerie Jarrett, and I boarded Marine One.

And then the president sang "Amazing Grace."

Photos of the White House lit up like a rainbow went viral immediately. But I've always liked this one best. It shows my colleagues enjoying the moment together. There were at least two marriage proposals that night.

I missed it, though. I was asleep by eight o'clock. Kristen took this shot when she arrived home five hours later.

At the White House on our wedding day, July 3, 2016. We told our families and wedding party that Obama was golfing and wouldn't be there. After they regained their composure, he posed for photos with everyone and offered some words of wisdom.

Putting the finishing touches on Obama's 2016 Democratic National Convention speech about an hour before we had to depart for Philadelphia. He was always most relaxed on gameday.

The people I missed most whenever I was writing: Kristen; my sister, Carly; and my parents, Marilyn and Steve, who made this wild journey possible.

Day Six

Monday, June 22, 2015

1

"OKAY, PEOPLE, WE'VE GOT A LOT OF WOOD TO CHOP THIS WEEK."

Denis McDonough's upbringing in Stillwater, Minnesota, a town known for its Lumberjack Days, had made him a library of folksy metaphors—and someone who loathed a logjam. A one-man receiving line, he slapped backs and pounded fists as the president's senior team filed into his office at 7:45 on Monday morning, cajoling the twenty-five of us to take our seats around the long table in his corner office that boasted even more floor-to-ceiling windows than the Oval.

I swigged black coffee as each of the president's senior advisors took turns updating everyone else on what their team was doing to keep the workstreams moving.

The ink wasn't yet dry on Obama's legislative obituaries as the congressional affairs team reported that trade legislation he wanted looked to be resurrected and on the verge of passing the Senate. The national security team was finalizing long-needed reforms to U.S. hostage policy. On the heels of a new scientific study warning that Earth was on the brink of a sixth mass extinction event if we didn't act more aggressively to curb climate change, the climate team was sweating new fuel-efficiency rules for heavy-duty trucks and limits on methane emissions, and the economic team was hours away from releasing the first-ever White House report on the costs and benefits of combating the crisis, with detailed repudiations of Republican climate deniers and the fossil-fuel industry funding their campaigns.

Critical issues all, and yet the restless unease in the West Wing air had everything to do with the fact that SCOTUS week was here. The Supreme Court was running out of days before its summer recess to issue rulings on nearly a dozen cases, including the blockbuster decisions on the ACA and marriage equality. The health care team, emitting an electricity I hadn't felt since the last time the ACA was on the docket, in 2012, was busy buttressing contingency plans to protect the millions who might lose their insurance in a matter of days, and the counsel's office was sketching out strategies to shore up rights for same-sex couples should marriage equality be snuffed out.

As for the speechwriting team, which had to write remarks for all of it—on the economy, national security, climate change, health care, and equal justice—it suddenly appeared as if Obama was going to speak in Charleston after all.

A few minutes earlier, Valerie Jarrett had grabbed me as I was walking into the morning meeting. I liked Valerie; with an unfailingly warm demeanor, she was easy to talk to, especially when we'd daydream about our plans to return to Chicago someday soon—glossing over our mutual knowledge that neither of us would depart the White House before the final day. She was born in Iran to African American parents who'd both been trailblazers in their fields, her father in pathology, her mother in early childhood education. Valerie chose public service and a career with the City of Chicago, where she hired a young lawyer named Michelle Robinson—and struck up a friendship with her fiancé, Barack.

In the White House, she wore two hats—one as the president's close advisor and "older sister," as he called her; and one as head of the Office of Public Engagement, a conduit for advocates and activists to feel heard within the White House. I didn't envy her for it; the roles often seemed at odds to me. She was intensely loyal to the president and protective of his reputation and his best interests, and the bane of anyone who wasn't. But she also had to cater to constituency groups whose agendas sometimes ran contrary to the president's best interests. It can't have been easy.

And sometimes, it felt like it suddenly fell to a speech to sort it out.

"I read an interesting piece this weekend on the meaning of the Black church, if POTUS is looking for a different message for the funeral. I'll send it to you."

"What?"

"For the eulogy on Friday."

My mouth hung open. I couldn't tell if this meant that it had been decided that Obama would be giving the eulogy and nobody had told me, or if Valerie had decided it without telling anybody.

Anita Decker Breckenridge brushed past and tilted her head as if to say "Come with me." As Denis started the meeting, I sat next to her at the far end of the table, and she passed me a note.

> P now thinking it will look bad if he doesn't go. Came up after dinner on Saturday. Tried to spare your Sunday. But he still doesn't want to speak.

I scribbled underneath and slid the note back.

> VJ seems to think he is.

Anita shrugged.

When the meeting turned to Charleston, though, it didn't sound like a done deal at all. The communications team hadn't heard from Obama that he wanted to go, or that he wanted to speak. Nor had the scheduling and advance teams. A lot went into scheduling a trip like that—advance teams would have to deploy to scout the location, Secret Service would have to deploy to scout the president's movements, the motorcade would have to deploy to be ready for his arrival. We could pull off a trip with as little as one day's notice, but even with several it was never easy.

I stared into the center of the table for most of the meeting, avoiding everyone's glance. When Denis called on me to speak for the speechwriting team, I ticked through the eight speeches we were working on with everyone's teams, including versions for all possible outcomes at the Supreme Court. I did not suggest that we were preparing anything for Charleston.

"I think he has to go speak in Charleston," Valerie offered. "People will expect him to."

"That's not a good reason," I countered. "And before my team starts working on a eulogy that may or may not happen, I need to talk with him."

As the meeting broke, I intercepted the president's diligent and wryly funny scheduler, Chase Cushman, a friend with whom I sat elbow to elbow on barstools to watch Big Ten football on fall Saturdays. Like Denis, he was a Minnesotan, but one who hadn't spent twenty years in Washington. The outdoors was fresher on him. The longer any meeting went on, the more his tie came undone and his permanent five o'clock shadow darkened, his gaze almost willing the conference table to morph into a firepit or an ice-fishing hole. He had entered politics shortly before the 2008 campaign and planned to return to Minnesota when the second term ended.

"Speaking of chopping wood," I asked him, "what's the earliest I can see the boss today?"

"I'll get you in as soon as I can, my man," he grunted.

My world felt totally upended. Even if a visit hadn't been decided yet, with Valerie pushing it, the odds were better than even that it would happen. She may have balanced competing interests at times, but she still put the president's interests first when it mattered most—and I couldn't imagine she'd press for a eulogy without Obama's buy-in.

I trudged back downstairs and stopped at Susannah's desk. "Morning. Can you assemble the team in my office at nine? It looks like we're going to Charleston." Her eyes opened wide. "And can you pull together a short bio for each of the victims with a little color about their lives? Things that will make people smile are always a bonus. Use the Tucson eulogy as a guide."

She swiveled to her screen. "I'm on it."

The monitor behind her showed groups of dueling protesters outside the Supreme Court with a chyron that blared SUPREME COURT POISED TO RULE ON HEALTH, MARRIAGE. I checked my watch. We still had an hour and a half before ten o'clock, when the first decisions might be announced. While it was unlikely the marquee cases would be among them today, it wasn't impossible.

My team materialized in my office at 9:00 on the dot, clutching coffees, teas, and breakfast burritos, ready to recap our weekends and speculate about the week ahead.

By virtue of my position, they always assumed I knew more than I did. I spoiled those hopes right away. Cultivating that assumption, giving off an air that you're perpetually in the know, was an intoxicating perfume huffed by many in Washington who rose the ranks that way. But sooner or later, the smell of bullshit always took over. I got my kicks by reminding the team that not only did I not know anything, but anybody who said they did was full of it.

"It would be nice if SCOTUS ruled on marriage before the Pride reception remarks this Wednesday," I said. "Would make for a heck of a party." I knew Sarada hadn't finished both sets of remarks for the marriage equality ruling, and as her spine straightened, I finished my thought. "But nobody seems to think they will."

She melted back into the couch. "Oh, thank God."

A smile crept across my face. "But who knows? They could."

Tyler, who could read me well, intervened with some glee. "Stop," he said, drawing out the word. "He's just kidding."

"Or am I?" I replied. My team booed. "Really, nobody knows. It does sound, though, like we might be going to Charleston after all. I have no idea what I'd write. I'm going to talk with Obama today. But we'll know about the Supreme Court before we know about that. Any minute now, in fact."

2

THE ANTICIPATION OF A SCOTUS RULING WAS THE HARDEST PART—and the most annoying.

Obama had likened it to waiting for the results of a biopsy. You've either got cancer or you don't. There's nothing you can do about it at this point but wait for the answer.

The Court had always been an intentionally impenetrable place with intentionally mysterious rules. It announced which cases it would consider each year and tended to save the most highly anticipated decisions for the end of each session but didn't hint at which might arrive when. The 2012 ACA decision, for example, arrived on the session's final day.

Adding to its enigmatic nature, while the other two branches of government had long since built their own broadcast facilities, the Court still didn't allow video or live audio of its decisions, nor did it allow electronic devices in the courtroom.

I could see how barring electronic devices during the actual arguments was a prudent decision in an age of social media. In 2012, Obama's solicitor general, Don Verrilli, was widely derided as "losing" his argument for the Affordable Care Act, and video to go with the apocalyptic opinion pieces would have driven progressives to despair. But his argument delivered the only thing that mattered—a win.

On decision days, though, the Court's recalcitrance was exasperating to those of us who had to respond to its rulings and excruciating to the millions of Americans whose lives might change because of those rulings. The justices probably considered this closed-door process a highbrow means to uphold quaint tradition and preserve their Delphic status. We found it absurdly anachronistic. And yet, we were on the edge of our seats, waiting and hoping that the black-robed gods of Olympus would find in our favor.

While nobody knew for certain what the outcome of either case would be, inside the White House, we were more nervous about the ACA. Few "experts" were making bold predictions. I read one opinion piece speculating that Chief Justice Roberts would "save" the law again, but one particularly gloomy lawyer in the White House counsel's office warned me against getting my hopes up.

A loss would feel catastrophic to the millions of Americans who'd lose their insurance, to a health care system thrown into chaos, and to Obama's presidency. Technically speaking, he was already a "lame duck" in the fourth quarter of his tenure, even if we didn't feel that way.

In fact, this lame duck's feet were furiously busy under the water in ways that few outside the White House knew. For months, Ben Rhodes had been shuttling to Canada and the Vatican to run talks with representatives of the Cuban government. In a week's time, the president would extinguish one of the last embers of the Cold War by reestablishing diplomatic relations with Cuba and announcing the reopening of embassies in both countries. Two weeks after that, he'd announce a comprehensive, long-term deal with Iran, negotiated with allies over years, that would shut down its nuclear weapons program without firing a single shot. And after almost two full terms of strategic policies and shrewd diplomatic moves, he'd be able to finalize the most comprehensive climate accord ever reached in Paris just before Christmas.

But if Obamacare went down in flames this week, his lame-duck status would become very real.

The marriage case *felt* better. That didn't make us any less anxious about it. But I had to believe that the country had progressed to a point where that kind of step forward was inevitable.

In 2004, Republicans had used marriage equality as a wedge issue to scare their voters to the polls. By 2015, seven in ten Americans lived in states where same-sex marriage was legal, a story of freedom across the country. It was easy, of course, for a straight, cisgender man like me to be sanguine. I doubted that many LGBTQ Americans, especially any same-sex couples holding hands while hanging on every word of cable news that morning, felt the same way.

There was no preview of each day's decisions, no scoops handed out to the press, no heads-up for the White House, not even for the plaintiffs, like Jim Obergefell, who showed up in the courtroom every decision day of SCOTUS week wearing a fresh outfit and mustering fresh optimism.

The only thing we knew for certain was that decisions were announced starting at 10:00 A.M.

At 9:59, I'd turn the volume up on MSNBC. It was a little like waiting for the white smoke that announced a new pope—only more chaotic and less definitive.

A reporter inside the Court would relay the immediate decision to his or her producer, but without the full text of the decision. Then, in the race to be first, a breathless reporter outside the Court or in the studio might interpret the decision incorrectly. Such an error happened in 2012, when CNN and Fox News embarrassingly declared the Affordable Care Act dead even as our lawyers were telling us that it was in fact quite alive. For a full six minutes, CNN's screen blared INDIVIDUAL MANDATE STRUCK DOWN: SUPREME COURT FINDS MEASURE UNCONSTITUTIONAL.

But that wasn't what the Supreme Court did at all. CNN quickly posted an all-time ass-covering: CORRECTION: THE SUPREME COURT BACKS ALL PARTS OF PRESIDENT OBAMA'S SIGNATURE HEALTH CARE LAW. The network ultimately issued a statement regretting and apologizing for the error.

Fox News, which had broadcast the same wrong interpretation, did not.

Within minutes of each verdict, a Supreme Court clerk would deliver boxes full of the lengthy written decisions to the Court chamber, and the farcical ritual known as the Running of the Interns would begin. A group of young journalism interns carrying copies would explode from the Court in a race across the plaza to be first to deliver it to their network's on-air reporter. You could tell which interns had limited themselves to debate society in high school and which had run track too.

Cable news might be the fastest way to get an answer, but for precision, we waited for the White House lawyers in the courtroom to interpret the white smoke for us. They'd pore over the decisions, then go outside and phone them into the White House counsel's office, who'd then email all of us to summarize the pages and pages of each decision.

The best mix of speed and accuracy, though, belonged to a website called SCOTUSblog. It placed a constitutional lawyer in the press room at the Supreme Court, who'd phone in the verdict to SCOTUSblog reporters, who'd share it in telegraphic live blurbs viewed by hundreds of thousands of people, each update accompanied by a "clickety-CLACK" sound.

Each alert was a pure jolt of adrenaline. Clickety-CLACK. On Monday morning, three cases were decided, one limiting law enforcement's ability to conduct warrantless searches of hotels and motels, one clarifying standards of excessive force claims by pretrial detainees against corrections officers, and one having something to do with royalties and Spider-Man. I kept listening for more. At each signal, my attention darted from television screen to computer monitor.

Clickety-CLACK.

We have the fourth and last opinion. *Horne v. Department of Agriculture.*

It was a case essentially striking down a federal agriculture program created during the Great Depression. Our lawyers had been right—our cases would wait. But for how long? Twenty-four hours? Four days?

Clickety-CLACK.

We are now waiting to hear . . . what the Marshal says about when the Court will next sit.

Agonizing minutes went by.

Clickety-CLACK.

Still waiting on the next opinion day.

I suddenly started to fret, against all advice, that the ACA II and marriage equality would come the next day and we'd have only hours to get the president's statements ready to go.

Clickety-CLACK.

Finally, official word that the Court will be in session to hand out opinions again on Thursday.

I exhaled. So we had until Thursday. I could practically hear Sarada doing the same from her office across the driveway.

Terry poked his head around the doorframe between our offices. He was always such a reassuring presence, a constant, an even keel when life got choppy.

"Hey, man. No big cases?"

"No big cases."

"You got time to look at these hostage policy remarks?"

"Of course."

"How was the wedding?" Terry had gotten to know the groom through their shared portfolio of foreign policy speechwriting.

"Really nice. God, it was good to get out of town for a couple days."

"I bet. You told me over the weekend that Obama wasn't going to give a eulogy. What happened?"

"I don't know."

"So he's really speaking in Charleston?"

"It feels like it's trending that way."

"I thought he didn't want to do these anymore."

"I don't think he does."

"I mean, what else is there to possibly say?"

"I don't know."

"Okay, good talk," he said. We both laughed.

"Sorry. I felt like I was off the hook for two blissful days, now I have to panic again."

"Have you talked to him yet?" He meant Obama.

I stood up to put on my coat. "I'm about to right now, as a matter of fact."

3

CHASE, WORKING WITH FERIAL, HAD DELIVERED AS PROMISED, securing me some time with Obama that morning. In a mix of fair play and self-interest, I'd emailed Josh Earnest, Jen Psaki, and Valerie Jarrett to invite them to join and get everybody on the same page—Josh and Jen for our message strategy, Valerie to take the spears in case Obama still didn't want to speak.

Ferial asked us to wait in the hallway until Obama had finished his presidential daily briefing. I took a high-backed chair and closed my eyes so that I wouldn't have to make small talk. A few minutes later, his team of national security briefers filed out, the looks on their faces matching the content of the document, a smorgasbord of whatever terrible threats lurked out there in the world. Rhodes brought up the rear.

"Hey, what are you in for?" he asked me.

I opened my eyes. "Charleston."

"Oh, Jesus. Good luck with that."

Obama's baritone rang from the Oval Office: "Come on in, people." I led the way, fluffed two pillows, placed them behind me, and plopped onto the couch opposite the Rose Garden, the fireplace to my left, the Resolute Desk to my right. Jen and Valerie took the couch opposite me, Jen closest to the fireplace, Valerie closest to the Resolute Desk and Obama. Josh stood behind them.

The president was standing behind his desk in shirtsleeves, organizing some papers. Were it winter, the sun would be streaming in at a low angle from behind him. But one day after the summer solstice, the sun was bathing from on high the collection of maples, elms, oaks, and magnolia trees that ringed and shaded the lush South Lawn. Two oil paintings of barns by Edward Hopper hung to his right, Childe Hassam's impressionist painting of American flags lining a rainy Fifth Avenue to his left.

"So, look," he said, "I've come around to the idea that I have to go to Reverend Pinckney's service in Charleston to pay my respects. I want to hug those families. But I don't really want to talk."

Valerie objected. "Mr. President, they'll expect you to speak."

Obama raised his arms in an exaggerated shrug. "I have nothing left to say!" He let them fall dramatically until his palms slapped his thighs. Then he looked at me. "Do you?"

I shook my head. "No, sir."

With his left hand, he pointed at me. "See? Cody doesn't know what to say either. We have run out of words." It was, I thought, the first time he'd used me as a human shield. I preferred it to being a punching bag. "I have done this too many times. And it doesn't have any impact. And I don't want to perpetrate this notion that, somehow, it's okay that this is normal."

If he was adamantly against speaking, though, he would have put his foot down by now. I knew him too well. I was starting to sense that this was one of Obama's setups where he already knew what was going to happen but feigned befuddlement to force his staff into making the argument for it.

Josh Earnest was too, well, earnest for games. He looked for the best in every situation.

"Mr. President," he said, "I think what the families of the victims did on Friday was pretty extraordinary. That's something you could talk about if you speak."

Obama had seen the video of the Charleston families while in California. His shoulders relaxed a bit and he walked around to the front of his desk, sat against it, and crossed his arms.

"Their actions shouldn't be a surprise," he said. "I've got some experience in the AME Church. Grace and forgiveness are tenets of the AME Church. But I found it very moving. People could learn something from that." Arms still crossed, he lifted his left forearm to emphasize a point. "But I don't think people need me to tell them that."

"You'll have to say something," Valerie protested again.

My cheeks were burning. I'd be the one up all night trying to figure out what to say.

But only one person got to vent in the Oval Office. And that was Obama.

"We don't need to have another 'conversation about race,'" he said, opening the steam valve a little. "I'm tired of hearing that. We've been having that conversation for four hundred years. We talk about race all the time. I gave a whole speech on it in Philadelphia, remember?"

He was referring to the "race speech" he delivered in March of 2008, honestly laying out America's long racial stalemate in a successful attempt to cool passions in the heat of the campaign.

"We don't need another race speech," he continued. "One thing we can do is take down that flag."

Jen Psaki seconded the idea. "You could explicitly call for the flag to come down."

Obama had said before that the Confederate flag belonged in a museum, not in public. And just two days earlier, he'd seconded Mitt Romney's similar stance. To say it again this week struck me as both a big deal and a half measure at once. It would be a big symbolic gesture for the South Carolina legislature to remove the battle flag from its grounds, removing some of its legitimacy and the pain it caused Americans who saw it every day, but it wouldn't solve the larger problem.

What's more, removing the flag from the grounds of the state capitol would require a two-thirds majority in both chambers of the South Carolina legislature, and they were nowhere near that number yet. Some members were dug in, either defending the flag or protesting that they'd already removed it from the capitol dome in 2000, placing it out front instead.

Newly surfaced photos over the weekend of Dylann Roof waving the Confederate flag softened those positions, or at least made them quieter. Obama taking a stand might harden them again, diminishing the chance for change.

"I think people know where I stand on that," Obama said. "But let's take on the notion of the flag as tradition. What history, exactly, are we celebrating here?"

He teed himself up to answer his own question. "The Confederacy formed with the explicit purpose of preserving slavery and all it entailed.

They felt so strongly about maintaining chattel slavery that they were willing to break up the Union and go to war. Hundreds of thousands of Americans died. And in the wake of that, during the process of Reconstruction, an entire apparatus of the Klan, Black Codes, sharecropping, Jim Crow, and redlining were explicitly designed to continue de facto subjugation as it existed previously to terrorize citizens.

"Is *that* the tradition that we're celebrating? What am I missing?"

They were rhetorical questions, but in my first year or two of working for him, I would have been nervous enough to try and fill the silence with an answer. *Don't look at me,* I instead thought to myself. *I don't want to do a eulogy either.*

I was enjoying the soliloquy, though. One of Obama's talents I always appreciated was his ability to summarize history pithily. And, as always, spinning him up was a great way to extract some ideas from his brain.

The release valve was fully opened now. "Tradition? They put the flag up at the state capitol in 1961! As a symbol of resistance to integration! It's not subtle. Black folks have to walk past it every day. How would a Jewish community feel if people hung a swastika somewhere? The flag isn't an embrace of history. That's a talking point. Come on, people."

I would have loved to use all that in a speech. Sensing that, Obama smirked at me. "Obviously, we shouldn't say that."

As he vented, I considered that the public debates around guns, race, even the Confederate flag had been unfolding in a more thoughtful and mature way than usual since Wednesday's massacre. There had been fewer Ted Cruzes grasping for relevancy or retweets. It was possible that Obama's initial statement about the shooting on Thursday, maybe even his speech about guns to the mayors in San Francisco on Friday, had helped set the national tone from the top, inspiring some empathy and reconciliation. It was also possible that the flag's defenders were quieter than usual simply because the terror attack was overtly carried out under their banner. The NRA was always quiet after a mass shooting, its social media account conveniently taking a sabbatical after each one.

But it was more likely that the goodwill, generosity, and grace the families of the victims showed with their act of forgiveness had rubbed off on everybody in a profound way. It felt as if we were all walking in a different direction than usual, as if their actions had bent history just a little bit, as if maybe they'd opened a brief window in time when we could all be a little better.

A window where maybe, as Obama had said in Selma three months earlier, the South could rise again—not by reasserting the past but by transcending it.

"It wouldn't hurt to make folks feel good about what those families did," Obama said. "To show that they ushered in the opposite of what the killer intended.

"If I'm going to do this," he continued, "that's what I want to talk about. The concept of grace."

It was clear now that I'd be writing the eulogy whether I wanted to or not. But I still had little to go on. What I needed out of this meeting was some sort of writing prompt, some lead to follow. I made a mental note to call Joshua DuBois and ask him to explain the concept of grace as the parishioners understood it.

"But let's use it as a challenge," Obama continued. "I don't want to congratulate ourselves too much when we as Americans just allow this shit to keep happening. Talk about guns. Talk about the flag. Talk about the way hundreds of years of racial subjugation and segregation still shape the present. But leave room for the possibility of progress. Leave room for grace."

Then he pointed at me. "Write it up. Pour a drink and let it rip. If you need some inspiration, read some James Baldwin. Then give it to me, and I'll work on it if the muse hits. All right?"

4

SOON AFTER HE MADE ME HIS CHIEF SPEECHWRITER, OBAMA offered some sound advice: "Read James Baldwin when you're stuck. Listen to John Coltrane when you're not."

Obama was my introduction to Coltrane. There was an effortless cool to his music that lent me the sense that I knew what I was doing, a secret language coming from his saxophone that entered my ears and exited my fingers, that made me type faster, that fueled a sense of flow.

Baldwin was harder. His writing was something you had to commit to. But his moral clarity and righteous anger cut through bullshit like a laser through butter. Baldwin was a reminder to write what was true.

The muse was a different story. I loathed the muse.

Obama first mentioned the muse in 2013, during a stretch in which he was slated to deliver speeches paying tribute to the 150th anniversary of the Gettysburg Address and the 50th anniversary of the March on Washington.

Publicly, he expressed humility. "Well, first of all, let's stipulate that my speech will not be as good," he laughed in response to a reporter's question. "You cannot win in that situation. Two of the greatest speeches ever given in the English language happen to fall this year, and I'm supposed to mark them in some way."

Seven days before Obama's speech paying tribute to the March on Washington, I brought Kyle O'Connor, our campaign intern in 2008 and by 2013 a senior speechwriter, with me to the Oval Office. I asked Obama if he'd given any thought to the remarks he was scheduled to give on the steps of the Lincoln Memorial, fifty years to the day that Martin Luther King Jr. delivered his "I Have a Dream" speech from the same spot.

"Look," he said, "I don't know what I want to say. Sometimes, the muse doesn't strike. And if that's the case, we'll just go with whatever you guys draft. The truth is, I don't want to be doing this. I'd rather be hanging out with my girls, or playing golf, or drinking a martini."

"And they say you're not American," I joked.

He let loose with a genuine laugh. But the joke was to cover for the frustration I couldn't let him see. It was our job to come up with something, I knew that—but I'd still hoped that the finest orator of our time, a self-professed better speechwriter than his speechwriters, would offer us a starting point. And while ultimately the muse did strike, and he did take a draft that we had labored over to a higher place, Kyle and I spent days in the Speechcave first, twisted into pretzels of self-loathing.

There was a gap between the public perception of my job and the hidden agony of it. Political junkies who'd consumed every episode of *The West Wing* presumed that being chief speechwriter for Barack Obama must be the coolest job in the world. Sometimes they were right! Most of the time, though, I was sitting alone at the computer, bereft of sunlight, freaking out about what to write, stewing in a toxic mix of pressure, stress, and self-doubt.

It was the best and worst job in the West Wing.

5

FIVE MINUTES AFTER OUR MEETING WITH OBAMA, AN EMAIL FROM Valerie underscored the worst aspects of the job.

"I know this is painful and you're on empty, but it is a moment POTUS cannot miss."

The reminder didn't help. But at that moment, things could have been worse still—I could have been Josh Earnest, who was about to begin his daily briefing to a press corps that was more stimulated than usual.

Three days earlier, at the start of his California trip, Obama sat down in the cluttered Los Angeles garage of an astute and acerbic comedian named Marc Maron to record an episode of *WTF,* one of the most listened-to podcasts in America.

The choice of interviewer was intentional, part of a strategy initiated by Dan Pfeiffer to bypass political reporters who covered politics like a game of who's up and who's down by going to the outlets most people watched and listened to. Whereas an actual political headline on Friday morning read CHARLESTON REMINDS "YES WE CAN" OBAMA OF HIS LIMITED POWER (which is not what

Charleston made Obama think about), Maron came across as a normal guy who'd ask questions in line with what most Americans would want to ask the president. He was also as charmingly nervous as any American who got to interview the president in their garage would be.

"This horrible thing happens Wednesday," Maron said as they were recording. "And you have these police actions in Baltimore and Ferguson. Coming from where you came from, and trying to define yourself in terms of the African American community and in terms of racial relations, where are we with that in terms of when you come in, in your mind?"

It was a lot of words to say "Make race make sense." But I'd heard clumsier ways of asking why, considering Obama's victories, we didn't live in a post-racial society yet.

Obama began with an on-brand answer. "I always tell young people in particular, 'Do not say that nothing has changed when it comes to race in America unless you've lived through being a Black man in the 1950s or '60s or '70s.' It is incontrovertible that race relations have improved significantly during my lifetime and yours, and that opportunities have opened up and that attitudes have changed. That is a fact. What is also true is that the legacy of slavery, Jim Crow, discrimination in almost every institution of our lives—that casts a long shadow and that's still part of our DNA that's passed on. We're not cured of it."

"Racism."

"Racism," Obama affirmed. "We are not cured of it."

"Clearly."

"And it's not just a matter of it not being polite to say 'nigger' in public."

I had been listening on speakerphone back at my desk in the White House, and the jolt of that word straightened me in my chair. I stared at my phone as if that would confirm what I'd heard.

"That's not the measure of whether racism still exists or not," Obama continued. "It's not just a matter of overt discrimination. Societies don't, overnight, completely erase everything that happened two hundred to three hundred years prior . . . Rather than just say that nothing has changed, we have to say, 'Wow, we've actually made significant progress over the last fifty years.' If we made as much progress over the next ten years as we have over the last fifty, things would be better. And that's within our grasp. It's available to us . . . But when it gets translated into politics it gets all confused. And trying to bridge that gap between I think the good impulses of the overwhelming majority of Americans and how our politics expresses itself continues to be the biggest challenge."

It was quintessential Obama, and emblematic of the rhetorical tightrope he continued to walk on race. Politicians said provocative things on race all the time. When Obama did, it was usually the most provocative thing of all: the truth. He was always careful with his words; if he said the one word you can't say, it was to shock people not only into listening but to think and engage before the national moment passed us by.

The podcast became available to the public on Monday morning. Within two days, it would be downloaded almost one million times. I saw that as nothing but good.

Political reporters, however, already annoyed that some comedian in his garage got the interview they wanted, were busy working overtime trying to create drama. As Josh called on them one by one from the podium in the Briefing Room, they asked more than a dozen variations of the same question for over an hour.

"Josh, given the reaction, does he in any way regret using it?"

"Josh, did the president intend to say what he did?"

"Josh, does the president condone the use of that word at home?"

"Josh, I want to follow up on something a lot of people have been talking about, and that's the use of the 'n-word.'"

Just watching it exhausted me. Once the briefing ended, I walked upstairs and into Josh's office down the hall from the Oval.

"Hey, I liked the part where they asked you about 'the n-word.'"

He laughed. "Jeez," he said. "That was a little much."

I'd long tried to get Josh to institute a new dunce cap rule: The most intentionally obtuse or performative question of the day gets you ejected from the Briefing Room for forty-eight hours. But he was someone who never held a grudge, always looking for the best in every situation.

"Hey, I really appreciated you including me in your discussion with POTUS earlier," Josh said. "It was very helpful prep for today's briefing and made my life easier, so thanks."

"I'm glad it made someone's life easier! I don't know what to do here. A eulogy like this can't be a half swing. That would be worse than saying nothing."

"I don't envy you. Guns, race, the flag, and you have to pay respect to the nine people who died too—this isn't an easy task. I really was struck by those families, though. They offered forgiveness, expecting nothing in return. That's the grace that we all seek from God. That's what Christ did. It's the whole 'Forgive them, Lord, for they know not what they do' thing."

Josh was a religious man. I rarely thought about faith while drafting speeches that weren't eulogies. He and Denis were often the ones who asked me to add some nod to people's faith in big speeches beyond the boilerplate "God Bless America" at the end.

"Anyway," he concluded, "I feel like I haven't been helpful here."

I was just about to tell him he'd been more helpful than Obama when a breathless Susannah poked her head through Josh's door. "Hey—the boss is looking for you."

"That's my cue," I said, following Susannah out the door. "Thanks, Josh."

"Hey, brother." Obama's feet were on the Resolute Desk as he swiped at something on his iPad. "Look, I realize I didn't give you much to go on. I just don't know what to say here. What you and I *want* to say is not the same thing as what we *can* say. That's why neither of us wants to do this."

"Sounds about right."

"Just do your best. Give me something when you can, and I'll play with it. And keep it short, and mostly focused on the reverend. I feel like I've mostly said my piece on guns and on race. I don't want to give a long speech there."

"Yes, sir."

A presidential eulogy was now a fait accompli. I emailed Kristen and asked if she'd walk with me to the Starbucks across the street from the White House. She met me out on the driveway, and we strolled through the big iron gate onto Pennsylvania Avenue.

"Well, it's happening. He's going to speak on Friday, even if he doesn't want to."

"Okay, first of all, you need to give the health care and marriage remarks to someone else."

"I'm almost done with the health care ones. I gave the marriage ones to Sarada."

"Good. Then you need to remember that you can do this. Did he give you any guidance?"

"Not really. I mean, this isn't 'just' a mass shooting; it's a mass shooting by a fucking white supremacist. I don't even know if it's possible for the first Black president to calm rather than inflame tensions. And even if it is, I don't think I can write something that gets him there."

"Ohh-kay," she said, shushing me. "Take a breath." She began to deliver her usual wise counsel and reassurance that goes deeper than a standard "You can do it." She reminded me of the times I'd had similar freak-outs before writing a speech, pulling them out of her memory like a perfectly organized filing cabinet. She told me to kick my bad habit of trying to please every individual audience and focus instead on what I'd want a future generation to hear Obama say about this moment. And, as someone who at times thought more highly of the American people than I did, she reminded me that most of the country would root for Obama to succeed in such a situation—which meant, by extension if not by name, they were rooting for me.

"Yeah, okay." I didn't have any counterargument. She was good.

"I'm proud of you. Remember that."

I considered "I'm proud of you" as flattery that too often sounded artificial, the Swarovski crystal of compliments. But from Kristen, it was always the real McCoy—a diamond. It mattered. I believed it. I believed her.

Then she stopped walking in the middle of Pennsylvania Avenue and threw her hands up, exasperated, even though I hadn't said anything. "And if *that* doesn't work, you should be proud of yourself. You're good at this job. Favs and Obama trained you well. And people trust you to get it right, *especially* the boss, or you wouldn't still be here. The only person who thinks you'll fail is you. So stop being so hard on yourself."

"Okay, okay." What I really wanted to do was hug her, but even though we were engaged to be married, she still felt uneasy about public displays of affection when colleagues could be anywhere. So I had some fun with her instead. I put my hand on her arm and asked intently, "Will you still love me if I fail?"

She groaned loudly and pushed me away. "Oh my gawwwwd, will you stahhhp already?" Her Staten Island accent only emerged when she was annoyed or when she was visiting Staten Island.

"Fine." I laughed. "I probably won't be home for dinner tonight."

"Good," she said. "Then I can get tacos just for me."

6

BY THE TIME I GOT BACK TO MY DESK, THE NEWS WAS OUT—THE press office had announced that Obama would travel to Charleston and deliver the eulogy. My inbox had filled with people piggybacking on the news. Reporters asked, "What's he going to say?" Staff who had no overlap between their jobs and the eulogy offered ideas and asked if they could be involved. Samantha Power chimed in with, "Wow. Can only imagine what you will do with this one."

The *New York Times* had already written up its story.

> The president's decision to travel to Charleston will place him in the role of national eulogist at the center of a national tragedy, much as he has done in other occasions such as after the massacre at a school in Newtown, Conn., in December 2012. This time it

comes freighted with the questions of race and hatred in a country that has elected an African American as president but still struggles with the legacy of division.

I sent that paragraph to Terry. Moments later, I heard him yell through the wall, "Oh, is that all?"

Sometimes, only speechwriters understood speechwriters. Vinay Reddy, Vice President Biden's kind, gentle, and talented chief speechwriter, a first-generation American, sent a note: "Always admire your heart and compassion. Thinking of you and the president as you find meaning for yet another tragedy. Good luck for Friday."

It really was the most honest, helpful message of all: *This shit's hard, good luck.*

I was about to turn off the television and get to work when I saw a gaggle of South Carolina politicians on the screen: Republican governor Nikki Haley and the state's two Republican U.S. senators—the only Black Republican member of the Senate, Tim Scott, and one of its most dedicated opportunists, Lindsey Graham—along with several others. I turned up the volume.

"This has been a very difficult time for our state," Governor Haley said. "Our state is grieving, but we are also coming together . . . It's time to move the flag from the capitol grounds."

Well, I'll be damned, I thought. Maybe the families really did start something.

The letters that the president had been receiving suggested the same. The director of presidential correspondence, Fiona Reeves, and her stellar team of staff and volunteers, sometimes thirty a day, had been setting aside a selection of emails coming in through the White House website.

A woman from San Antonio wrote:

I'm pretty sure you aren't the first President to use the 'n' word in the White house, sir, and I found your honesty refreshing. I hope you continue to be honest about your personal feelings/experiences. I wish I were a fly on the wall.

Another from Nashville added:

> I am a white southern woman in her mid-60s who grew up with overt racism. Now I see hidden or covert racism all around. White folks think by not using the N word they are not racist, white people think because they know black folks they are not racist. None of this means their racist feelings are gone or as you said 'cured.' Hidden racism thrives and your using the N word to some folks is unacceptable . . . but it is unacceptable to those who still harbor racist views . . . views hidden but not gone.

I forwarded that one to Josh.

And a remarkable letter came from Philadelphia:

> With your election . . . I could hope for progress, but what has actually happened has surpassed what I dared to hope. I'm a gay woman. I came out in Utah, in 1980. I didn't expect to see marriage as a possibility . . .

She also had metastatic cancer.

> I have Medicare now, but I know future Americans will have access to Obamacare . . . your hard slog with Congress transformed lives, and I'm grateful for the many who will benefit—and pray these gains won't be eroded. It's hard to express how profoundly these two signature gestures of yours have affected my life . . . Out here in America many are having some of the most searching conversations about racism that I have heard. It feels as though there is a moment now for us to move closer to a better place, despite or because of the wrenching deaths we've seen. For my part, as a gay woman who has seen more change than I could've hoped for, I will do what I can to challenge fear, hatred, and misinformation—in myself and others.

I marveled at what one letter could do for my spirits. A woman from Philadelphia had just convinced me that we could move closer to a better place—because she'd seen it in her own life. She'd lived it. And maybe that was all Obama had to do on Friday—remind people that something better was possible.

I turned off the television and started reading through Susannah's good research about the nine victims and their lives. She included a note:

> I know you can't read everything, so there's no more than two thirds of a page on each person. I know you are writing maybe one sentence at most, but there are two or three people where two or three details could work, and I wanted you to be able to pick.

I smiled. She was good.

7

PREPARING FOR A LATE NIGHT IN THE SPEECHCAVE, I ORDERED THE dinner of champions from the Navy Mess—chicken tenders and a large coffee—just before the takeout window closed at eight o'clock.

The Mess was half a flight of stairs down from my office, named for the facilities on bases or ships where members of the military could eat and hang out. Ours was operated by culinary specialists in the United States Navy who prepared three full menus a day, either to pick up from the wood-paneled antechamber, where you might make small talk with other staffers waiting for their food, or to sit and enjoy in the ornamental dining room with paintings of famous warships on its walls hidden behind the galley kitchen. (We paid for all our food; itemized bills arrived at the end of each month.) To be able to take your parents for a seated lunch in the Mess was a rite of passage, a way to say, "Look Ma, I made it."

Settling in with my chicken and caffeine, I turned on the television to watch the president speak at the Iftar dinner, the post-sundown meal with which Muslims end their daily fast during Ramadan. It was one of several religious dinners he hosted every year, from a Seder to Diwali to Christmas, signaling that all faiths were welcome in the White House, and in America.

As famished guests dug into their meal carefully curated by the White House chefs—vegetable salad with rosemary pita chips, lemon lamb, crushed peanut potatoes, French beans, chocolate flourless cake with cherry compote, yogurt sorbet, and chai tea—Obama approached the lectern.

> Tonight, our prayers remain with Charleston and Mother Emanuel church. As Americans, we insist that nobody should be targeted because of who they are, or what they look like, who they love, how they worship. We stand united against these hateful acts. These are the freedoms and the ideals and the values that we uphold. And it's more important than ever. Because around the world and here at home, there are those who seek to divide us by religion or race or sect.

After that ominous note, he shared a story as uplifting as the letter I'd read earlier.

> Here in America, many people personally don't know someone who is Muslim. They mostly hear about Muslims in the news—and that can obviously lead to a very distorted impression.
>
> We saw this play out recently at a mosque in Arizona. A group of protesters gathered outside with offensive signs against Islam and Muslims. And then the mosque's leaders invited them inside to share in the evening prayer. One demonstrator, who accepted the invitation, later described how the experience changed him; how he finally saw the Muslim American community for what it is: peaceful and welcoming.

That's what can happen when we stop yelling and start listening. That's why it's so important always to lift up the stories and voices of proud Americans who are contributing to our country every day.

By our seventh year in the White House, my team and I had worked hundreds if not thousands of happy endings into speeches, endings powered by some wonderful daily story that came to us from out there in any one of the "real Americas." I'd written and read so many that few of them moved me anymore. The tipping point on my emotions had moved so far down the spectrum that it required something truly extraordinary.

But Obama really did believe in the American people, and he thought it was important to share those stories whenever we could. And if those families in Charleston and that demonstrator in Arizona could show an open heart, maybe more Americans could too.

Susannah poked her head through the door. "Okay if I go home?"

"It's after nine o'clock! I insist you do. Thanks for everything today."

She beamed. "My pleasure!"

Two minutes later, as I heard her keys jingle and the door close behind her, a parting email from Susannah showed up in my inbox with the subject line "James Baldwin."

> There is never time in the future in which we will work out our salvation. The challenge is in the moment, the time is always now.

The next four days would be a minefield of unknowns—whether the tone the Charleston families had set would hold, where the debates over guns and the Confederate flag would go, which ways the Supreme Court would rule on health care and marriage equality. Four days that might determine whether or not our side in the clash of ideas would win out. It could end up the most consequential week of Obama's presidency—and I was staring at a blank page.

7

Day Seven

Tuesday, June 23, 2015

1

NOT YET SEVEN FORTY-FIVE IN THE MORNING, THE MERCURY WAS already pushing ninety on its way to ninety-seven when I parked my car on the driveway between the West Wing and the Executive Office Building. Washington summer was back with a vengeance. It was the time of year when I kept my suit jackets and ties in the office and didn't put them on until I had to.

I said good morning to the Secret Service agent on my way into the West Wing, then I saw Jen Psaki down the hall to my right, picking up her breakfast at the Navy Mess window. She was wearing a black dress that made her hair seem a more saturated shade of red than usual.

I walked over and down the six steps to pour a coffee. "How are you feeling?"

"I'm ready not to be pregnant anymore." She laughed, rubbing her belly. "How are *you* feeling?"

"I'm good. Thanks for helping with the incoming." I'd been forwarding Jen emails from a hungry press corps looking for any morsel about the speech, some asking for examples of times Obama had talked about race, others even asking if it was the most important speech of the presidency.

"I've been telling them off the record that this isn't a big moment," she said. "He's not going to make a big policy statement on guns or race, and what they should expect is a brief and personal set of remarks about the pastor. That sound right?"

"That's what we're going for. You know him, though—it might change the night before."

"Your fiancée helped us pull a bunch of passages from previous speeches where he talks about race that we'll give to reporters, everything from the statement he made last Thursday after the shooting to the speech he gave in Philadelphia in 2008."

"You mean . . . the speech everybody calls 'The *Race* Speech?'"

"That's the one."

"People in this town have the memory of fruit flies."

"We're also pulling together a list of all the states and cities that have acted on guns since the president's push in 2013."

"Oh, that's a great idea," I said. After the Newtown school shooting in December 2012, Obama had pushed not only for universal background checks before gun purchases, but also for a reinstatement of the ban on assault weapons, a ban on high-capacity magazines, and a ban on armor-piercing bullets beyond the military or law enforcement. He also called for resources to bolster school safety, mental health services, and more. The NRA blasted each proposal, calling instead to put armed officers in every school in America (which, conveniently, would sell more guns).

Obama knew the odds of his proposals making it through a Republican Senate were long, and he was clear in every speech he gave that change would happen only when we started electing enough people who'd be willing to do something about gun legislation.

But while Republicans had been a noisy failure by quashing any attempt at change from the Senate, state legislatures and mayors around the country had been quietly enacting tougher gun reforms. In the six months after Newtown, the states of Connecticut, New York, and Maryland all toughened their assault weapons bans and banned high-capacity magazines like the ones used in that massacre, and Colorado and Delaware passed universal background check laws.

It was worth reminding people that even if Republicans stymied progress in Washington, it was possible elsewhere.

In fact, beyond the gates of the White House, events of the week kept surprising, as if the political tide had gone out and everyone was trying to do the right thing for once before it came back in.

Senators Pat Toomey, a conservative Republican from Pennsylvania, and Joe Manchin, a conservative Democrat from West Virginia, were reviving their post-Newtown 2013 attempt at bipartisan gun reforms.

Walmart, Amazon, and Sears announced they were pulling all Confederate flag merchandise from their physical and digital shelves, and NASCAR put out a statement reminding Americans that it already had a policy prohibiting the banner in any official capacity.

Paul Thurmond, a Republican legislator in South Carolina and son of Strom Thurmond, a longtime South Carolina senator who once ran for president on a platform of segregation, bucked his own late father to denounce the Confederate flag, saying he'd vote to remove it from the statehouse grounds. "Our ancestors were literally fighting to keep human beings as slaves," he acknowledged, "and to continue the unimaginable acts that occur when someone is held against their will. I am not proud of this heritage."

They were welcome advances, but I didn't hold my breath for a full-fledged national reckoning. Politico, of course, covered Republicans calling for the flag to come down in a section of its morning tipsheet called "How It's Playing"—the outlet's daily reminder that doing the right thing doesn't matter; getting the best coverage does.

Jen climbed the stairs to her office, and I dropped my backpack in mine. Obama wasn't scheduled to say a word in public this Tuesday, and I was looking forward to a more or less quiet day to write—something that rarely happened. I needed to see a clear runway of at least an hour or two to feel like I could really get going on a big speech. It's just the way my brain worked.

That's not to say I wasn't a world-class procrastinator. I could waste a half hour spelunking in a YouTube black hole of movie trailers and

Russian car-crash videos with the best of them. If it was fifty-one minutes past the hour, I'd justify spending the next nine minutes scrolling through Twitter for things to read before *really* getting to work.

There was something almost subconscious about it—as if wasting time was actually a prudent way to create the pressure I needed to do my best work.

Just as I started browsing ESPN Chicago, Valerie poked her head around my doorway. That was unusual. I couldn't remember her ever coming to my office before.

"Good morning," she said.

"Hey," I said with a dash of affability. Even if she'd facilitated my own private misery for the week, I still liked her. I also respected the fact that she cared more about what Obama needed than she cared about being anyone's work bestie. She was savvy enough in this case to know what I was feeling, and skilled enough at diplomatic jujitsu to swing my momentum in a direction that delivered results for the president.

"Anything I can do to help? I know I'm the one who advocated for him to go and speak. I still think it's his only option, but I want you to know I'm not leaving you hanging. I'm happy to help however I can."

"I never thought that," I fibbed. "But I appreciate you saying that." That part was true.

"I think you can tell the truth," Valerie said. "Just do it in the context of our better angels."

Valerie's advice was both correct and obvious, and I thanked her. The right would pounce at any chance to accuse Obama of being divisive, because they knew his political goodwill with the American public was built on him being the opposite. If there was a model for the sweet spot, it would be the Selma speech. She asked if I wanted to walk with her to the 7:45 meeting in Denis's office, but I told her I was going to skip it and try to write.

She smiled and left, and Terry sidled from his office to mine. One of the perks of sitting in the lowest dungeon of them all was that he could eavesdrop on every conversation I had.

"Hey, man," he said with a broad grin and his sleeves rolled up. "Is it Lincolnesque yet?"

"Well, I stayed until midnight, and I've got about a page of loose thoughts to show for it, half of which is an unusable screed about the Confederate flag. You know, Gettysburg Address stuff."

"Seems ahead of schedule!" Obama hadn't given me a deadline beyond "when you can." For most speeches, receiving a draft the night before suited him fine. For speeches like Selma or Charleston, I'd aim for three nights before. I'd often miss.

Right now, we were three days out. I had seventy-two hours until the speech. I needed ninety-six.

"It would help a little if I knew which way these court cases were going to go," I said. "Imagine if he gives this eulogy the day the ACA gets gutted? It'll be covered like he's giving his own eulogy."

"I'd rather not," Terry replied. "But imagine if he gives this eulogy the day the ACA and marriage equality are *upheld*. You should write it as if that's what's going to happen no matter what. Make him confident in America and what we can do. Make it a rallying cry."

It was a good idea. I recalled the speech Obama delivered after losing the New Hampshire primary in early 2008. Favs had written it as a victory speech on the heels of Obama's massive victory in the Iowa caucus just days before. When it became clear that Hillary was going to eke out a win, he added one line congratulating her but left the rest of the speech intact. Had you tuned into the speech twenty seconds late, you'd have thought Obama won. It was hopeful, optimistic, forward looking, and ended on a "Yes We Can" riff that was made into a pop song and a rallying cry for the rest of the campaign.

Terry returned to his office, and I turned to my prewriting rituals.

Research was key to making a speech colorful and memorable, to making a good speech great. I had Susannah's research into the victims and their lives. To add something beyond Scripture, I'd also asked Sarada, a musician, for any suggestions from old Black spirituals, gospel hymns, or even some blues. She delivered, sending an emotional menu with several deep cuts from all three genres. Martin Luther King Jr.'s favorite tune, "Take My Hand, Precious Lord," was the only one with which I was familiar.

Beyond such requests, I tended to do my own research—and to do too much of it, compiling massive documents filled with interesting thoughts from stories I'd read and notes I'd emailed to myself from the shower, from my commute, from meetings. Now I rifled through the research document I'd been preparing for the eulogy, which had already ballooned to twenty somewhat organized pages. Unlike Obama, who preferred to make detailed outlines, I tended to work out the structure of a speech in my head. He could probably tell.

I also needed music. Coltrane didn't apply here, because I still wasn't sure what I was going to write, and he wasn't really my favorite anyway. What I listened to depended on whether I wanted lyrics. If I really had to think, lyrics got in the way. That's when film soundtracks worked well—orchestral super-heroics from *The Dark Knight* or *Man of Steel*, or Trent Reznor and Atticus Ross's moody ambient backdrop to *The Social Network*.

Dark and broody when stuck, soaring when not.

When my mental traffic jam cleared, and I had enough neurons to process someone else's words in my ear at the same time I was putting my own on the page, I wanted something that matched the mood of what I was writing: Bruce Springsteen for a gritty economic speech, a crash course from Kristen in Taylor Swift for an upbeat 2015 State of the Union Address.

The Boss offered moral clarity in some of his songs. Rap sometimes offered more. When it came to rap, though, I was a dilettante. My closest friend with an encyclopedic knowledge of rap was Dan Pfeiffer, who'd left the White House three months earlier. I texted him to ask what might help me find some moral courage with Charleston.

Right away, he suggested Kendrick Lamar's fearless opus "To Pimp a Butterfly," but also a specific song by Lupe Fiasco called "Jonylah Forever." The beat was mesmerizing, but the lyrics were what made it searingly topical.

It was a song about Jonylah Watkins, a six-month-old who was shot on the South Side of Chicago while in her father's arms and died after a day in the hospital. The song imagined a world where she took her first steps, spoke and read her first words, discovered that Chicago was bigger than the South Side and the world bigger still, became a doctor who turned down lucrative offers to set up in her old neighborhood instead—and bumped into an art teacher named Hadiya Pendleton. It painted a picture of a world where both of them had lived.

I listened to it three times. "Holy shit," I texted.

"Show people a better world," he wrote back. That was about as emotional as Dan got.

As I was about to start writing, there was a knock on the door to my office. Kristen tiptoed in, holding a coffee in one hand and pulling the door shut behind her with the other. She was wearing a sleeveless gray sheath dress, black belt, and black heels.

"You don't have to knock."

"I know, but what if you were in the middle of a sentence? Sometimes you're mean when you're in the middle of a sentence."

I had started a new document, relegating what I'd written the night before to a document titled "cutting room floor." I swiveled the monitor to show her a blank page with nothing more than a heading:

REMARKS OF PRESIDENT BARACK OBAMA
Charleston, South Carolina
June 26, 2015

"Oh no."

"Well, the good news is, I have now read everything there is to read, and I have nineteen pages of notes."

"Start writing! You can do it!"

"Okay."

She set the coffee on my desk. "That's for you."

"Thank you. I think I'm probably going to stay late tonight too."

"Okay, then I'll go to yoga and eat pasta and catch up on *The Bachelorette*."

"That's your perfect night."

"Yep! Might as well enjoy it now before we have to stay here all night fact-checking all your speeches."

"I'm sorry."

"I'm kidding. What's really bothering you? What's the holdup?"

I confessed that I was afraid that I wouldn't write a good speech when it mattered most.

"So, the usual," she said. I never revealed that fear to anybody else. But she'd heard it from me before, and every time a speech went well, she'd say, "See?"

"Yeah, but there's one thing more I keep thinking about. I've never had to worry about anything I'm writing about this week. I don't have to worry about being attacked because of the color of my skin. I don't have to see a symbol every day that's designed to remind me of my place. I don't have to worry about losing my health care. I don't have to worry that someone will tell you and me that we can't get married. If shit goes sideways this week, Obama has to show people he understands all that."

"When has that ever stopped you from writing before? You can't change a tire, but you can write a speech that brings autoworkers to their feet."

"I can change a ti—"

"You know what I mean! You can't be all those people, Cody, and you don't have to be. Aren't you the one always telling people that empathy is the most important quality in a speechwriter?"

Other than being able to string a sentence together, empathy *is* the most important quality in a speechwriter. The ability or at least the attempt to understand your audience, to walk in their shoes for a little while, even if empathy will never be a perfect match for experience.

"You're pushing something off that you don't want to do," Kristen added. "That's all it is. Take a quick walk. Clear your head. Find the silences!" She smiled at me. "Have you tried finding the silences?"

2

THE STATE OF THE UNION ADDRESS IS A SPEECH THAT EVERY speechwriter dreams of writing until they get to do it, a Frankenstein's Monster that requires stitching together forty or fifty or more different policy ideas into one coherent narrative.

By January 2015, I'd ruined three consecutive Christmases trying to do just that. But for the first time, I felt I finally had a draft worth showing Obama eight days before the speech—a new record! I included it in his evening briefing materials and expected to hear something the next morning. The morning came and went, and nothing.

Finally, a little after noon, Ferial called and asked me to come upstairs. When she did that, it wasn't so the president could give you a gold star and send you on your way. As I tossed on my jacket and trudged upstairs, I worried that I'd have to rework a seven-thousand-word speech.

The president wasn't in the Oval Office. "He's having lunch and wants you to join him," Ferial said. That was unusual. I crossed the empty Oval Office, mentally preparing myself for an all-night rewrite, thinking through all the meetings I'd have to convene to come up with new policies.

I entered the small hallway of his private sanctum, passing his bathroom on the right and his study stuffed with family photos and a computer on the left, and poked my head into the small dining room at the end of the hall where Obama was sitting alone at the head of a six-seat table under a brass chandelier. Across the table from me, Muhammad Ali's boxing gloves, signed for Obama, sat on a buffet table under *The Peacemakers,* a painting of Lincoln, Grant, General William T. Sherman, and Rear Admiral David D. Porter, who commanded Union fleets, strategizing at the end of the Civil War.

"Hey," he said, crunching on some baby carrots. "Sit down."

Now I truly felt screwed.

"So," he said, picking up his knife to cut a piece of chicken, "how you doing?"

"I'm fine, sir," I replied, screaming internally, *Oh my God, just tell me if the speech is okay!*

"Look, I think the speech is in the best shape one of these has ever been a week out." Everything in my body relaxed. "I actually think I could deliver this as is." I tensed up again. He never meant it. "But we have a week, so let's make it even better.

"Here's the thing. Everything is in here," he continued, tapping the draft State of the Union Address on the table with his right middle finger. "Every sentence says something. Every word means something." Raising his hand, palm down as if he were showing how tall you must be to ride this ride, he said, "The entire speech is up here at ten." He pushed his hand down. "I need some of it down here, at six, seven, eight. You following me?"

"Yeah. I mean, that's the thing about State of the Union Addresses—everything *is* in there."

He took a swig of unsweetened iced tea and sat forward. "Let me put it another way. You listen to Miles Davis?"

I worried this was a test to see if I'd followed John Coltrane down the rabbit hole. I said yes.

"You know what they say about Miles Davis?"

I did not.

"It's the notes you don't play. It's the silences. That's what made him so good. I need a speech with some pauses, and some quiet moments, because they say something too. You feel me?"

By that point, I did. I knew exactly what he was talking about. What brief pride I'd felt in a speech that was in the best shape it had ever been a week ahead of time was quickly replaced by regret—regret that I'd been so consumed with making sure *everything* was in there that it made him complain that everything was in there.

"Good," he finished. "Like I said, we're in great shape. I don't want you to do any work tonight. I want you to go home, pour yourself a drink, and listen to some Miles Davis. And tomorrow, take another swing at it."

He pointed his fork at me. "Find me some silences."

From then on, I thought about that all the time. Finding the silences. In a speech, in life, in the moments of mental stress and emotional dread when I didn't think I could meet the moment.

Take a breath. Pour a drink if you've got one. Focus on finding the silences.

Day Eight

Wednesday, June 24, 2015

1

SHORTLY AFTER EIGHT O'CLOCK ON WEDNESDAY MORNING, THE Confederate battle flag on the grounds of the Alabama state capitol building was quietly lowered and taken away, along with three other flags from the era. A reporter asked Governor Robert Bentley, a Republican, if he'd ordered them removed. He answered with a simple "Yes I did."

Everyone, it seemed, was making progress but me. I didn't find the silences after all; I had left the office around two thirty in the morning with only a roughly sketched page and a half of the eulogy that Obama had to deliver in just two days' time. It was barely good enough for an op-ed.

To make up for the late night, I slept through the morning meeting. As I pulled into a parking spot outside the West Wing shortly after nine o'clock, an email arrived from someone on Valerie's staff with a draft program for Reverend Pinckney's memorial service.

The program led with a touching message from his wife and wrenching messages from his young daughters about all that had been taken away, and all that Clem Pinckney had given and left behind. The rest of the service looked to be carefully curated with reflections, readings, songs, and hymns.

And then I saw something that almost made me paint the exterior wall of the West Wing with the large iced coffee I'd picked up on the way to work.

WORDS FOR THE HEALING OF THE NATION—
BY BARACK OBAMA

I set the coffee on the roof of my car and forwarded the email to Valerie, Jen Psaki, and Josh Earnest, pecking on the screen as angrily as one's thumbs can peck. "So much for expectations setting."

Valerie replied quickly: "I'll ask them to change it to say 'Eulogy.'"

"If they don't," I pecked back, "I'm going to call the United Nations and make them title Rhodes's next UN General Assembly speech '*World Peace by Barack Obama.*'"

My coffee left behind a ring of condensation that I watched dribble down to the door seam, a moment of zen before walking into the ground level of the West Wing and trying to reach the safety of the Speechcave without catching anyone's attention.

"Hey, Cody!" For the second day in a row, Jen was the first person I saw at work. Everyone should be so lucky. Even nine months pregnant, she was a bolt of cheer. She'd just picked up her breakfast and was carefully climbing the steps from the Navy Mess to the ground-floor lobby.

"We missed you this morning," she said.

"I bet. Why, is something going on?"

"Well . . ." she said, in a way that suggested there was something I didn't know about.

"Oh my God."

"No, no, it's fine," Jen jumped in. "Let's go to your office." We marched with our coffees past Pete Souza's photography office on the left, Ben Rhodes's office on the right, then turned into the outer chamber of the Speechcave complex, said hello to an eager Susannah at her desk, and continued into my office, where I motioned for

Jen to take any seat she liked while I dropped my backpack on the floor and docked my laptop.

"We discussed the location and timing of all the president's statements this week," Jen said, taking the chair in front of my desk.

"What do you mean? Supreme Court rules, he goes out. No?" I'd just assumed the cases get decided at ten, Obama speaks around eleven.

"Well, yeah, but here's what we're thinking." She opened the lid to her fruit. "On the ACA, if we win, he speaks in the Rose Garden."

"Great."

"But if it's on Friday," she said, "when he has to travel to Charleston, then we'll only have about five minutes before he boards Marine One."

"Great, fine, short remarks are good."

"And if we lose," she said, stabbing a strawberry with her fork for emphasis, "he speaks in the Briefing Room."

"The place where hope goes to die. Sounds right," I replied.

"Marriage." She munched on her strawberry. "If we win, he speaks in the Rose Garden. If we lose, he doesn't."

All of this sounded reasonable. Then something hit me. "What if they're both the same day?" Jen was already nodding. "If we win both, great," I continued. "If we lose both, I'll just go out and light myself on fire on the North Lawn."

"I'd join you, but, you know," she said, pointing to her belly.

Behind Jen, Sarada had walked into my office with a puzzled look on her face. "Do I even want to know?"

I was just beginning to process that there could be an even more complex scenario. "If we win one and lose one on the same day," I continued, "that's a real weird set of remarks." How had that not occurred to me before? "How many more statements can we write?"

Sarada chimed in. "Funny you should ask. The lawyers emailed me this morning that there are actually several different possibilities on marriage."

"No, that's for the ACA case," I said.

"Yeah. And marriage."

"What?"

"Four scenarios," Sarada started to explain. "One is your epic win: SCOTUS requires states to recognize marriages licensed by other states *and* recognizes the right to marry for everyone. Two is still a win: SCOTUS requires every state to recognize marriages licensed by other states but doesn't rule on the right to marry for everyone."

"What does that mean?"

"It means that states won't be *required* to offer marriage licenses," Jen offered. "The ones that want to, can. The ones that don't want to, don't have to. But they *will* have to recognize marriages from other states." She tossed a grape into her mouth.

"Three," Sarada continued, "is very similar: SCOTUS requires states to recognize marriages licensed by other states but rules *against* a constitutional right to marry for everyone. So in two and three, states would have to recognize marriages performed in other states, but there would *not* be a national requirement that every state has to offer marriage licenses."

The speechwriter's portion of my brain was processing midstream, focusing on what any one of these scenarios would mean for the culture wars. The first was a clear win for equal rights. The second and third, a mix. But all three would be seen by opponents as "forcing" people in states that had decided against marriage equality to recognize same-sex marriage, fanning resentment and fueling the "states' rights" argument that Confederate dead-enders had hung on to for 150 years as their rationale for a failed rebellion.

I sighed. "I think I know what four is."

"Four: We lose on both counts. The states that have marriage equality can keep it, but other states don't have to recognize those marriages—and opponents of marriage equality in the states that *have* marriage equality have new ammunition to fight to get it overturned."

Jen turned from Sarada to look at me. "The question is whether we treat the first three options as wins. I think he speaks on one and two. Three is more challenging. And if it's the fourth scenario, and we lose on both counts, I don't think he has to go out. What do you guys think?"

"I don't know," I said. "I agree he shouldn't own a bad decision like it's a blow to him when it's a blow to everyone. But it *is* a blow to everyone. I think he should say something if we lose."

"There's an argument for speaking on three too," Sarada said. The lawyers had laid out the difference between ruling and not ruling on marriage equality as small, she said, but significant. Ruling against a constitutional right to marry for everyone would wipe out marriage in the states where it was decided by judges—but then those states could pass a law affirming same-sex marriage.

"In that case," I said, "it would be useful for Obama to go out and fire people up for a fight."

"I like that," Jen said.

"So, doing some quick math," I said, while pretending to count on my fingers, "if both decisions come on the same day, with four possibilities on marriage and three for the ACA—win, lose, and something in between—that's a lot of different possibilities for one statement."

Jen pushed herself up and parted with her usual mirth. "Okay, well, I'll leave you guys to that!"

"Hey thanks, Jen, it's been a blast."

Sarada stayed behind. "Did you have a chance to look at tonight's Pride reception remarks?"

I had. Sarada's draft was mostly good and hit all the right notes, but parts of it didn't sound like Sarada or Obama. I could tell that Valerie's team in the Office of Public Engagement had inserted themselves, larding up the remarks with an activist wish list. Parts of it read like a Fox News tirade against a strawman caricature of a liberal designed to terrify voters in the run-up to an election year.

Obama was already the first president to come out for marriage equality, to mention gay Americans in an inaugural address, even to say the word "transgender"—symbolic gestures to be sure, but they were backed up by his administration's accomplishments thus far.

The draft as it was, though, would make Obama lead with his chin in a way that might doom the policies the activists wanted.

The administration was already working, for example, to end the military's ban on openly transgender service members. There was a successful blueprint here: In December 2010, when Obama's signature repealed Don't Ask, Don't Tell, the military's ban on openly gay service members, the president and his LGBTQ liaisons had endured two years of relentless criticism from advocates who demanded he overturn the policy right away—even though it could have alienated the military. But by taking the time to work with each branch of the military, change took hold with a higher likelihood of success—and by late 2011, Obama had troops under his command who could serve openly because of it.

Many of Valerie's staff, then and now, had been activists before joining the White House, and they still thought of themselves that way. And for them to take slings and arrows from their fellow activists, who now saw them as standing in the way of change, must have been painful.

"Tone it down," I told Sarada anyway. "It's more effective when he gives people the space to come around than when it sounds like he's forcing change on them."

I wasn't proud of myself for telling Sarada to tone it down. It marked the latest scar in a conflict between activists and speechwriters. Activists rightly want everything right away. They wouldn't be good activists if they didn't. And America was on the cusp of two milestone victories because of the tireless, decades-long work of activists.

But speechwriters have to remain true to the things our boss believes and says consistently, and to take into account political capital and realities like whether the votes are there. I had to make sure that some brief remarks at an evening reception with canapes didn't blow up the president's agenda. How to run a complicated policy process with the military wasn't up to me. What was up to me was making sure staffers didn't try to use a speech to circumvent that complicated policy process without coordinating with the president or the Pentagon first.

There was no handed-down briefing book to help the first Black president find the sweet spot between ineffective prodding and forcing change that half the country wasn't ready for. Activists would rage at this approach, dismissing "incrementalism" as cowardice. I empathized with that point of view. Slow progress could wear you down almost as much as no progress at all. I just disagreed with it. If someone was convinced that cutting the uninsured rate in half was a failure because we couldn't cut it to zero immediately, I couldn't help them. Progress, however unfinished, was still better than huffing the self-satisfied fumes of purity.

Progress for the gay rights community was by no means finished, but they had run up a string of victories with Obama. He'd spent a lot of political capital to help. One thing that sometimes irked Obama about gay advocacy groups was that, even though they were more successful and better funded than many other activist communities, they didn't always stand up for other marginalized communities when they needed allies.

I suggested that Sarada add something about that into the remarks. "Include a broader call for the LGBTQ community to engage in the fight for equal rights for everybody. Disability rights. Immigrant rights. Voting rights. Whatever. We can't just play for our own teams here. A vibrant democracy depends on it. He doesn't have to chastise the audience, but I want him to see some light bulbs going off over their heads."

"You got it," she replied. "One other thing: I wonder if, in the SCOTUS remarks, he should acknowledge that it's sensitive and there are Americans who aren't on board yet, but he hopes they'll come around. I get that this is a big victory lap. But he's the president of everybody, and he's come around from his own old positions."

I told her I thought it was a great idea. And it happened to be true.

2

IN 2004, SAME-SEX MARRIAGE WAS SOMETHING REPUBLICANS RAN against and Democrats ran from. Just a decade later, same-sex marriage was something that Democrats, and even a few Republicans, ran on. When Obama took office in 2009, it was legal in two states. By 2015, it was legal in thirty-seven plus D.C. It was an extraordinary evolution in a relatively short time.

Same-sex marriage was an evolution for Obama too. In 2008, when running for president, he'd endorsed civil unions and all the benefits that come with them but said that he was not in favor of gay marriage. To support civil unions was the unsatisfying but safe option, one that would prevent the need to fight what was still framed as a religious battle. I always thought—but never wanted to ask and find out—that he'd compromised his personal views for political expediency. For someone proud that he'd generally said what he thought, I assumed that it gnawed at him. I know Obama's decision disheartened, even disillusioned, his LGBTQ staffers.

Once in office, though, he enacted important policies that moved the ball forward on LGBTQ issues. The biggest successes were ending Don't Ask, Don't Tell and seizing the opportunity to stop defending the Defense of Marriage Act in federal court. Along with those came a volley of progress: signing a hate-crimes bill into law, lifting a Reagan-era ban on allowing foreigners with HIV to travel to the United States, adding LGBTQ protections to the Violence Against Women Act, prohibiting federal contractors from discriminating on the basis of sexual orientation or gender identity, requiring hospitals receiving federal funding to treat LGBTQ patients the same as everyone else. Finally, thanks to the ACA, insurance companies could no longer deny coverage to LGBTQ Americans.

When it came to marriage equality, the most important dynamic in Obama's mind was the generational tide. His own daughters and their friends had grown up in a country where differences in sexual orientation weren't a big deal. It didn't make sense to them that same-sex couples would be treated differently. People coming out—to their parents, to their friends—had changed perspectives on a massive scale. It's one reason the country moved so far so fast—people listened to their kids. I couldn't imagine that coming out to one's parents would ever be easy—but I had to believe that most parents found it harder to remain homophobic after their child said *"This is who I am."*

Prejudice and bigotry would never fully vanish. But when Obama framed his shift in a 2010 interview by saying "attitudes evolve, including mine," lots of people could sympathize.

And there was a marriage equality strategy in the works. Not around *whether* Obama would come out in support of marriage equality but *when*—before or after the 2012 reelection campaign.

But then Vice President Joe Biden blew up that strategy like the Kool-Aid Man smashing through a wall. In May of 2012, a week or two after Obama officially kicked off the reelection campaign, Biden was asked about Obama's "evolution." And in his typically blunt and honest fashion, he became the highest-ranking politician in America—and probably the most prominent Catholic—to endorse marriage equality.

"I am absolutely comfortable," he told host David Gregory on NBC's *Meet the Press,* "with the fact that men marrying men, women marrying women, and heterosexual men and women marrying another are entitled to the same exact rights, all the civil rights, all the civil liberties. And quite frankly, I don't see much of a distinction beyond that."

Biden being Biden, he then told a story about kids he met who loved their two dads. And Washington being Washington, political reporters went into a frenzy as to whether there was some rift between Obama and Biden, or whether Biden's getting out in front of the president was a calculated trial balloon on behalf of the president.

The truth is, it was just Joe. He'd just been with a group of LGBTQ supporters a couple of weeks before the interview, and they'd asked him about marriage. He realized he couldn't be coy about it anymore. And that was contagious.

Obama decided, *Fuck it. Let's do it.* Three days later, on May 9, 2012, he walked through the outer Oval to the Cabinet Room for a live interview with Robin Roberts, one of the anchors of ABC's *Good Morning America,* a Black woman who had grown up in the deep South and spent most of her career as a stellar sportscaster. She wasn't publicly out when she and Obama sat down, though she had been in a committed relationship with a woman for several years.

She didn't waste time. Her first question was: "So, Mr. President, are you still opposed to same-sex marriage?"

There was a drawback to Obama's disdain for sound bites: It led to long answers.

> I've stood on the side of broader equality for the LGBT community. And I had hesitated on gay marriage in part because I thought civil unions would be sufficient. That [it] was something that would give people hospital visitation rights and other elements that we take for granted. And I was sensitive to the fact that—for a lot of people, you know, the word "marriage" was something that evokes very powerful traditions, religious beliefs, and so forth.
>
> But I have to tell you that, over the course of several years, as I talk to friends and family and neighbors, when I think about members of my own staff who are incredibly committed, in monogamous relationships, same-sex relationships, who are raising kids together, when I think about those soldiers or airmen or Marines or sailors who are out there fighting on my behalf, and yet feel constrained, even now that Don't Ask, Don't Tell is gone, because they're not able to commit themselves in a marriage.
>
> At a certain point, I've just concluded that for me personally, it is important for me to go ahead and affirm that I think same-sex couples should be able to get married.

For all the strategizing and handwringing among the communications team, there wasn't any blowback. The country was already ahead of Obama: Americans' support for same-sex marriage surpassed opposition in 2011 and steadily climbed from there. Anyone who'd be angry with Obama for his stance probably wasn't going to vote to reelect him anyway.

In 2013, he became the first president to call for marriage equality in an inaugural address:

> We the People declare today that the most evident of truths—that all of us are created equal—is the star that guides us still; just as it guided our forebears through Seneca Falls, and Selma, and Stonewall; just as it guided all those men and women, sung and unsung, who left footprints along this great Mall, to hear a preacher say that we cannot walk alone; to hear a King proclaim that our individual freedom is inextricably bound to the freedom of every soul on Earth.
>
> It is now our generation's task to carry on what those pioneers began . . . Our journey is not complete until our gay brothers and sisters are treated like anyone else under the law—for if we are truly created equal, then surely the love we commit to one another must be equal as well.

And in the 2015 State of the Union Address, he endorsed marriage equality as a civil right, saying, "I've seen something like gay marriage go from a wedge issue used to drive us apart to a story of freedom across our country, a civil right now legal in states that seven in ten Americans call home."

A president calling same-sex marriage a civil right and an equal right on the two grandest stages in politics was a big deal—even if a slim majority of the country already agreed.

Too often in politics, telling the truth that most people already know passes for radical.

3

BY NOON ON WEDNESDAY, WITH LITTLE MORE PROGRESS TO SHOW, I switched from the eulogy to the ACA remarks. Working on another speech felt less like procrastination when it was something I had to do anyway.

Before leaving the office for home at two thirty that morning, I'd sent three versions of the ACA remarks—win, lose, and something in between—to a small group of staff for their approval.

One of the lawyers wrote back around six that morning: "It's been pretty grim preparing for the decision . . . but your victory speech just brought tears to my eyes. Win or lose, thank you for that."

A note like that was always welcome, especially after receiving comments from the policy wonks and fact-checkers.

When drafting a policy speech, we often sat down with brilliant, bookish experts from the National Economic Council, Domestic Policy Council, or any of the cabinet agencies to absorb their encyclopedic knowledge of the given policy. When we returned to our computers, though, our task as speechwriters was to translate that policy into something simple, memorable, and sticky enough for an audience to consume and remember. The press office would make sure that all the numbers and nuances were in a fact sheet that was sent to reporters the morning of the speech to help them write their stories, and those fact sheets were then sent to the wider world as soon as the president started speaking.

The wonks might object that we'd "dumbed down" the policy they'd worked so hard on. I sympathized. But I still instructed my team of speechwriters to distill a policy down to the way they'd describe it to a friend at a bar: in colloquial English.

The battles with the fact-checkers, though—those were slugfests.

Fact-checkers had a different target than the policy nerds. They didn't care about the speechwriters getting it right as much as they cared about Obama not being perceived as getting it wrong. It was their job to make sure the speech was bulletproof, that nothing could be construed as a lie, an inconsistency, or just plain inaccurate.

I sympathized with that too—it's important! The problem, though, is that absolute factual accuracy can turn a speech into unintelligible mush. A speech can still be factually honest by deploying simile, metaphor, and rounding rather than absolute, soulless precision.

One of the journalistic fact-checking operations judged political statements on a spectrum of verdicts from "True" all the way to "Pants on Fire." I often joked with Kristen that "Mostly True" was my wheelhouse. She never laughed.

When a first draft was finished, we'd send it to the fact-checkers. Kristen and her team would return every draft highlighted with errors and riddled with footnotes and sources that we speechwriters hadn't supplied. It was impressive. But even though they made it clear that it was their job to overanalyze Obama's words, to give us zero wiggle room for nonfactual exaggeration, we took it personally every time. I spoiled the first half of Kristen's twenty-eighth birthday—a Saturday—with my objections over her rigorous fact-checks to the climate change–focused college commencement address that Obama was delivering that afternoon. (Fortunately, we weren't living together yet, so we could take a few hours to cool off before her birthday dinner.)

I was feistier than usual today because I was mad at myself about my lack of progress on the eulogy, annoyed that the day was already full of interruption, and prickly that, after seven years in the White House, I was preconditioned to anticipate the policy and fact-checking quibbles, so I'd already written around them—which nobody even seemed to appreciate.

One passage, for example, touting the successes of the Affordable Care Act, seemed simple enough:

> This law has helped hold the growth of health care prices to its lowest level in fifty years. If your family gets your insurance through your job, you're paying about $1,800 less per year on average than you would be if we hadn't done anything.

I didn't love either sentence in terms of sheer prose, and the first statement wasn't true in absolute terms—health care is subject to inflation like everything else. But it was true that costs were rising at the lowest rate in fifty years. "Has helped" was a way to avoid getting dinged for claiming that the law was entirely responsible. (Technically, we couldn't say health care "costs" but "prices," a distinction I never really cared about, but I gave up after the full weight of the Council of Economic Advisors came down on me.) Nor was it true for every single American—that's why the second sentence specified employer-based coverage and included the words "on average."

Like I said, unintelligible mush.

And when the wonks and fact-checkers made it even mushier, that's when I could turn into a real jerk.

Matt Fiedler, the chief economist on the president's Council of Economic Advisors, was the resident health care economist supergenius and looked the part: tall and lanky, with a shyly crooked smile and hair that fell across his forehead as if he'd been too busy reading to bother sweeping it back. He'd asked me to change "than you would be if we hadn't done anything" at the end of the second sentence to "than you would be if trends over the decade before this law had continued."

I was incredulous. "That says the same thing as 'if we hadn't done anything'!"

"The $1800 reflects the broader slowdown in employer premium growth, which in turn reflects factors other than the law itself."

"Look, man, an asteroid could have changed the trends in health care costs too! But my job is to make Obama sound like a human. We have fact sheets for the rest." I won the fight.

Then Kristen tapped in.

On the draft I sent around in case of a loss on the ACA, I had Obama rip Republicans a new one for finally achieving their long-sought goal after fifty repeal votes, legal briefs, and lawsuits aimed at tossing millions off their health insurance.

> While I'm sure some Republicans think that tearing down this law is good politics that plays well with the base, I'd point out that about two thirds of the people who will be immediately harmed by this decision live in Republican congressional districts. And robbing people of their health care isn't good politics. Jacking up costs on working folks isn't good politics. Making a mother on chemotherapy worry that she'll have to stop her treatment early isn't good politics. Going back to days when families had to choose between paying for health insurance and feeding their kids isn't what this country is about.

Kristen had assumed I was writing about a real person rather than a hypothetical one. She'd found a story about a woman who'd been in the news recently and fit the profile. "One flag to be aware of," she noted, was that the woman had posted on Facebook criticizing the ACA while noting that she was grateful it had helped her.

I wrote back, "Hey, look, she's happy that she got affordable health care. That's great. The bad news is, I have no idea who this woman is."

"Cool," Kristen wrote back. "Glad we wasted our time on that."

From my standpoint, everything about the day felt like wasted time. Edits, interruptions, emails—there was no undisturbed stretch of time when I could think and write. My patience with everyone and everything was wearing thin, making me gruffer and meaner than usual.

That afternoon, the Senate renewed what was known as trade promotion authority (TPA), which gave Obama more power to negotiate trade agreements on his own, something you couldn't pay me enough to care about. I despised writing about trade.

Around two o'clock, I ran into economics advisor Brian Deese while grabbing a sandwich from the Navy Mess window. "Hey man," he said, "it's probably our biggest legislative victory of the year. Any other week, this would be the biggest news."

"Sure." I laughed. "Too bad that Obamacare, marriage equality, and the Confederate flag coming down across the South rained on your parade."

Of all the president's economic advisors, Brian had the most political sense, and while he was happy about the win, he also knew it wasn't something that Obama needed to comment on that week. There was a reason it was a bipartisan piece of legislation—Republicans liked trade more than Democrats did, and they were better at demagoguing it in the run-up to an election year. Republicans voted for trade agreements, then blamed them on Democrats. Most Americans loosely grasped the concept that trade is why televisions are cheap, but they knew damn well it was why the manufacturing base in their hometown had been hollowed out.

One minute later, carrying my turkey on rye from the Mess window, I saw the president's top trade advisor, Mike Froman, walking out of the dining room with two well-heeled types. A former Citigroup executive who did not share Deese's political finesse, Froman was the only person who would barge through my closed door during State of the Union time demanding to see if I'd put his issue in the speech.

He rubbed his hands together and asked with a big grin, "Any chance you can work TPA into some of the president's remarks this week?"

I kept walking. "Nope," I shouted over my shoulder.

4

KRISTEN AND I NEVER WENT TO BED ANGRY ABOUT A FACT-CHECK battle. From her office across West Executive Avenue, she called my desk phone shortly after five o'clock.

"Are you watching this?"

"Watching what?"

"The Pride reception remarks."

I turned on the television and flipped to the internal White House channel. The president had barely begun his remarks in the East Room of the Residence.

"Okay, you know what, no, no, no, no, no, no, no. No, no, no, no, no."

My heart leaped to my throat—did he not have the speech in front of him? Did Sarada not send it? Did Brian not print it? Was it the wrong speech? It was like living my nightmares.

"Listen, you're in my house," Obama said as the crowd cheered. I could not for the life of me figure out what the hell was going on.

Kristen caught me up. "It's a heckler."

"Oh, come on," I replied. "About what?" She didn't know. It was hard to hear the heckler without a microphone, and the camera remained on Obama, so we couldn't figure out who the heckler was or what they wanted. I was pissed.

Obama could handle a heckler, but, like he said, it shouldn't happen in his own house. "You're not going to get a good response from me by interrupting me like this," he said.

The rest of the crowd started chanting "Obama! Obama! Obama!" to drown out the heckler. What a mess.

"Why isn't someone leading them out?" Kristen asked over the phone.

Obama was wondering the same thing. "All right, can we have this person removed, please? Come on. I'm just going to wait until we get this done." He looked like an exasperated schoolteacher. Vice President Biden was at his side, glaring like a chained attack dog at the heckler in the back of the room.

Finally, the heckler was removed, and Obama continued. "Okay, where was I? So as a general rule, I am just fine with a few hecklers, but not when I'm up in my own house. You know what I mean?" The crowd was laughing and applauding throughout this improvised comedy bit. "You know, my attitude is, if you're eating the hors d'oeuvres . . . You know what I'm saying?"

Biden leaned in and slapped Obama on the back. "I do."

Obama laughed. "Okay. And drinking the booze . . . Anyway, where was I?"

A guest in the crowd yelled, "We love you!"

"I love you back. Anyway, so the civil rights of LGBT Americans. This is an issue whose time has come."

We later found out that the heckler was an undocumented transgender woman who'd planned the interruption with a simultaneous press release about deportations. One could forgive her for not partaking in the champagne. To be transgender was to be an often-overlooked part of the LGBTQ community, not to mention the country—and to be undocumented was to be often unwelcome in the country entirely. Obama had taken actions to lift the shadow of deportation from hundreds of thousands of undocumented young people (known as Dreamers), along with certain undocumented parents, and he wanted a pathway to citizenship for the 11 million or so undocumented—but without action from Congress, it wasn't going to happen. Heckling him, rather than hectoring the Republicans actually standing in the way of reform, wouldn't change that.

"Those of us who know freedom and opportunity, thanks to the toil and blood of those who came before us—we have an extra responsibility to extend freedom and opportunity to other people who are still marginalized and still facing injustice," Obama continued. "Working families who aren't getting paid a living wage. Women who aren't getting paid equally for their efforts. Immigrants who deserve to have a pathway to be able to get right with the law. Anybody who is treated differently because of the color of their skin or the nature of their faith. Anybody whose right to vote is threatened."

He leaned in for the finish, and I wondered if the possibility of a Supreme Court ruling the next morning was in the back of his mind. "But if the people in this room and our friends and allies across the country have proven anything, it's that even in the toughest of circumstances, against the greatest possible odds, in America, change is possible. It's in our hands. Together, I know we'll get there. Look how far we've already come."

The response was rapturous. "The transsexuals love you," yelled a guest.

"Well, that's the kind of heckling I can always accept." Obama laughed.

I piled on. "Hey, I love you," I told Kristen, who had stayed on the line so we could watch together. "Sorry about before."

"Me too," she replied. Once the White House stenographers had finished transcribing the president's remarks as he delivered them and circulated the transcript, Kristen emailed me a line from the early minutes:

> THE PRESIDENT: Okay, you know what -- no, no, no, no, no, no, no. No, no, no, no, no.

"This is you to our fact-checks."

"That's you to our good speeches!"

"Someone should make it into an autotune song immediately."

And we were a happy couple again.

On the periphery of my vision, I saw Sarada's head poke through my door. "Hey, I've got the title for his memoir. 'Don't Drink My Booze and Heckle Me: The Story of an Unlikely President.'"

I laughed. "Hey, great job. Those remarks were excellent."

"Thanks. You good?"

"It's been a long day of interruptions and I'm finally about to start working on the eulogy again."

"Can I help?"

"No, I just need to tune everything out and actually finish a draft tonight, however long it takes."

"Good luck. I'll be online tonight if you need me."

The entrance to my office was like a conveyor belt. Shortly after Sarada left, a smiling Valerie walked into my office holding some papers and dropped them on my desk. It was a revised copy of the program for the memorial service. I flipped to the back.

EULOGY: PRESIDENT BARACK OBAMA

"Well, that's better. Now I just have to make sure he has one."

She turned to leave. "You'll get it done. You always do."

Susannah, sensing the mood, ran in on her tiptoes. "Hi, I assume you're going to stay late in this tiny box of interruptions." She was speaking even more quickly than usual, presumably because she was nervous that I was close to snapping and would throw her out. "I am very happy to stay late just in case the opportunity arises to be helpful, or just to keep you company beyond the mice in the ceiling. But I also recognize you might want to be alone with your own thoughts. But I also just wanted to check."

I laughed. "Thank you. That's very nice of you to offer. I appreciate all your help so far." She beamed. "I'll email you if I need anything else. Have a good night."

The scene was approaching parody as Terry emerged from his office with his briefcase. "Are you telling me you're not done yet?"

I knew he was kidding, but I groaned anyway. "Today was not supposed to be like this. I'm still on page two, and I'm already tired. I keep getting tripped up on structure and keep rearranging what I've got."

"Just like you did with Selma." His smile turned serious. "You kept rewriting and rearranging, and you produced amazing stuff. I bet it's better than you think. Maybe the best structure is the simplest: the tribute to the reverend, the meaning of this moment, the lessons we take from it as a country."

"Easier said than done. Time is my enemy and my friend at this point, if that makes any sense. I don't have enough, which is bad; but that's forcing me into some panic writing, which is good."

"Time's the worst. Holler if I can help!" He left for dinner with his wife and kids and shut the door behind him.

I was finally alone. Over the next forty-eight hours, Obama would speak on the fate of marriage equality and the Affordable Care Act, and deliver a eulogy to a national audience. The outcome of the cases wasn't in our control. The eulogy was entirely in our hands. Everybody assumed I was locked away in my office making magic. And I was terrified that I was going to let them down.

Day Nine

Thursday, June 25, 2015

1

A TWENTY-MINUTE SPEECH ISN'T LONG ON PAPER. ABOUT TWO thousand words. About five hundred words per page. Four pages.

When you *have* to, when there's been a disaster or an attack and the president needs to say something as soon as possible, you'd be surprised how quickly you can bang out a page.

But when you've got *time*—when you're overthinking a speech, intimidated by it, aware everybody wants to see it, your elbows are on your desk and you're breathing through your hands while you stare at it—an empty page feels like an eternity. Four pages an infinite void.

Staring into that void, I reminded myself that I knew how to do this, that there was a structure to follow and that I already had pieces written. I knew to begin with something from Scripture. But it had to be something powerfully relevant; there could be no faking it at a reverend's memorial. I knew to have the president speak to the front row first, to the bereaved who'd lost the most—Reverend Pinckney's widow and his children. Then to those in the next rows, who felt their own loss—Pinckney's friends, his congregation, his community, his constituents, the people who knew him personally. And only then to the world beyond the pews, to the battery of unblinking lenses that would be broadcasting live on every channel and to all posterity that might someday read these blank pages begging to be filled.

Using Susannah's research, I had already put words down in an attempt to sum up Clem Pinckney's life. I knew this couldn't be mere biography, not a Wikipedia page. I had to find a way for the president to show what made him unique, to tell listeners why he mattered, to try and make sense of a cruel and violent end. Then, if I could, I would try to bring people back to the moment by making them laugh. Clem Pinckney's life wasn't sad. A eulogy shouldn't be either.

Finally, I would have to turn those small truths into the big bang—as Terry put it, the meaning of this moment, the lessons we should take from it as a country—in order to draw an elegant conclusion from the reverend's existence that challenged everyone, now that this man of worth was gone, to fill the void by expanding our own moral imaginations, by rediscovering our obligations to ourselves and to each other.

And that's where, at one o'clock in the morning, my pages were still blank.

I cracked my fingers and quickly cycled through the five stages of speechwriting neurosis.

> Denial. *It's only four pages! And there's a formula to it! Just write something down, revise it a bit, and give it to the boss—if he changes it, no big deal. Been there, done that. This is easy, you'll be done in two hours.*
>
> Anger. *How did you let three full days go by with nothing to show for it? Why did you waste so much time preparing nineteen pages of notes? Nineteen pages for a four-page speech! What the fuck is wrong with you?*
>
> Bargaining. *Maybe someone else wants to do this. Litt said he wanted to do it. I wonder if he's still awake.*
>
> Depression. *I am fucked. I can't do this. He's going to be so pissed. Everyone's finally going to figure out that I'm a fraud.*
>
> Acceptance: *Okay, it's probably time to get to work.*

I added page numbers to the document and saved it as a new version. Feeling like I'd accomplished something without even adding a word, I rewarded myself by pulling a cigarette from my desk drawer and standing up with a stretch to go walk outside.

The West Wing is a strange place after the witching hour. You'd expect a stillness to settle over the building. But the hum of a minifridge and computer equipment, unnoticed during the day, become impossible to ignore. Mice scurry through the jungle of wiring in the ceiling above, the scrabbling of their feet betraying their precise location. The muffled whir of a vacuum ebbs and flows through the closed doors to the hallway, reminding you that you're not alone.

The president's staff may be gone, but there's a support crew on duty, a different one than in the daytime. A new custodian comes in to empty the trash and jumps at the sight of you, then vanishes without showing you photos of her kids like Lawanda and Terri do at lunchtime. Equally startled is the unfamiliar officer who enters to collect "burn bags" of classified documents. He asks for your badge as proof that you're allowed to be there. Strange faces from the Situation Room's night watch sidle up next to you in the bathroom, wondering just who the heck *you* are. New Secret Service agents stare at you as you walk by. "Just going to have a smoke," you say, as if it makes you any less suspicious.

Then to walk out the double doors, to be surprised by the darkness after leaving an office where the light never changes, to breathe fresh air for the first time in hours and bathe in the silence of downtown Washington—it felt like freedom, even if I knew a dozen hidden eyes were trained on me as soon as I stepped outside.

Leaving the compound was too time consuming, but there was a concealed smoking area under one of the paved courtyards of the Eisenhower Executive Office Building, just down a flight of metal stairs that were death traps in the winter and through a narrow corridor lined with pipes and used as access for the hulking structure's mechanical equipment.

I justified the pilgrimage to light up as giving myself a change of scenery, a quick rewiring of the brain, even though a smoke-free walk would probably accomplish the same without the health risks. I enjoyed these smoking runs most on frigid nights during the State of the Union process, when I'd purposely go out in shirtsleeves to scare off sleepiness, shivering and taking a long, slow pull of poison cut with polar air. Sometimes inspiration didn't strike, and I'd return to my desk with nothing to show for it but stinking clothes. But sometimes it did—a new line would unspool in my head, a new argument would reveal itself, the structure I'd been searching for would emerge from a fog. I'd quickly email such revelations to myself before I lost them again.

Some of my greatest hits came from that smokers' pit.

That wasn't the case that very early morning. The only emails I sent myself on that break read "SHORT SHORT SHORT" and "stop rewriting the same shit"; one offered a weak structure for the second half of the eulogy: "grace, reconciliation/change, flag, racism, guns, call to action, ending???"

Things weren't going well, and the eulogy was now technically tomorrow.

The first two pages felt fine. The Scripture had been easy enough. I'd considered a slate of suggestions that Joshua DuBois had emailed and gone with something from the Book of Hebrews:

> They were still living by faith when they died. They did not receive the things promised; they only saw them and welcomed them from a distance, admitting that they were foreigners and strangers on Earth.

The first sentence struck me as literally true. The second, I thought, applied to both the Reverend and the Representative Pinckney—a man of the cloth and a man of democracy, someone who put his faith into action both for our individual and our collective salvation, someone who once described his calling as "not just within the walls of the congregation, but . . . the life and community in which our congregation resides."

For the summary of his life, I'd been struck earlier in the week by the way a friend of Reverend Pinckney had described him. That when he entered the room, it was like the future arrived. It was both an extraordinary thing to say about somebody and a way to drive home the depth of his loss. I'd written it down immediately, knowing right away that it belonged in the eulogy.

To illustrate that Pinckney came from a family of preachers, I alluded to more Scripture, from Proverbs, and suggested that he had lived by their teaching. I deployed some alliteration to highlight his shockingly young ascent—to the pulpit by thirteen, a pastor by eighteen, a public servant by twenty-three—and another allusion to Scripture to defend that fast rise:

> Don't let anyone look down on you because you are young, but set an example for the believers in speech, in conduct, in love, in faith, and in purity.

I described the way he approached his career in the state legislature, with a collegial, collaborative, empathetic manner not unlike that of the man who would eulogize him. I capped this off with something Reverend Pinckney once said, another sentence I knew belonged in the eulogy from the first time I saw it:

> Across the South, we have a deep appreciation of history—we haven't always had a deep appreciation of each other's histories.

The transition to the world beyond the pews was blunt and unsubtle, but a suitable placeholder for now:

> What a life he lived. What an example he set. What a model for how to conduct ourselves.

Expanding the sermon, I added what I'd learned—from Joshua DuBois, from the president, and from a lot of reading—about how the Black church had been a haven throughout history for African

Americans to call their own, and how often it had been attacked for that very reason. I added a line about the killer's foul motivation but kept the emphasis on the families of the victims, the grace they showed in parrying that attack, with praise for how the church, Charleston, and the country had conducted itself all week. These were all important points leading up to something, even if I hadn't figured out what.

Grace was what Obama wanted to talk about. It would be the opening to the eulogy's big bang. Joshua DuBois had described the concept to me over the phone as "the act of extending unmerited love, favor, and goodwill to someone else." My first attempt to get words on a page was to use a longer rumination that he had offered via email: a delineation of the quiet grace that sets a louder example than any shout of hatred, the active grace that announces, in AME tradition every Sunday, that "the doors of the church are open," and the amazing grace that can drive hatred from our own hearts and heal the hearts of others. The grace we're shown even when we haven't earned it. The grace we *can* earn, even cultivate, by making the effort to see ourselves in each other, something that stirs souls into the most unexpected of mercies, like whites and Blacks, Republicans and Democrats, coming together on a mission to remove the Confederate flag, a searing reminder of systematic oppression, violence, and degradation over generations, from our public places.

It still felt like I was building a bridge as I was walking across it, unable to see safe anchor on the other side. I had my structure, but there was too much to cover, a confluence of too many strands in our society to braid into it. Effortlessly accessible guns. The easy self-radicalization of enraged white supremacists. Injustice rooted throughout our institutions such that we couldn't look at this massacre in isolation—not after Trayvon Martin, not after Freddie Gray and Baltimore, not after Michael Brown in Ferguson and the slew of constitutional rights violations uncovered under the stone of its police department. People in power too timid to seize the solutions that were right there for the taking. And an angry subset of Americans who didn't want them to.

It was too much. I went out into the night to have another cigarette.

I emailed myself from the pit: "symbolic vs. substantial reconciliation." Back in the Speechcave, I wrote a passage about how, while removing the Confederate flag from the grounds of the state capitol would be a quick solution, no act alone, no matter how positive, would absolve us of our collective responsibility for what happened in Charleston unless we prevented it from happening again. I was channeling my own anger from past eulogies that were followed by too little action on guns. Reconciliation at the expense of lasting change, lasting justice—that isn't reconciliation at all. But I was also mindful to write about the flag in a way that wouldn't earn me a do-over from Obama. To hell with the flag and what it stood for—but a more graceful note from him, I knew, would go a longer way in the city where the first shots of the Civil War were fired.

Then again, I thought, *if I'm too soft, he might tear this page up and call me a Confederate sympathizer, so just keep going.*

I wrote about gun violence, about the absurdity of some unwritten rule that says it's impolite to politicize these catastrophes, when it's merely admitting reality, as uncomfortable as it may be. That avoiding discussion of the ideology that leads to such violence, and the easy access to weapons that make such violence possible on a massive scale—those are political choices too. That suggesting we do nothing in the face of such horror robs us of our own agency.

And surely, if Reverend Pinckney could partner with other legislators to move the ball forward, if he could seek that deeper appreciation of each other's histories, then we could do the same. We could see that to be Black in America often means being looked at with suspicion or not at all; we could imagine the shame a Black father feels when he has to sit his son down and tell him there's a certain way he has to carry himself in public; we could understand the lump a white mother feels in her throat when she has to tell her daughter, who's barely old enough to understand, what to do if a gunman invades her school.

To forgive, I wrote, was the families' right. But to change is our responsibility. I added the James Baldwin quote that Susannah had sent me four days earlier, on Monday: "There is never time in the future in which we will work out our salvation. The challenge is in the moment, the time is always now." That, in turn, inspired a riff: There is no more time for cruelty. There is no more time for greed or shortsighted self-interest. There is no more time to fight each other. We do not have enough days together. The time is always now.

And I ended the draft eulogy with a prayer that Reverend Pinckney used to offer:

> We thank you, God, for all who come seeking to expand their horizons, and seeking to learn more about what our country's made of and what makes us who we are. We pray for their safe return as they go back home. We pray that our time spent here today will be seen as an act of love as well as an act of righteous indignation in the face of injustice.

I saved drafts at one, three, and five o'clock. It got better each time, but I knew it was still just . . . fine. Full of platitudes. Fine for someone else. Not for Obama. "This is well written," he might say, "but . . ."

It felt like my muscles weren't working, like my body wasn't mine. The fear of the half swing—the fear of failing him—was the only reason I was still awake.

I needed coffee. But it was 5:45, and the Mess didn't open until 6:00. So I went for another cigarette to pass the time. It was light outside. Birds were chirping. It was always jarring to leave my windowless office to discover that night had fallen without my knowledge; it was even weirder now to see that day had broken before I had even slept.

2

DOWN IN THE PIT, I TRIED TO TRICK MY MIND INTO ACCEPTING that it was Thursday now. The morning meeting in Denis's office started in an hour and a half. The Supreme Court might rule on either or both big cases two and a half hours after that. Obama could ask for the eulogy at any time. I had to be ready for all of it.

At 0600, the men and women of the United States Navy set out the coffee urn. It was as good as Reveille. I filled my mug, nodding at staffers arriving for the day, none of whom noticed I was wearing the same clothes I had the morning before.

When I returned to my desk, Kristen had emailed, saying she'd just woken up on the couch where she'd fallen asleep waiting for me to come home. "Are you okay?"

"I am a wreck."

"I was hoping you'd come home at some point. I bought you dark chocolate." I loved dark chocolate. "Did you sleep?"

"No. My brain is at like 15 percent."

"Go take a shower in the gym. I'll bring you clean clothes."

I loved her.

I took a shower and, unwilling to answer questions about the speech drafts, skipped the 7:45 meeting again, positive I'd fall asleep in it. Instead, I kept revising the speech from start to finish, polishing lines and buffing paragraphs but failing to come up with any new ideas for the second half. I kept my door closed, my final-days-of-the-State-of-the-Union move, my passive-aggressive way of telling everybody "I'm working on it."

Susannah, who had full access privileges, sang "Good morning" as she proactively brought me another coffee around eight o'clock. It was a thoughtful gesture. She was rooting for me. It made me feel guilty. So I took care not to ruin her idealism by devolving into a feral animal with no people skills and, instead, made a big deal of lowering my shoulders and sighing a heartfelt "Thank you" rather than grunting one.

Minutes later, I nodded to Terry as he crept through my office as quietly as possible without asking how the speech was going. We knew better than to interrupt one another while typing. That too made me feel bad. He more than anybody else had rescued my drafts before. And he as much as anybody other than Kristen had listened to me complain and let me bounce ideas off him all week.

"It's not great, Terry," I offered as acknowledgment.

He froze halfway through his door and craned his head back through the doorway to look at me. "Hey, man. Can I help?"

"Not yet, but thanks." Time always sped up as I was writing. Hours could go by before I realized it. That morning, I forgot to worry about what it would mean if 20 million Americans lost their health care because we lost our biggest achievement. I forgot to worry about what it would mean if gay Americans—our own friends and colleagues—were deemed second-class citizens.

I even forgot to turn on the television at ten o'clock.

I found out at 10:09 A.M., when an email arrived from Sarada with the subject line "fuck yeah." A whoop echoed from the hallway. A muffled "Yes!" issued from Terry's office. I turned on the television. It *looked* like the Supreme Court had ruled for us on Obamacare!

Unwilling to trust the TV drama, I pulled up SCOTUSblog, scrolling furiously for the latest.

Clickety-CLACK.

> 10:08 AM Healthcare!
>
> 10:08 AM Decision of the Fourth Circuit is affirmed in *King v. Burwell*. 6-3.

The 6-3 decision made it a bigger victory than the 5-4 victory in 2012.

> 10:09 AM Chief Justice writes for the Court.

Not only did the chief justice "save" Obamacare a second time, he wrote the opinion: "Congress passed the Affordable Care Act to improve health insurance markets, not to destroy them."

> 10:09 AM Holding: Subsidies are available.

10:09 AM This means that individuals who get their health insurance through an exchange established by the federal government will be eligible for tax subsidies.

The Court, or at least two thirds of it, had seen through the bullshit lawsuit to what the law intended: that the ACA's subsidies could go to Americans who needed them, wherever they lived, including in the thirty-four states where Republicans refused to set up insurance exchanges.

Clickety-CLACK.

10:10 AM Administration wins, to put it another way.

Clickety-CLACK.

10:10 AM Short story is a victory for the ACA and the Obama Administration.

Loved it. What about marriage?

Clickety-CLACK.

10:11 AM This was the last opinion of the day, so we will have to wait for tomorrow for the remaining five decisions, including SSM.

Same-sex marriage—and the eulogy—would have to wait. The boss couldn't. I pulled up the Epic Win version of the ACA remarks to take a final read-through just as Kristie Canegallo emailed almost a hundred staffers about the decision.

Kristie was my age, but she'd reached the White House in a very different way—a stint at the Pentagon, postings in Afghanistan and Iraq, and an appointment to the National Security Council that began in the final year of the Bush administration and ultimately brought her under Denis's wing. In 2014, he promoted her to deputy chief of staff for policy implementation, a role that required her to keep dozens of plates spinning at once—including the ACA.

We had an easy camaraderie and possessed a shared mantra, even if I sometimes violated its second directive in a taxing week like this one: Work hard and don't be an asshole.

"Early read is we won 6-3," Kristie wrote. "We have NOT read the decision yet. Issue no comment from the WH. Will email next steps shortly."

I replied to all immediately. I couldn't help it.

"But I can light the drafts of the 'defeat' remarks on fire, right?"

I walked around my desk and into Terry's office to celebrate and tell him about what I had and hadn't accomplished during the all-nighter. He again offered to look over and edit the eulogy if I wanted him to. While I was in there, I missed Kristie's reply, just to me: "Lawyers are reading now but we are about to tell P if you want to join."

As soon as I saw her email, I took the stairs two at a time to find Kristie, Denis, and Neil Eggleston, the top White House lawyer, just exiting the Oval. They'd interrupted the president's daily briefing to give Obama the news.

"It's a clear win for us," Kristie said, with a smile so broad it scrunched her eyes. "Epic win statement is a go."

"Congratulations, buster," Denis said, biting his lower lip while punching me on the shoulder. I hadn't done anything to sway the Supreme Court; he was almost certainly doing that to everybody. "We're having a small senior advisors huddle in my office at eleven, okay?"

I winced. "Do you need me? If people start weighing in on Obama's statement more than a day after I circulated it, I might fall apart."

"Well, don't do that," Denis replied.

"The statement is excellent," Kristie said. "I'll tell people to back off."

As they peeled away, the national security briefers filed out of the Oval. "Fuck yeah," Ben Rhodes said with a fist pound. "Obama actually did a little dance. You look like hell. Want to go have a cigarette?"

I did, but I needed to see if Obama had edited the remarks he would deliver within the hour. I entered the outer Oval just as Ferial hung up her phone after connecting Obama to the solicitor general, Don Verrilli, so that the president could congratulate him on back-to-back victories, in 2012 and 2015, defending the ACA before the Supreme Court.

Ferial handed me a folder with her trademark smile, the kind you can't fake. "He made a few edits to the victory version. He didn't edit the other versions."

"I knew it," I said. Just like in 2012, he'd been confident all along that we would prevail. He hadn't even looked at the defeat versions. It wasn't his style. That was glass he wouldn't break.

"He did write something on the defeat one, though," she said.

"What?" Confused, I flipped open the folder.

Across the top, he'd written in large handwriting, "Didn't need this, brother!" He also signed it for posterity. I laughed at that. But what a keepsake. "That was nice of him."

"Oh, and he hasn't asked about the eulogy yet."

"Thank God." I'd kept blowing through self-imposed deadlines and the man kept showing me grace, even though we'd be leaving for Charleston in about twenty-five hours.

I had thirty minutes to make Obama's edits to the victory speech and run them by the fact-checkers.

"Hey guys," I emailed Kristen and Matt Fiedler, the health care economist brainiac. "He added that the uninsured rate in America is the lowest since we began to keep records. That's true, right?"

"Totally," wrote Matt.

One of the other fact-checkers on Kristen's team, Bart Jackson, sent an email beginning with another passage:

> "For all the misinformation campaigns and doomsday predictions; for all the talk of death panels and job destruction; for all the repeal attempts—this law is helping tens of millions of Americans. As many have told me poignantly, it has changed their lives for the better. And it's going to keep doing just that."

Bart added, "Just wanted to say that while it's true there are still no 'death panels,' that line killed me."

I appreciated that. For one day, the policy wonks, fact-checkers, and speechwriters were all getting along.

I sent the final speech to a hundred or so people, including the advance team that printed the remarks and the military communications team that loaded them into the teleprompter, with my customary sign-off, "This is final," and sat back in my chair and exhaled. One down.

I took a quick glance at Twitter, actually looking forward to it for once.

Right off the bat, I saw a reporter tweet a nerdy joke that Republican budget cuts had eliminated money for droppable mics, creating a real challenge for Obama's speechwriters. Favs, from his new home in California, tweeted at him that Obama did still have his own brass band. I laughed in my office, alone, wishing a bunch of the people who'd left were still around to celebrate with.

Just then, Favs forwarded an email he'd received from a CNN producer to me, Ben Rhodes, Dan Pfeiffer, and former roommate and NSC spokesperson Tommy Vietor.

"Cody, don't read this until the speech is done or your head will explode," Favs wrote.

I didn't have the willpower to ignore a tease like that. I kept reading.

> Hi Jon! How are you? I'd love to see if you might be available for an interview TONIGHT as we discuss an idea: Obama's defining moment—won the battle for healthcare—and now tomorrow he comes here to South Carolina and talks about race—can he make changes on that too—one major issue down, another to go.
>
> Can the first Black president solve race? What will be his legacy?

Cable news had too many hours to fill.

I traveled with Obama often, but I rarely watched him deliver speeches in person when he delivered them from the White House. I had gone to the East Room when he delivered remarks the night the House of Representatives passed the ACA, and for his statement after the Supreme Court upheld it in 2012. I figured I'd go to this one too and celebrate a three-peat of sorts.

It was a gorgeous morning in the Rose Garden. Skies were gray, but it somehow felt sunny, with the air at eighty degrees and the humidity low, our bodies casting faint shadows on the ground. The rosebushes were in full June bloom. I walked down the Colonnade just after eleven thirty, content to watch from the far end behind staff who'd gotten there early.

Obama emerged from the Oval Office with Vice President Biden, a Cheshire cat grin on his face, at his side. I leaned against a column and enjoyed the moment.

"Today," Obama said, "after more than fifty votes in Congress to repeal or weaken this law, after a presidential election based in part on preserving or repealing this law, after multiple challenges to this law before the Supreme Court—the Affordable Care Act is here to stay."

I'd tried to root the ending of the remarks in what I hoped was shaping up to be the larger arc of the week.

"That's when America soars. When we look out for one another. When we take care of each other. When we root for one another's success. When we strive to do better and to *be* better than the generation that came before us and try to build something better for generations to come."

Obama made one final edit in real time, adlibbing a line to the end of the speech: "This was a good day for America. Let's get back to work."

Biden cracked to Obama, with an even bigger grin than the one he bore walking out, "This is a bigger deal."

His comment harkened back to five years earlier, the day Obama signed the Affordable Care Act into law. That morning, in the East Room, Vice President Biden had introduced the president. As Obama and Biden hugged, Biden said, "We did it, buddy." Obama smiled. As the crowd whooped, Biden leaned around to Obama's left ear, away from the audience, and said, "This is a biiiig fuckin' deal." The microphone picked it up, and Obama pursed his lips, as if to express disappointment with the VP's choice of words. I never understood why. Behind closed doors, Obama cursed all the time. And it *was* a big fuckin' deal! The phrase made it onto T-shirts in time for the reelection campaign.

I appreciated the vice president's commitment to the bit: He'd waited five years for the right moment to unleash the sequel! But once again, Obama didn't smile—he just clapped Biden on the back, and they walked back into the Oval Office together.

Get back to work, huh? I thought. *Some of us haven't stopped.* I left everyone to celebrate while I slipped back downstairs to my office—but not before taking a photo for posterity of the "Didn't need this, brother!" speech draft with the event in the Rose Garden as background.

At my desk, I saw that Kristen had sent me an email with the subject line "Spotted!" A reporter had tweeted, "Lots of WH staffers on hand to see POTUS ACA remarks, inc speechwriter Cody Keenan, who is working w O on SC eulogy."

"Fact-check: half true!" I wrote back. "I haven't given it to Obama yet, so it's hard to say we're working together."

"How are you," Kristen asked. "Can I help?"

"Usually, my problem is letting the perfect be the enemy of the good," I replied. "But I'm not even sure if this is good."

"Send it to him! He can work on it."

"He's not free until five thirty." It wasn't even noon. "So I might as well work on it until then."

But then Ferial's name lit up on my desk phone. "Scratch that, Kristen—I'll call you back."

Ferial's cheerful voice chirped in my ear. "Hi, can you come up?" She always asked it the same way. It was never really a question. So much for having until five thirty.

"How's it going, brother," Obama boomed, his feet up on his desk, face buried behind his iPad. "I haven't seen anything yet, so I'm just making sure you're okay."

"Sorry, sir. It's getting there. Good shit on health care."

Obama pursed his lips and cocked his head around the iPad as if to say *"Bitch, please."* "There was never any question we were going to win this one."

Tell that to your staff, I thought. Collectively, we'd spent thousands of hours preparing for every outcome.

"It feels good, though," he said, cracking a huge smile. "Those fuckers."

It was a relief to see him loose. *Jesus,* I thought. *Imagine how this conversation would go if we'd lost.*

"What are you stuck on?" he asked. "I just want to make sure I don't get jammed tonight."

It was a fair concern. For a speech that everyone seemed to be amped up about, I should have gotten him something on Tuesday or Wednesday. I told him where I was struggling. He set the iPad on the desk and wrapped his hands behind his head.

"Well," he said, "here's what I think you say," and he proceeded to dictate something pretty close to what I already had.

Son of a bitch, I thought, *Maybe I got it right after all!* I told him we were in good shape, then, and he'd have something before he went home.

I felt lighter than I had in days. Everyone seemed to be feeling the same. Walking out of the Oval, I saw that the television in the outer Oval was tuned to Josh's daily press briefing, taking place just thirty feet away. He was cracking jokes in the style of Obama's most recent White House Correspondents' Dinner comedy bit, where we'd used "bucket" as shorthand for "fuck it."

Obama had joked that night, just two months earlier, "I'm determined to make the most of every moment I have left. After the midterm elections, my advisors asked me, 'Mr. President, do you have a bucket list?' And I said, 'Well, I have something that *rhymes* with bucket list.' Take action on immigration? Bucket. Let's go for it. New climate regulations? Bucket! It's the right thing to do . . . Anyway, being president is never easy. I still have to fix a broken immigration system, issue veto threats, negotiate with Iran—all while finding the time to pray five times a day."

On the television, a reporter asked Josh, "Do you think we're going to see more bucket list–type policy and verbiage use?"

"Yes," Josh said with a smile, "I think you will."

Grinning at the screen, and with a fresh spritz of courage after Obama's tentative imprimatur, I decided it was time to share the draft with Terry for his thoughts and with Kristen's team so they could start fact-checking.

"Here's what I've got," I wrote them. "I'm going to give it to POTUS before he goes home. My gut is he keeps pages 1–2 and changes pages 3–4. But Team Research: pages 1–2 are the facty ones."

Terry suggested some helpful edits, saying he thought the eulogy was sound. I plugged them into the draft, played with it for four hours that passed like mere minutes, gave it a quick scan for embarrassing grammar issues, left in the embarrassing prose, printed it out, and delivered it to the outer Oval at five thirty where Ferial shot me a sympathetic look.

Obama was standing by her desk flipping through a copy of *Sports Illustrated*. "How do you feel about it?"

I told him that, at minimum, it was ready for him to look at.

"All right, I'll take a look," he said. I couldn't see myself in the mirror, but I assumed I looked more haggard than usual. He looked me up and down and added, "You go get some sleep."

That was the plan, but first I swung by Denis's office down the hall from the Oval to see if he had any beer. He did, in a big bucket of ice on his patio through tall French doors, and the health care team was enjoying it in an echo of Obama's 2010 Truman Balcony party. I grabbed a bottle, wiped it off, and clinked it with a couple of the wonks who couldn't stop grinning.

"Hey, buster," Denis said again, almost too vigorously clinking his beer to my own. "You hanging in there?" I updated him on the speech and told him it was in Obama's hands now.

"Impossible task, even for you," he replied. "Don't sweat this." On the day the ACA survived the Supreme Court, nothing could bring Denis down.

"There was only one impossible speech," I deflected. "When the Packers won the Super Bowl. I gave it to Tyler and took the afternoon off."

He laughed. He was a Vikings fan, I was a Bears fan, but when it came to the Green Bay Packers, we were united in our animus.

I made the rounds, hugging and congratulating the policy wonks, lawyers, and comms staff who'd lived and breathed health care—some, like Jeanne Lambrew, who'd done it for decades. Her dad was a doctor, her mom a nurse. She'd inherited the healing gene, but her fear of needles and blood pushed her to study public health policy. She then toiled in the legislative and fiscal trenches for decades before joining the Obama White House on a mission to finally get the job done. She knew more about the law than anyone in Washington—and with her sweet and shy disposition, she was the world's most pleasant encyclopedia to consult. She was exactly what a public servant should be. I was as happy for her as I was for anybody on that day.

My back was to the building, but I noticed the air shift, along with everyone's gaze, as Obama stepped onto the patio. Some of the policy specialists had barely interacted with him before. He gave a quick toast, telling everybody how proud he was of them, then hugged each one in turn.

When he got to me and Denis, he said, "I don't need to hug you guys."

Turning to me, he said, "So, I read the speech. It's well written." I knew what came next. "The front half is fine. The back half isn't quite there. So I'm going to work on it and leave it for you to pick up in the morning."

At least my assessment was right. "Want me to come back tonight and grab your edits?"

"Nah, I don't think that's necessary. Seriously," he said, pointing at my chest, then pointing out toward the larger world, "go home."

It was only six o'clock, but I wasn't going to argue. First, though, I wanted to see Kristen. In the ongoing cruelty of our professional relationship, my work on the speech might have been done for the night, but hers was just beginning.

I left the chief of staff's patio and exited the building one level below, crossed the driveway that cut between the West Wing and the Eisenhower Executive Office Building, climbed the curved staircase to the first floor, and walked down the long hallway with black-and-white checkered floor and twenty-foot ceilings to the research suite of offices on the north side of the building.

I briefed Kristen and Alexandra Platkin, the leader of the team, within earshot of five or six other researchers at their desks in the open floorplan. "The good news is, it's not so bad that it requires serious triage. I don't *think*. The bad news is, it's just good enough that his plan is to leave me edits in the morning. So we'll have some work to do then. Sorry, guys."

"No problem," Kristen said. "We'll split the first two pages and we'll send flags on those tonight. We haven't touched the part he's going to change. Just send us the edits in the morning, and we'll crash on them. It may be a highwire act if marriage comes down, but at least the ACA is out of the way. Now listen to the boss and go home!"

I wanted to kiss her but refrained with her colleagues in the room.

Before going home, I needed to do one last thing: write a mea culpa to the other staffers who should have seen a draft by now. The eulogy was twenty-one hours away, and I'd only shared it with the president, Terry, and Kristen. A group of readers that small, that soon before a speech, was unprecedented.

> I confess I've been struggling with tomorrow's eulogy, which is why none of you have seen it. POTUS asked for the draft before he went home and looked it over and said he's going to work

on it tonight and have his edits ready for me early tomorrow morning.

Press team—I don't know what he's going to do, and I know that complicates your interactions with reporters who all want to know if he views this as the most important speech of his presidency. I suggest we largely mirror what Josh has been saying to them:

It's a memorial, so POTUS will mostly stay focused on the victims.

He will, of course, address racism and gun violence—it would be inappropriate if he didn't.

But I would tamp down expectations that this is some major race speech.

The good news is, it's completely accurate to tell reporters that POTUS spent a lot of time working on this one himself!

As I was packing up to leave the compound for the first time in thirty-six hours, Valerie walked into my office for the third time that week. I wasn't used to it.

"Hey, you," she said. "I saw your email. Don't sweat it. It was an impossible assignment." It was precisely the same platitude as the one delivered by Denis, which made me wonder if they'd been talking.

"Selma was much easier."

"Well, of course. You had something to go on. And because of Selma and Beau's eulogy, expectations are high. Success raises the bar. It's unfair, and you should get a pass. But that's not how this place works."

The president had eulogized the vice president's son, Beau Biden, not even three weeks earlier. His death from brain cancer, at just forty-six years old, knocked the entire White House staff off kilter. Beau was a rising star in politics, a genuinely good man with few detractors—someone who, like Clem Pinckney, when he walked into a room, it felt like the future arrived. The eulogy for him was one our finest pieces of writing, another collaboration between Obama and me that improved the remarks exponentially.

"Fortunately, he's no slouch," Valerie added of Obama. "If we had lost today, it might have been hard for him to dig deep tonight. But he is in pretty darn good spirits. He'll figure it out."

I hoped so.

3

ARRIVING HOME, I'D RARELY FELT SO GRATEFUL TO TAKE OFF A suit, put on jeans, and flop onto the couch.

With some shame, I ordered a pepperoni pizza from Domino's. Hitting my version of culinary rock bottom, I remembered a comedian's routine that began with "I ate at Subway today . . . because I gave up." I laughed, alone, and considered going to sleep right there, pizza on my chest.

Just as I was drifting off, my cellphone rang. UNKNOWN CALLER.

It was just after nine o'clock. On the television, the Cubs were losing, 1-0. I answered the phone, and a woman's voice said, as matter-of-factly as possible, "Please hold for the president."

"Okay." Five long seconds of silence passed.

"Hey."

"Hey."

"I'm done working, but it might take you some time to make my edits, so why don't you come by at ten and I'll walk you through them."

"I'll be there."

We hung up. I called Kristen, still at the White House, to let her know. "I'm coming back. Want a ride home?"

"Ugh, we're just about to send you our flags and I just want to go home. That okay?"

"Of course."

"I'll meet you outside and give you a hug."

I didn't bother putting a suit on, just a collared shirt and blazer, and drove back down 14th Street to the White House. Kristen was waiting where I usually parked.

"Hi!"

"We've got to stop meeting like this. There's pizza on the counter."

"My hero."

"It's Domino's."

"Oh."

"I'll let you know how it goes."

I passed the unfamiliar Secret Service agent and the unfamiliar cleaning crew and dropped off my backpack and laptop in my office. I climbed the stairs, but rather than make a U-turn toward the Oval Office, I hung a right and walked down the Colonnade, along the Rose Garden still in full bloom, past the point from which I'd watched Obama speak ten hours before, and through the double doors of the Residence.

Walking down the red carpet of the center hall, I showed my badge to another unfamiliar agent, took a left at the president's elevator, and walked up a hidden stairwell that led to the private residence. Rather than continue up to his quarters, I stopped on the first floor. He almost always came down to meet me in the office that the White House ushers used, along the North Portico, across from the Red Room, nestled between the old family dining room and the central foyer where presidents and First Ladies would make their grand entrance for state dinners.

Obama never snuck up on me. I could hear the flip-flop of the leather sandals he wore when off duty coming down the marble stairs for a good ten seconds before he appeared.

"Hey, brother." He was wearing gray jeans and a white polo shirt, and he was carrying the gray folder in which I'd put his remarks. His briefing folders were color-coded; speech drafts went into gray manila folders emblazoned with PRESIDENTIAL STATEMENT across the front. "Have a seat."

He pulled out a stack of papers. He'd edited the first two pages of my four-page draft by hand, a little heavier than usual, with a few deletions and more additions. Pages three and four were untouched—save for a giant line through each, from the lower left corner to upper right.

He'd deleted both pages in their entirety. He'd never done that to me before. Ever.

In their place, he handed me three yellow legal pages filled with his handwriting. The muse had hit, and hard. It was the first time I could remember him whipping out the legal pad since his 2013 speech at the fiftieth anniversary of the March on Washington.

He'd erased an all-nighter's worth of work in two seconds and rewritten it in two hours.

Over fifteen minutes, he walked me through his edits and his writing, his long finger tracing each line from an addition to its new home in the text. That wasn't novel—the most powerful man in the world always took the time to explain his work to his speechwriters, and we always appreciated it.

He asked me to have a new version incorporating his edits and his guidance ready for him by nine in the morning and stood up to leave. He was cool about it and didn't seem the least bit disappointed. He almost never did, but it felt strange that he didn't this time, after I'd had a whole four days to write.

I followed him out toward the Cross Hall and stopped him when he was about three steps up the stairs.

"Hey. I'm sorry I couldn't get this right." I felt I'd failed him, more than I had in a long while. He turned and looked at me, walked back down the three steps, and did something rare: He rested a hand on my shoulder.

"Brother, we're collaborators. You gave me the scaffolding I needed to build something here. You'll recognize your work in what I wrote. And trust me, when you've been thinking about this stuff for forty years, you'll know what you want to say too. All right?"

"All right."

Grace, it appeared, was contagious.

I wound back through the Residence to the West Wing, past the unfamiliar officers who wondered why someone was wandering around in jeans at ten thirty, and called Kristen.

"Wow," she said.

"Yeah. It's fair to say the reflections of a fifty-three-year-old Black man on this are more meaningful than mine."

"I love you and want to wait for you. But I have to get up early to work on whatever you're working on."

It would take me about an hour to make his edits, another hour or two to make some additions based on his guidance. I sat in my desk chair for about three seconds before deciding I couldn't work in that office anymore. I drove home for the second time that evening, kissed a sleeping Kristen, and opened my laptop at the dining table pushed up against our apartment's floor-to-ceiling windows overlooking 14th Street. I liked working there, especially when Kristen was asleep in the next room. It was the opposite of my office. I'd sit facing those windows and write, catching up on the world I'd missed while trapped in the Speechcave.

A couple of minutes after I sat down, my phone dinged with a text message from Bobby Schmuck, a convivial coworker, friend, and fellow Northwestern Wildcat.

"By chance are you up late in your window writing a eulogy?"

"Yes, why?"

"We're outside waving. Just heading home from the bar. Good luck, bud."

I looked down and waved back, feeling pangs of gratitude and guilt. Gratitude for good friends, great colleagues, a thoughtful boss, and a spectacular fiancée. Guilt for my own shortcomings and shortsightedness. I'd never been alone; everyone who mattered in my world was rooting for me.

I poured a bourbon and opened the gray manila folder of edits.

What he'd done to the speech was extraordinary. And he'd said he had nothing to say.

It took me three hours to make his changes.

Day Ten

Friday, June 26, 2015

1

I'D GONE TO BED AT THREE AND WOKEN UP AT SIX. THREE HOURS of sleep in the past forty-eight.

The boss was right—a lot of what I'd written in my bumpy draft was still present in his rewrite. He'd used the meditation on grace as a transition to turn from the eulogy for Pinckney to the second half of the remarks on the vexing issues of guns, racial inequity, the flag, and our moral obligations—and crafted it into a beautiful emotional nexus, one that offered the chance for people to change their minds.

It was less of a speech now than it was a sermon.

Arriving at the White House by six thirty, I learned that Obama had asked to pull down his in-person national security briefing for the day (he would read the briefing himself) so that he could continue to work on the eulogy. I spent an hour or so giving it another polish, emailed it to Kristen and her team so that they could start fact-checking the pages he'd added, then printed it for the president before he finished his morning workout. I trudged upstairs, half an hour late to the 7:45 meeting. I figured people deserved an explanation for why they hadn't even seen a draft yet, with the departure for Charleston scheduled just three hours from now.

But nobody gave me a hard time. People seemed looser than usual, relieved after Thursday's midnight pardon of the Affordable Care Act.

Anita Decker Breckenridge passed me a note.

I'm moving you to M1 today.

I winked a "Thank you" at her. If you were traveling with the president on Air Force One, there were two means of travel to Joint Base Andrews. You could navigate traffic for forty minutes in one of four vans filled with aides and support staff, or you could hitch a seven-minute ride from the South Lawn on Marine One.

Six of the ten seats were always spoken for by the president, two Secret Service agents, the military aide with the nuclear football, the president's doctor, and whichever personal aide was traveling with the president that day. That left four seats for senior staff. Since becoming chief speechwriter, I'd accompanied the president on Marine One maybe once every two or three months, usually on big speech gamedays or whenever Obama wanted to talk.

In the years of the first term, though, it had been a rare privilege, and for a speechwriter, there were two ways it came about: by nailing a speech, or by failing a speech.

My first trip was in September 2009, after Obama was impressed by a eulogy in New York City. Nailed it. My second was in December of the same year, after Obama didn't like the draft of an economic speech, and a morning reshuffling of the manifest put me on Marine One to take down his guidance and rewrite the remarks on the plane. Failed it.

It was an open question as to which way today would go. But with the president still working on the eulogy himself, it made more sense to keep me nearby.

I took the long way back to my office after the meeting, walking past the Roosevelt Room, packed with a larger, younger contingent of staff ready for their 8:30 meeting to start. I noticed bigger smiles than usual, a crackle of nervous energy, certainly a louder buzz of chitchat than most mornings. People were convinced that the marriage equality decision would come today. It was Friday; surely the Supreme Court justices who, despite their practiced dispassion, liked to make a splash, wouldn't make everyone endure three more days waiting for a Monday ruling.

I emailed Sarada on the way back to my desk. "You ready to rock if marriage comes down this a.m.?"

"Yep."

"Every version?"

"Yes!"

Maybe it came from thirty-four years of Chicago sports fandom, but my instinct was to protect myself by assuming the worst. If I put my armor up, I wouldn't be let down. Besides, if we won, we still had to go give a eulogy for a promising young civil rights leader slain in a racist massacre. If we lost, millions of Americans would be deemed second-class citizens *and* we still had to go give a eulogy for a promising young civil rights leader slain in a racist massacre.

Still, I couldn't help it—I felt a tug of nervous anticipation usually reserved for election night. There was a chance that something extraordinary could happen.

It was, in fact, the same feeling I'd had five weeks earlier, when I'd proposed to Kristen.

It was an elaborate ruse. I wanted to propose to Kristen atop Rockefeller Center, with a view of her native Staten Island in the distance. I'd been asked to deliver the convocation address at New York University's Wagner School of Public Service. That was my excuse to get her to New York City. But to get her to the top of Rockefeller Center without suspecting a proposal—that was harder.

In April, *Saturday Night Live*'s Cecily Strong had served as the entertainment at the annual White House Correspondents' Dinner. I had coordinated with her to make sure her jokes and the president's didn't overlap, and I emailed her a few weeks later to ask if she'd help with my scheme. She gleefully agreed, emailing Kristen and me to ask if we could come to *SNL* as her guests and visit the roof of Rockefeller Center beforehand, supposedly to watch some cast members film a prerecorded skit for the show. We were greeted at the door, whisked to the top floor, taken to a cordoned-off half of the rooftop, and—in front of a hundred confused tourists and my friend and first roommate in Washington, Nick Ehrmann, who was hidden in the crowd to take photos—I dropped to my knee at sunset and proposed.

My new fiancée had suspected nothing. After the shock wore off, Kristen had even asked, "Are we still going to *Saturday Night Live*?" (We were not; I had our families and friends waiting at a nearby bar to celebrate.)

Kristen and I would be able to marry whatever the Supreme Court decided. Why shouldn't everyone get to experience such happiness? Why shouldn't everyone have the same right to equality and basic fairness?

Jim Obergefell had been in the courtroom every decision day that week, waiting for an answer to that question. He wasn't demanding special treatment. He just wanted his marriage to matter; he yearned for the same equal treatment under the law as anybody else. By 2015, his husband had died—but Jim was still living up to the promises they'd made to love, honor, and protect one another. If opponents were truly concerned about the sanctity of marriage, Mr. Obergefell was reason not to worry.

It struck me, though, as a long, lonely journey. He wasn't an activist when he filed his case. But he was now on the cusp of making change in his own quiet way. After decades of such advocacy, organizing, and struggle, progress had finally begun piling up for same-sex couples—hospital visitation rights; changes to health care; tax laws; immigration status for noncitizens in relationships—but so many same-sex marriages still didn't matter under the law. The Supreme Court's decision in *Obergefell* could put an emphatic stamp of approval on that progress or dispatch activists back to the trenches.

That contrast inspired me to add one thing to Sarada's otherwise beautiful set of remarks.

She'd opened the draft by writing:

Our nation was founded on a bedrock principle: that we are all created equal. The project of each generation is to make those words real in the lives of every American, and that progress often comes in small increments. But today, we take a historic step forward.

I thought we could expand on that idea of slow progress and quick payoff. Back in the Speechcave, I typed:

Our nation was founded on a bedrock principle: that we are all created equal.

The project of each generation is to bridge the meaning of those founding words with the realities of changing times—a never-ending quest to ensure those words ring true for every single American.

Progress on this journey often comes in small increments, often two steps forward for every step back, propelled by the effort of persistent, dedicated citizens.

But sometimes, there are days like this—days when that slow, steady effort is rewarded with justice that arrives like a thunderbolt.

And toward the end:

Change, for many of our LGBT brothers and sisters, must have seemed so slow for so long. But compared to so many other issues, America's shift has been so quick. I know that Americans continue to hold a wide range of views on this issue, based on sincere and deeply held beliefs. All of us who welcome today's news should be mindful of that fact. We respect different viewpoints and revere our deep commitment to religious freedom. But today should also give us hope that on the many issues with which we grapple, often painfully—real change is possible. A shift in hearts and minds is possible. And those who have come so far on their journey to equality have a responsibility to reach back and help others join them.

I sent it back to Sarada. "OK? (I know, I'm a monstrous hypocrite when it comes to keeping things short.)" I'd told her to keep the remarks to a page, and here I was extending them beyond that.

"Yes," she replied. "But this is great!"

For a moment, I didn't know what to do with myself. After going at full throttle for four days, all there was to do was wait—wait for a decision, wait for Obama's edits.

Then Lisa Monaco walked into my office with a dour expression on her face.

"Oh my God," I said, "what? What is it?"

"We have to add an update to the hostage policy review to the top of the president's remarks today," she said.

My great relief that there wasn't some new terrorism concern gave way to indignation. And the whiplash kept me from thinking clearly about the logic of her intrusion. "What! We're on the cusp of a landmark civil rights moment, and you're telling me you want Obama to cede wall-to-wall coverage for an update from a staff meeting? Are you out of your—"

She couldn't keep a straight face any longer. "You're too easy."

I couldn't help it; I chuckled too. "Oh, for fuck's sake, Lisa. Not this week!"

Terry was hooting with laughter on the other side of the wall we shared.

It was a testament to how highly I thought of Lisa that I had believed her. Without standing up, I reached across the desk to give her a half-assed high five before she turned and left.

I knew there were gatherings going on all over the West Wing and Executive Office Building. People wanted to watch any announcement together. In moments like this, I preferred to be alone—to exhale and reflect if we won, to seethe and mourn if we didn't.

We didn't have to wait long.

Clickety-CLACK.

10:01 AM Marriage.

Here we go!

Clickety-CLACK.

10:01 AM Kennedy has the opinion.

I hoped that boded well. Justice Anthony Kennedy had written the opinions in *Lawrence v. Texas* and *United States v. Windsor,* two earlier cases that brought LGBTQ Americans closer to full equality under the law. Kind of tough to advance equal rights twice, then set a limit on them. Besides, everybody liked a trilogy.

Clickety-CLACK.

10:01 AM Holding: Fourteenth Amendment requires a state to license a marriage between two people of the same sex.

I reflexively shouted, "Yes!"

"Did we get it?" shouted Terry through the wall.

"Yes!"

On MSNBC, the anchor broke into coverage and threw it to a reporter at the Supreme Court with the fastest interns already appearing behind him. "I'm speaking to you from the Supreme Court, we have read from the bench, there is a right to marriage equality—I repeat, speaking to you from the steps of the Supreme Court, there is a right to marriage equality read just from the bench now, [we're] waiting to get the opinions as they come running out of the Court."

The crowd that had started gathering behind the barricades just after dawn was straining to hear what the reporter was saying. They looked around, confused, expectant, checking their phones, and ultimately breaking into cheers. Whoops and yelps throughout the West Wing turned it into surround sound.

Clickety-CLACK.

10:02 AM And to recognize a marriage between two people of the same sex when a marriage was lawfully licensed and performed out of state.

Clickety-CLACK.

10:02 AM It's 5-4.

The justice correspondent for NBC was on the screen now. "This is a total victory for the advocates of same-sex marriage . . . The Court has gone the *whole* way, said there is an absolute constitutional right to same-sex marriage. Now, what this means is that it is now the law of the land."

The chyron on the bottom of the screen finally changed from SUPREME COURT DECISION ON MARRIAGE EQUALITY to SUPREME COURT RULES IN FAVOR OF MARRIAGE EQUALITY.

I picked up my landline phone and called Kristen at her desk to tell her I loved her.

"Oh," she said, "I thought you were calling about the marriage remarks. I'm still fact-checking them. I love you too!"

"Well, you only have to look at the 'total fucking victory' version now!"

I sat back and took in the joy on television. Ebullient couples were jumping up and down on the steps of the Supreme Court, embracing, waving American flags, celebrating that their love had been declared equal to everybody else's. My throat tightened a bit.

Terry poked his head around the corner and caught me. "You too?"

"I mean—" My voice cracked and I had to clear my throat. Terry laughed. "I mean, how can you watch this and not feel happy?"

"It's incredible!" Terry exclaimed, walking farther into my office so that he could see my television. "Think about it. If someone had told you back in 2007 that a Black guy would be elected president, end DOMA and Don't Ask, Don't Tell, and that gay marriage would become the law of the land—in less than a decade—you'd think that person was crazy."

"And killing bin Laden," I added.

"And killing bin Laden."

"But yeah."

"That's not just historic change, that's historically *fast* change."

"Yeah," I said, staring at the jubilation on TV. "Maybe the Cubs will win the World Series!"

Clickety-CLACK.

10:06 AM It is actually eerily quiet here in the Court's cafeteria, but I imagine it's about to get crazy outside.

I hoped it was crazy everywhere.

I read that many of the Supreme Court justices' clerks had sat in the courtroom to hear the decision. That was unusual, allegedly—I wouldn't know—but I knew the same thing would happen in the Rose Garden in less than an hour: Every young staffer in the building would be there.

I bounded up the stairs to see if Obama was in the office yet and if he'd had a chance to look at the statement he was about to deliver. Walking into the outer Oval, I saw Brian Mosteller doing something rare behind his desk: He was smiling.

"Congrats, brother," I shouted at him. Brian had met his partner, Joe Mahshie, almost a year earlier, on the Fourth of July. They'd begun talking about marriage but hadn't wanted to do it until it was valid everywhere. Joe worked for the First Lady, and I was sure that Brian had called him once the decision came down, just as I'd called Kristen.

"Congrats to all of us," he replied. It was about as much emotion as you'd get out of the guy. I hugged him anyway.

Ferial was beaming. "Cody, he's still in the Residence working on the eulogy."

"Oh well, that's just fucking great," I replied, hugging her too. "I assume he knows. Somebody told him, right?"

"He knows. Let's just call the marriage statement final, he'll be good with it."

"Right on." After working on the eulogy, he probably hadn't looked at the marriage equality statement. I was sure he hadn't looked at the adverse-decision versions.

I bounced back downstairs. Sarada was standing at my desk in a black suit, head craned up toward the television, delighted at the scenes of waving American and rainbow flags. She turned to me. "Holy shit!"

"Right?" We hugged too.

"Is he making edits?"

"Not to yours," I replied. "You're good to go. He's still at home working on mine."

"Oh no!" Sarada laughed. "I saw you just sent something around, but I haven't gotten to look at it yet." I'd decided it was time to get the draft of the Charleston eulogy to a wider list and had clicked SEND just minutes after the marriage ruling came down.

"Remember where I wrote the words 'Amazing Grace'? He crossed out *everything* after that and used it as a unifying theme. Even wrote out the lyrics later on."

Sarada's face fell. "Oh my God. When you asked me for that list of hymns and spirituals, 'Amazing Grace' never crossed my mind. I can't believe it. I'm so embarrassed."

"I didn't use it as a song either! I wrote the two words at the end of a fumbling riff," I told her. "He added the lyrics."

2

THE DISSENTING OPINIONS OF THE JUSTICES QUICKLY MADE THEIR way around. Clarence Thomas howled about "inestimable consequences for our Constitution and our society." Samuel Alito fretted that anyone who opposed same-sex marriage would be branded a bigot. Even Chief Justice John Roberts, while writing that people should feel free to celebrate the decision even though he thought it unconstitutional, bemoaned the national hubris in allowing "five lawyers" to rewrite the rules of a social ritual that had been around since the time of the Hans, the Carthaginians, and the Aztecs. (None of whom were quite the Cleavers. As it turns out, every society is a little bit *Modern Family*.)

"Just who do we think we are?" Roberts wrote.

We're Americans, I thought. *We change.* Emperors and kings were once the basis of human society. We cast that off. Slavery and legal segregation were once the basis of American society. We cast those off too—even if the journey to full equality was unfinished, even if we were still waiting, and might wait forever, for more moments of victory like the scene unfolding at the Supreme Court that morning.

But while the dissenters seethed, Kennedy's majority opinion soared:

> No union is more profound than marriage, for it embodies the highest ideals of love, fidelity, devotion, sacrifice, and family. In forming a marital union, two people become something greater than once they were. As some of the petitioners in these cases demonstrate, marriage embodies a love that may endure even past death. It would misunderstand these men and women to say they disrespect the idea of marriage. Their plea is that they do respect it, respect it so deeply that they seek to find its fulfillment for themselves. Their hope is not to be condemned to live in loneliness, excluded from one of civilization's oldest institutions. They ask for equal dignity in the eyes of the law. The Constitution grants them that right.

People would no doubt incorporate that part of Justice Kennedy's opinion into their wedding ceremonies for years to come. But I found other passages more interesting:

> The nature of injustice is that we may not always see it in our own times. The generations that wrote and ratified the Bill of Rights and the Fourteenth Amendment did not presume to know the extent of freedom in all of its dimensions, and so they entrusted to future generations a charter protecting the right of all persons

> to enjoy liberty as we learn its meaning . . . Indeed, in interpreting the Equal Protection Clause, the Court has recognized that new insights and societal understandings can reveal unjustified inequality within our most fundamental institutions that once passed unnoticed and unchallenged.

Put more simply, and to answer the question Justice Roberts posed: America is great because America can change.

The notion was the underpinning of so many of President Obama's speeches, and it was how he was poised to open his remarks in just minutes:

> Our nation was founded on a bedrock principle: that we are all created equal. The project of each generation is to bridge the meaning of those founding words with the realities of changing times—a never-ending quest to ensure those words ring true for every single American.

For the second time in less than twenty-four hours, I strolled out into the Rose Garden to watch him, taking a deep breath of the fresh, fragrant air. The rows of chairs were completely full of guests; there appeared to be more cameras than usual behind them. The sun was trying and failing to break through the clouds, but you wouldn't know it from the smiles on people's faces.

The Colonnade was filled with young, happy staff. I leaned against a column at the far end of the Rose Garden from the president's lectern, trying to stay as far out of sight as I could, taking it all in. Big victories—clear, indisputable ones—don't come along all that often in politics. November nights in Chicago in 2008 and 2012. The Sunday night in March 2009 when the Affordable Care Act eked out enough votes to pass the House. The Sunday night in May 2011 when Obama announced that Navy SEALs had smoked bin Laden. Nights when you'd been pushing the world for so long—and it finally moved.

We racked up little victories all the time—executive orders that pulled the lever on some progressive or worker-friendly change, symbolic gestures that some group or other had long fought for—but most of the 2,922 nights in the Obama White House, we went home happy if we'd moved the ball forward just a little bit. And we'd return the next morning to do it again.

This, though—this was worth savoring. Millions of lives had changed for the better just like *that*.

Like a thunderbolt.

Denis approached with a shit-eating grin on his face and offered a fist pound. "Pretty rad, huh?"

"Unreal, man," I replied.

"Hey, keep this between us, but this evening, rather than land directly on the lawn, the helo is going to swoop around the front of the house so POTUS and the First Lady can see the front of the house all lit up like a rainbow."

In the events of the week, I had forgotten all about the plan to splash the Pride flag across the White House, the brainchild of a bespectacled, quick-to-smile thirty-two-year-old press aide named Jeff Tiller. With a lot of spadework from the First Lady's chief of staff, Tina Tchen, Jeff had secured the necessary approvals and worked out the logistics with Residence staff, White House electricians, and the Secret Service—and found funding so that taxpayers wouldn't be on the hook. He just needed to wait for the Supreme Court to rule.

When he'd first come up with the idea, Jen Psaki asked him what would happen if, after all the effort to set up the lights, the Supreme Court ruled against marriage equality?

"Then it's even more important to light them up," Jeff had told her.

Now, back in the Rose Garden, I reacted to Denis's secret. "Get out of here. That is *awesome*. Can they drop bags of health care and marriage licenses on people too?"

Denis laughed. "Why not?" He slapped me on the back and walked off to make sure everybody else got a fist pound. I checked my watch, then my email, to convince myself that everything was still running smoothly. Sarada had returned to her office, and at 11:01, she sent the final remarks for Brian to print and for the teleprompter guys to load. At 11:02, she sent me a frantic response to her own email.

"It says 'good afternoon'! Shit!"

So it did. The first line of the remarks read, "Good afternoon." It was 11:03.

"I got it," I wrote back, ducking behind everybody and trying to stay out of sight on my way to the A/V equipment that was tucked into the northwest corner of the Rose Garden, just offstage. The president was smart enough to know what time of day it was and nimble enough to adlib "good morning" on the fly. But I never took any chances.

"Hey, sir," I whispered to the teleprompter operator, an active-duty military member of the White House Communications Agency. "Can you change 'Good afternoon' to 'Good morning'?"

"Already did, sir." I loved those guys. I thanked him and slowly stood up. Staying low hadn't worked—one photographer had his lens trained on me and several members of the press corps were staring, wondering what late-breaking change I'd made to the remarks. Was the president going to break some news? How exciting!

I winked at them and went back through the double doors into the West Wing, past the entrance to the Briefing Room, and looped around into the outer Oval Office. The "good afternoon" had to be changed in the printed remarks too. The shades were drawn on the floor-to-ceiling windows in preparation for Obama's remarks, which would offer a less distracting backdrop behind him than a glimpse into the Oval Office nerve center. It made it easy to forget that a couple of hundred people were waiting on the other side.

"Hey, Brian, can I make a quick change to page one?"

"Is it 'good morning'?"

"Yep."

"Already done."

Ferial was standing behind her desk with her phone to her ear. She shouted, "You ready, sir?" I craned my neck to look through the door to the Oval and saw Obama sitting behind the Resolute Desk in shirtsleeves, wearing a bright blue tie. I also noticed something else: another page of yellow legal paper in front of him. He was adding to the eulogy again!

"Yep," Obama shouted back. But he didn't move from behind his desk.

"What's going on?" I whispered to Brian.

"Check this out." He pointed a remote control at the small television on a side table next to the chair where the Obama family dog, Bo, usually curled up during the day, and he turned up the volume.

The screen was usually set to a quadbox of CNN, MSNBC, Fox News, and CNBC all playing at the same time. I thought it odd that it was showing only CNN. The chyron read AWAITING OBAMA STATEMENT FROM WHITE HOUSE. Onscreen, CNN anchor Jake Tapper was standing on what appeared to be the East Lawn of the Capitol Building, with the Supreme Court in the distance.

I heard Obama's voice from the Oval Office. "Hi, is this Jim?"

On television, Tapper said that Jim Obergefell was on the Supreme Court steps, "getting a phone call from a very important person."

I turned and grinned at Brian. "Oh, well done," I said, emphasizing every word. Brian nodded.

Coverage switched to the Supreme Court steps. I'd never seen Jim Obergefell before. His thinning, graying hair was contradicted by an unlined face. He was wearing a black suit and white shirt with a purple-and-white striped bowtie. His big black-framed glasses hung over dark irises that looked stunned at his victory only an hour before, a bit overwhelmed by being on live television, surrounded by revelers, and now confused by somebody offscreen handing him an iPhone. I noticed he was wearing his wedding ring and felt a now familiar lump rise in my throat. Obergefell bent down to put his ear to the phone, then straightened, noticing that it was set to speakerphone, trying to discern the phone number.

The reporter smiled into the camera. "Yes, and that very important person, Jake, is President Obama." Mr. Obergefell winced, his hands jolting like somebody had shocked him with a live wire. Eyes wide, he glanced at the acquaintance who had handed him the phone as if to ask, "What do I do?"

I suddenly worried this was a very cruel thing to do to a person. Then, in one fluid motion, Obergefell hushed the still-talking reporter with a stern glance and a raised finger. *Never mind,* I thought, *he's got this after all!*

"Hello?"

In real time, the conversation was already well underway in the Oval Office. But the television feed was several seconds behind. Brian turned the volume to the lowest level at which we could still hear both sides of the exchange. Obama's booming voice behind us kept interrupting Obama's delayed speakerphone voice onscreen.

"Hi, is this Jim?"

"Yes, it is, Mr. President."

"I just wanted to say congratulations."

"Thank you so much, sir," Obergefell said with an excited laugh.

"You know, your leadership on this has changed the country."

"I really appreciate that, Mr. President," Obergefell said. "It's really been an honor for me to be involved in this fight and to have been able to fight for my marriage and live up to my commitments to my husband. I appreciate everything you've done for the LGBT community, and it's really an honor to have become part of that fight."

"Well, I'm really proud of you, and just know that not only have you been a great example for people, you're also gonna bring about a lasting change in this country. And it's pretty rare where that happens. So I couldn't be prouder of you and your husband. God bless you."

"Thank you, sir, that means an incredible amount to me, and . . . yeah, thank you." He laughed nervously.

"All right. Take care." Obama was smiling.

"Thanks for the call, Mr. President."

"You bet, bye bye."

With more than decent aplomb, Obergefell had handled a phone call from the most powerful man in the world on live television.

Onscreen, he said, "Oh my God," and let loose with happy laughter and a whimper of relief, exhaling as if he'd never exhaled before. It looked like he was about to cry with joy and have a heart attack at once.

Sarada materialized in the doorway, panting. "Did you fix it?"

"All good," Brian said, holding up a binder filled with the president's remarks, double-spaced and in large type for easy reading. He slipped through one of the outer Oval doors, exposing us to the waiting throng outside, to put the speech on the president's lectern as he had done a hundred times. As usual, he was all business, expressionless in his impeccably tailored suit—but that morning, I swore I saw some extra pride in his step. Obama had given Brian a hug once he'd come to the Oval from the Residence, knowing what the decision meant to him. As he placed the binder on the lectern and opened it to page one, I imagined him thinking, *Boom!*

"Prompter's good too," I told Sarada. "You didn't have to run!"

"Dude, I ran like the *devil*. I've never been so happy to be a woman who doesn't believe in heels. I wasn't going to let the president reveal that he doesn't know what time of day it is!"

"You know who else caught it?" I asked her. "Nobody. There are bigger things happening. Come on, let's go watch." We took the long way, out into the hallway, back past the Briefing Room, to the double doors that opened onto the Colonnade. There was no sneaking out this time. The "Voice of God"—a staffer over the microphone—had already given the audience a two-minute warning, so everyone was hushed. Every pair of eyes shifted to us, reporters once again wondering what drama was unfolding with the remarks. It felt a little like we were disturbing church. I found an opening and leaned up against a column again.

Obama was already at the lectern. "Good morning," he began. I smirked at Sarada.

There were even more staff members packed along the Colonnade and on the grass, arms around each other, than for the ACA remarks the day before. I saw Kristen and her team—a rarity. Facts were going unchecked! It really was a big moment!

The staff watching the president was younger than it was the day before too. At thirty-four, I wasn't exactly old. But looking around the Rose Garden, I felt that way. It was plain to see how important this moment was to them, a big civil rights moment, history unfolding in real time. Young people, in so many ways, had nudged an older generation to get itself right on the issue. We had accelerated the entire country's evolution.

I thought of everyone who'd sacrificed so much for this day to come true: the protesters at the Stonewall Inn; generations of marchers and organizers who toiled to change an unjust status quo; every American who did the hard work of changing their own hearts when a loved one came out. To them, it must have felt like something that had taken so long, when to the rest of us, it felt like it had come so quickly.

"And then sometimes, there are days like this," Obama said, "when that slow, steady effort is rewarded with justice that arrives like a thunderbolt."

His delivery was appropriately lofty—cadence, pauses, and emphasis all on point. The two men who'd most recently sat at his desk had set back equality with Don't Ask, Don't Tell and the Defense of Marriage Act. In a few short years, Obama had flipped the script. Posterity would see him behind the lectern when the biggest moment came—and he wore the moment well.

One of the perks of being a speechwriter is that you know when the speech is about to end. I needed to get back inside as quickly as possible to collect my laptop and backpack. As soon as Obama finished his remarks, the military aide on duty would contact the pilots of Marine One, who were already in the air as Obama was speaking, and they'd be wheels down on the South Lawn precisely five minutes later.

As Obama began the final line, I prepared to move. "There's so much more work to be done to extend the full promise of America to every American. But today, we can say in no uncertain terms that we've made our union a little more perfect." Six and a half minutes. Nice and tight for once.

But he kept going. I cocked my head and watched. It wasn't rare that he would extemporize. He'd do it all the time. It *was* rare that he'd do it when there were no further words on the screen to return to. He was on his own here. I was curious as to where he'd fly and how he'd land this plane.

"That's the consequence of a decision from the Supreme Court—but more importantly, it is a consequence of the countless small acts of courage of millions of people, across decades, who stood up. Who came out. Who talked to parents. Parents who loved their children no matter what."

He was speaking slowly—even more so than usual—taking long pauses between every clause.

"Folks who were willing to endure bullying, and taunts, and stayed strong, and came to believe in themselves and who they were, and slowly made an entire country realize . . . that love is love."

I wondered if he was talking a bit about his own evolution. I knew he understood what the day meant to his staff.

"What an extraordinary achievement. What a vindication of the belief that ordinary people can do extraordinary things. What a reminder of what Bobby Kennedy once said about how small actions can be like pebbles being thrown into a still lake, and ripples of hope cascade outwards, and change the world.

"Those countless, often anonymous heroes—they deserve our thanks. They should be very proud. America should be very proud. Thank you."

Some months later, I asked Obama if his delivery that morning had been slow because he was moved by what had happened, by the pace of progress, by processing the realization that we had lived through a civil rights triumph in real time. He said no, he was just tired from working so late on the Charleston speech. But I knew that wasn't true—he'd given it back to me well before midnight.

As everyone applauded for the president and high fives broke out across the Rose Garden, I made a break for the West Wing. I noticed Jeff Tiller, who'd be responsible for the rainbow that evening, doing the same, and I wondered if, out of superstition, they hadn't set up the lights yet.

3

THE PRESIDENT'S HELICOPTER TOOK SHAPE IN THE DISTANCE, A speck rounding the Washington Monument, flanked by two decoys. Watching it land on the South Lawn never got old.

Marine One approaches the White House straight on and slowly, like a hulking, wingless goose gliding in for a landing, while the decoys speed up and pass directly over the White House. Once over the South Lawn, the helicopter makes the slightest left turn, beginning a meticulous arc that positions the fuselage parallel with the Residence. The trees lash like they're in a hurricane. It descends at less than a foot per second, methodically lining up the three tires with the X in the center of three circular panels temporarily placed on the lawn to protect the grass.

As the wheels touch ground, the pilots kill the blades but keep the engines running, ready for a quick takeoff. The instant the blades stop turning, a Marine in full dress uniform opens the front door, descends the steps, opens the rear door, then returns to attention at the front steps to await the president.

I loved flying on Marine One. I hated boarding it.

Generally, if the president was in the West Wing, he'd walk from the Oval Office to Marine One by himself, wave at a small group who'd been invited to watch, salute the Marine at the front steps of the chopper, and climb aboard, all while a gaggle of photographers snapped photos.

About ten seconds later, staff traveling with him would trail behind. With the president already onboard, all lenses were trained on us. Some staff loved it, smiling for the cameras or pretending to be deep in animated and very important conversation, knowing that any photos taken in that moment and published would be forever attached to their name. I despised the ritual, wishing I was invisible.

The few photos that exist of me making that perp walk reveal as much.

Fortunately, the walk this day would be shorter than usual.

The First Lady, who was right now in the Residence doing a Make-a-Wish visit with a child, would be joining the president for the trip to Charleston. Rather than have her walk to the West Wing and then across the lawn with the president, he had decided to "pick her up at home."

The Obamas exited the Residence, hand in hand, and elegantly strolled to the helicopter, waving to the crowd that had stuck around for the second half of a rare doubleheader: a speech *and* a Marine One landing. Ten seconds later, the rest of us followed from the Residence. Not only was it a shorter and less exposed walk from the Residence than from the Oval Office, but the camera angles were worse. Once you made it across the driveway, the only angle was the back of your head. Valerie led the way, with Denis and me following in tandem, me using him as a human shield. The First Lady's personal aide MacKenzie Smith walked just behind us, trailed by Major Wes Spurlock, one of the friendliest people ever to carry the controls to America's nuclear arsenal, and two of the First Family's favorite Secret Service agents, Robert Buster and Allen Taylor, the latter a gentle yet lethal bear of a man whom Malia and Sasha loved like family.

We boarded the helicopter through the back door and stooped under the low ceiling as we walked to our seats. Valerie, Denis, and I sat in the front, on the bench along the right side of the aircraft, our backs to the fuselage. The president and First Lady sat across from us, on the left side of the aircraft, in front- and rear-facing captain's seats. The president, facing forward, had the latest version of the eulogy on his lap, still marking it up in pen. The First Lady, facing backward, was resplendent in a black sleeveless dress and simple earrings, her hair pulled tight in a top bun. Her hands rested in her lap, her nails painted a bright seafoam.

"Hi, guys." She smiled at everyone.

The president looked at each of us in turn, almost as if he was curious to discover who was traveling with him, his gaze finally settling on me, sitting to his three o'clock. "You know Cody just got engaged?"

"Congratulations," the First Lady exclaimed. "Who is she?"

"She works for us," Obama interrupted. "Kristen fact-checks my speeches."

I deployed my most weathered joke about our professional partnership. "Yeah, she actually gets paid to tell me I'm wrong."

The First Lady pursed her lips. "Mmm-hmm, get used to *that*."

The president returned to his editing with a close-lipped smile. As Marine One lifted off the lawn, rotated south, and rounded the Washington Monument to fly southeast, the First Lady peppered me with questions: Did I ask her father first? When was the wedding? What was the venue? Did she have a dress?

I told her we hadn't even started to think about timing yet, but a weekend with no speeches would be good. I told her how, when I'd revealed the plan to propose to Kristen atop Rockefeller Center, the president's only advice was to bring an umbrella—and how annoying it was that he'd been right. Without looking up, he smiled again.

"If it's next year, maybe we'll come," he said. "If we're invited, I mean." Mrs. Obama clapped.

Surprised, I blurted out, "Well, yeah, if you want to." Regaining my composure, I issued a challenge: "As long as you like a good party."

"Oh!" they both exclaimed at once. "You're on," the First Lady added.

Seven minutes after we'd lifted off the White House lawn, Marine One touched down on the tarmac at Joint Base Andrews and taxied to a stop about fifty yards from the nose of Air Force One. Obama snapped the cap back on his pen, stacked the pages of the eulogy in his lap, and handed them to me. I quickly leafed through them. The first three pages had only several small, surgical insertions; the fourth and fifth pages had one long written insertion on each that I didn't have time to read just then. But it all looked to be in good shape, good enough that I was about to ask if he was done.

"Do one more version and let me see it one last time." I hated it when he did that. It meant more stress—spending the entire flight to Charleston frantically inputting the insertions; printing and delivering that new draft to him, then waiting for a final version that would arrive as we were landing; pecking in his edits at an awkward angle while sitting between two other staffers in a van; and praying the cellular coverage was good enough to email a final version of the speech to advance staff onsite who could load it into the teleprompter and print a copy for the podium before it was time for him to hit the stage. It was a multi-act play.

He stood up, ducking under the ceiling as he buttoned his coat. "You know, if it feels right, I might sing it."

Halfway through stuffing the pages into my backpack, I froze and looked up at him. I was pretty sure I'd just heard him say he might sing "Amazing Grace" during the eulogy. Usually, my inclination was to think of a reason why he *shouldn't* do or say something, a habit born of an instinct to protect him. But I wasn't about to tell him that singing was a risk; I knew he thought of himself as a good singer.

He was looking at me, waiting to see what I thought, while the engines thrummed, while another gaggle of photographers and another group of admirers and a 747 full of people were waiting for him to exit and board that aircraft. There was no time for a list of pros and cons. The week had been heavy. The day had already produced some joy. Why not?

Bone-tired, all I could come up with was a phrase he'd recently told me Sasha was fond of.

"You do you, man."

The president and First Lady disembarked via the front steps of the helicopter and strode to Air Force One, stopping to wave to a group of ROTC cadets that had gathered to watch outside the passenger terminal at Joint Base Andrews. Once the Obamas were thirty yards or so from the helicopter, the rest of us clambered out through the back, one at a time, and trailed behind, only boarding via the red-carpeted front stairs once the Obamas had waved and disappeared inside.

Much like Marine One, traveling on Air Force One never got old, and each flight had its own enduring routine.

Most of the traveling staff boards Air Force One about half an hour before the president arrives. They say hello to the crew, hang up their coats, settle into their seats, start up their laptops, and catch up with the stewards who bring around fresh coffee. Then they get to work, the high-pitched hum of the four idling General Electric engines broken only by the clatter of silverware from the galley, the "bong" of a call button, a burst of laughter, the rustle of a newspaper, and ultimately the crisp warning over the loudspeaker that the president is five minutes out.

But when you board with the president, the engines fire as soon as he takes his seat—so you'd better take yours.

By 2015, mine was typically in the senior staff cabin squeezed between the galley and the conference room, an eight-by-eight chamber with four high-backed seats that could swivel 360 degrees to face one other, or away from each other so each occupant could use an individual desk that folded down from the wall—or recline almost flat for sleep on intercontinental journeys.

The foursome that day was Denis, Valerie, the First Lady's chief of staff Tina Tchen, and me. I jacked in and began working the president's latest edits into the speech, sliding my laptop to the side of the desk and his pages to my lap when lunch came around.

The food on Air Force One was no joke. The chefs were active-duty Air Force and highly trained culinary specialists like their Navy counterparts in the West Wing. What they prepared at forty-five thousand feet was even more impressive considering that the galley was about the same size as the senior staff cabin.

Chefs prepared a unique menu for each flight, printed with the day's date on gold-leaf menu cards placed at every seat. Each meal featured three generous courses of high-calorie, all-American fare. A day might begin with eggs or pancakes and a fruit parfait for breakfast. Maybe a chicken Caesar sandwich, kettle chips, fresh fruit, and a lemon tart for lunch. For dinner, perhaps lasagna or beef medallions with green beans, mashed potatoes, heirloom tomato salad, and a slice of cheesecake with raspberry compote. All of it positioned to perfection on china with the White House seal and served with a drink of your choice in glassware etched with the same.

I did notice that the meals were always slightly healthier when the First Lady was on board. The president and his family could order off-menu. Obama, to his credit, almost always stuck to his nutritional pyramid–conforming meal of salmon or chicken, a whole grain, and steamed vegetables, even when his wife wasn't traveling. But even staff who tried to eat healthy usually surrendered upon seeing the menu. Buffalo wings on shorter flights were always crowd pleasers. People still recalled a breakfast leaving Denver: scrambled eggs and bacon served in a nest of crispy hash browns. In one extraordinary exception the year before, dinner after a speech in Austin, Texas, was purchased from the world-famous Franklin Barbecue—brisket, burnt ends, pulled pork, sausage, baked beans, and potato salad. Obama didn't have to wait in the daily six-hour line that stretched down the block, but he did have to hope he hadn't lost votes from the people at the end.

We were billed for each meal a day or two after we returned to Washington. We never complained.

I walked toward the rear of the plane to grab the fresh speech from the printer and noticed Congressman John Lewis, Speaker John Boehner, and a gaggle of other members of Congress eating their lunches in the guest cabin. Just the sight of Lewis, fifty years older but with every ounce of the purpose about him that he had as a young civil rights leader, made me pull myself a little straighter. I wanted to shake his hand but told myself to do it later.

I carried the warm pages to the conference room. Obama preferred to spend his inflight time there with his briefing books and a small group of aides who were ready to play cards whenever he was, rather than sit alone in the presidential suite with private office, bedroom, and full bathroom in the nose of the plane.

The conference room on Air Force One was a flying command center with eight seats around a central table, the president at the head, with the Air Force One seal on the wood-paneled wall behind him and a television on the wall facing him. Phones were attached to the table at each seat, and a couch with a phone of its own ran along one wall. Unlike in the movies, we experienced very little drama in the conference room, no high-tech terrorists hacking military video systems to make demands to a room packed with two dozen aides. At night (and, in March, during the day), the screens were turned to basketball.

Whenever a speechwriter entered the conference room to push back on something, Obama's comrades in cards—his talented and crustily funny photographer Pete Souza; his affable trip director, a 6'8" Canadian named Marvin Nicholson; his wry but good-natured personal aide Joe Paulsen; and Josh Earnest—usually glanced up from their hands and smirked as if to say "Good luck with that."

I dropped the speech next to Obama, pretending to study his hand, and raised my eyebrows even though I didn't understand the rules of spades. Then I returned to my cabin, broke the presidential seal around my napkin, and tucked into my lunch just as stewards were clearing everyone else's away.

I was intrigued by one of the additions Obama had made that morning, squeezed along the top and right margins of the page in his neat penmanship.

> That's what I've felt this week—an open heart. That, more than any particular policy or analysis, is what's called upon right now, what a friend of mine calls "that reservoir of goodness, beyond, and of another kind, that we are able to do each other in the ordinary course of things." If we can find that grace, anything is possible. If we can tap that grace, anything can change.

It was less an afterthought to his rewrite the night before, I thought, than an addition based on the flood of fellow feeling after that morning's Supreme Court decision.

The "friend" was a mystery, as was the quote. A Google search came up empty. I didn't really care at that point—I just wanted it to be a painless process through to the end.

I knew that wouldn't be enough for my fiancée, who'd already sent a fusillade of fact-checks during the flight. Kristen had cleverly caught several things I'd gotten slightly wrong, suggesting alternatives to make each line work as intended while reconciling each statement with reality. She also included her usual litany of overanxious concerns: Dr. King had been to Mother Emanuel but hadn't *literally* preached from its pulpit; we weren't *literally* blind to the unique mayhem of gun violence or the pain that the Confederate flag stirs in too many citizens. Those fell into the category of "I know you're not being literal, these are probably fine, but it's our job to point them out so that we can say we did."

ABF, she said. Always Be Fact-checking.

She was the best at what she did and had saved my ass more times than I could count, but she was like Obama—she wanted to work on a speech right up until delivery. I just wanted to be done. With time winding down, I parried each of her concerns with "It's fine." "It's fine." "It's fine."

Right on cue, as Air Force One landed with a jolt, Kristen emailed, copying Alex Platkin, the director of the research department, to ask about Obama's new "friend."

"Where's this quote from? I can't find it anywhere."

I replied honestly: "I have no idea."

"OK, well that scares us. If we get asked about it, we're going to have to ask POTUS who it's from."

She was right, as usual—a leader worth taking seriously couldn't just make stuff up and stiff-arm the press. As Air Force One taxied to the waiting motorcade, I went to find the president in the conference room.

Joe Paulsen, who was putting playing cards back in their box, pointed forward. "He's up front." I walked up to Obama's private office. The door was open; I rapped on the doorframe.

"Hey," Obama said. He was standing behind his desk, undoing his cobalt, maybe sapphire, blue tie so that he could retie it. His flight jacket with presidential seal was draped over the back of his seat. The First Lady was seated, touching up her makeup. I was intruding.

"I'm sorry to disturb you. The new quote at the end—who's it from?"

"That's from my friend Marilynne Robinson."

"Who's that?"

"You don't know Marilynne Robinson? She's a brilliant author. She writes about faith. She won the Pulitzer Prize for *Gilead*."

Later, I'd see how their kinship made sense—her characters often struggled to reconcile the kind of common sense and homespun values that he identified with from his own upbringing with the travails of the modern world. It echoed his frustration with the yawning gap between the goodness and decency he saw in most Americans and the dogmatic smallness of our political life.

But in the moment, I'd never heard of her or *Gilead*. My simmering fear of being exposed as a fraud in front of Obama was suddenly front and center. I'd walked right into it.

"Okay, but I can't find that quote anywhere. Is it from one of her books?"

"Well, you wouldn't find that quote anywhere."

This was starting to feel like a game. "Why not?"

"Because it's from one of her letters to me. She's my pen pal."

I cocked my head to the side. "You have a pen pal?"

He smiled like an excited kid as he fiddled with his four-in-hand knot. "Yeah, we write each other letters!" I looked at the First Lady. She just shrugged.

"Yeah, okay." I shrugged back and walked down the aisle to my seat to relay the news to Kristen and Alex.

"I love that POTUS has pen pals," Kristen wrote.

Alex Platkin, sitting just five feet from Kristen back in Washington, was more sanguine. "What! That's so awesome! I love her stuff." A voracious reader, Alex set a goal each year to read seventy-five books. Once she started working at the White House, she wisely lowered it to fifty. We worked the same hours, but I was lucky if I read a book a month.

"Anyway," I wrote them both, "I think that's a private thing we don't give to the press."

As Air Force One rolled to a stop and the president's motorcade appeared outside the plane's windows, everyone packed their bags and lined up to exit through the rear of the aircraft. Only the First Family and anyone chosen to ride with them in their limousine exited through the front. That day, the Obamas waved from the top of the stairs that had been backed up to the door, walked down to greet the commanders of Joint Base Charleston, which shared runways with Charleston International Airport, and climbed into the limo by themselves.

The president's motorcade is a constant of every presidential trip—a local police lead, two Cadillacs more like luxury tanks than limousines, armored SUVs, a small parade of locally rented Ford Econolines to carry the rest of the traveling circus, an ambulance, a hazmat vehicle, a communications vehicle, and an array of countermeasures to thwart any attack.

In Secret Service parlance, the president's limousine, whatever the model, is always dubbed *Stagecoach*, just like his helicopter, whatever the model, is always *Marine One*. The newest model of limousine, popularly known as "the Beast," went into service the same day he did, on January 20, 2009. Despite its badging as a Cadillac and only four large leather seats in the main cabin, it was neither a smooth nor a quiet ride: Once the Secret Service finished outfitting it with thicker bulletproof glass and more advanced offensive and defensive capabilities than its predecessors, it drove and sounded like its nickname, like a diesel truck. It's where we'd trade office gossip and share notes on what we were watching and listening to. It's where I forever lost my cultural credibility with Obama when I called the movie *Point Break* (the original, not the remake) a classic. I refused to back down from my review.

As the president reads or talks with other passengers, Stagecoach plays a shell game with Spare, the decoy limousine (that day carrying Pete Souza and the president's doctor); Halfback, the SUV carrying the president's protective detail; Control, the SUV carrying the president's national security advisor, military aide, and nuclear football; and a varying number of other SUVs loaded with heavily armored counterassault teams.

The vehicles ferrying staff are usually driven by local volunteers, who pretend they're unfazed by the whole thing while a member of the president's advance team riding shotgun barks at them to keep pace. Finally, the full motorcade is buzzed by a swarm of police motorcycles that rotate positions, speeding ahead to stop traffic as the motorcade rumbles by, then racing past the motorcade to do it again in a constant game of hot potato. There's nothing like it. It's an intricate dance between a 747, four helicopters, and dozens of vehicles—a menacing ballet that makes sure the president's home-court advantage travels with him wherever he goes.

If you missed the motorcade, you were on your own. So it was a strange feeling for me now to stand in the front door of the plane and watch the shiny procession pull away.

Obama had handed me his final edits just before stepping off the plane. I made the call not to follow my usual routine of pecking changes into the speech from the back of a van. The morning's remarks in the Rose Garden had us about twenty minutes behind schedule. Once the president arrived at the memorial service, he would have time only to greet the Pinckney family and AME Church leadership before joining the congregation. With a speech this high profile, I decided to stay behind on Air Force One and get the job done right away.

I leafed through the pages as I walked back to the senior staff cabin. Then I froze, along with my heart. The final two pages were missing. Fuck! I called Marvin Nicholson, who told me that Obama was still working on them several vehicles ahead in the Beast. Before I could object, he assured me he'd collect the pages from the president as soon as the motorcade arrived at the site and call me right away to read me the edits. Marvin delivered as always, and once I pecked in the few remaining edits—one of which was to add Marilynne Robinson's name—the speech was printed and loaded into the teleprompter before Obama took his seat at the service.

All the while, crews were busy getting Air Force One ready for the return trip, refueling, performing maintenance checks, vacuuming, restocking the galley, and tidying the cabin. Tanya, a steward with a short bob and a clipped, professional twang, came by and asked if she could get me anything. My work was done, everybody was gone, and it was after noon on Friday of a long week—I ordered a beer and then clicked SEND, distributing the final version of the eulogy to the widest list of staff.

Hundreds of people were about to read it for the first time. Minutes after that, the press corps would receive an embargoed copy of the text so they could begin writing their stories. And in less than an hour, millions would watch Obama deliver it live.

But the pressure was gone, released with a tap of my finger. It was the most taxing and intoxicating thing about being a speechwriter: For days, you are the most sought-after person on staff, on gameday the most essential, everyone desperate for a piece of you or a peek at what you've been toiling over, unaware of the solitary hours of writing and rewriting, the anxiety and doubt, all of which you leave behind as what you've created from a blank page is let loose on the world.

Nobody had to care about me anymore. I put my feet up, took a long swig of cold beer, and turned on the television.

4

AS THE PRESIDENT'S MOTORCADE ARRIVED, THE MEMORIAL SERVICE was already underway, just around the corner from Mother Emanuel, in the arena where the College of Charleston played basketball. The crowd of nearly six thousand applauded as the Obamas snuck to their seats. Every seat in the arena was full, additional folding chairs had been set up in the concourse, and still thousands more had been turned away. The crowd was diverse, mostly wearing its Sunday best even on a Friday afternoon, lots of women in fancy hats.

Glancing at the program for the memorial service, I guessed there was still half an hour before Obama would speak.

Alone on the plane, I emailed Kristen, Terry, and Ben Rhodes at their desks in the White House, who would all remain my watching buddies and color commentators throughout the afternoon ahead.

"P said he might sing 'Amazing Grace' in the eulogy."

"Um, what?" Terry replied.

"OMG," added Kristen.

"That would be the greatest thing ever," Ben wrote. "Such a good idea. People will love it."

After invocations, and anthems, and Scripture, and the Gospel, and a hymn, and an introduction from a bishop, Obama rose from his seat, climbed the steps, and crossed the stage.

The audience applauded, holding up their phones to document the moment as Obama shook hands with several members of the AME Church leadership. When he docked with the lectern, the audience burst into cheers.

A purple AME banner, the flags of all fifty states, and a regiment of AME bishops, each one clad in purple vestments, were lined up behind him. Reverend Pinckney's coffin, blanketed with red roses, lay before him.

Reverend Pinckney's memorial service was the third among those for the Charleston Nine. Three more would take place the next day, one more on Sunday, one on Monday, and the final one on Tuesday. The Mother Emanuel community must have been exhausted physically and emotionally. But the service was filled with the spirit. Even on television, you could hear members of the congregation calling out and punctuating each set of remarks with "Mmm-hmm" and "Amen."

Obama started speaking at 2:49 P.M., a little over an hour behind schedule.

"Giving all praise and honor to God," he adlibbed.

He didn't wait—he immediately adopted his preacher voice and cadence, drawing out the vowels, emphasizing the first syllable of certain words. The mourners applauded at the first line of Scripture, knowing it by heart.

"They were still living by faith when they died," Obama said. "They did not receive the things promised; they only saw them and welcomed them from a distance, admitting that they were foreigners and strangers on Earth."

He began eulogizing Reverend Pinckney, the clergy behind him peppering every pause and filling every space between every sentence with "My, my," "Mmm-hmm," "Uh-huh," "Yeah."

I knew Obama would feed on it. He'd said he'd have to see if singing would feel right in the moment. With a congregation like this one, I had suspected it would. Watching on TV, I was certain. He wouldn't be left to sing by himself.

"Man, at Mass, they'd whack us if we spoke," Terry wrote from his desk in the West Wing.

Kristen, unable to savor the moment until she was certain the remarks were completely fireproof, had found and shared another concern with the text, even though she too was watching the president round the corner onto the second page.

I told her I loved her and ordered another beer.

Obama improvised a bit more, echoing a part of his eulogy for Beau Biden a few weeks before.

"What a good man. Sometimes, I think that's the best thing to hope for when you're eulogized. After all the words, and recitations, and résumés are read, to just say somebody was a *good* man." The congregation applauded. He raised his voice above theirs, underscoring: "You don't have to be of high station to be a good man."

He continued with the prepared text.

"Preacher by thirteen. Pastor by eighteen. Public servant by twenty-three. What a life Clementa Pinckney lived. What an example he set. What a model for his faith.

"And then to *lose* him at forty-one—slain in his sanctuary with eight wonderful members of his flock, each at different stages in life, but bound together by a common commitment to God.

"Cynthia Hurd. Susie Jackson. Ethel Lance. DePayne Middleton-Doctor. Tywanza Sanders. Daniel L. Simmons Sr. Sharonda Coleman-Singleton. Myra Thompson.

"Good people. Decent people. God-fearing people. People so full of life, and so full of kindness, people who ran the race, who persevered, people of great faith."

He traveled through the Black Church's place in the center of African American life, using what I'd drafted as a starting point but elevating it as he brought all of America along for the journey, adlibbing an exaggerated "Hallelujah!" where necessary.

"They have been, and are, community centers where we organize for jobs and justice; places of scholarship and networking; places where children are loved and kept out of harm's way and told that they are beautiful and smart; taught that they matter.

"*That's* what the Black Church means. Our beating heart; the place where our dignity as a people is inviolate."

Through a verse on the history of Mother Emanuel and what it meant to abolitionists, to the civil rights movement, and to America as a whole, isolated shouts of "That's right," and "Amen, Mr. President," popped from each section of the arena.

"We do not know whether the killer of Reverend Pinckney and eight others knew all this history. But he surely sensed the meaning of his violent act. It was an act that drew on a long history of bombs, and arson, and shots fired at churches—not random, but as a means of control, a way to terrorize and oppress. An act that he imagined would incite fear and recrimination; violence and suspicion; an act that he presumed would deepen divisions that trace back to our nation's original sin."

"My Lord," a bishop behind him chimed in.

It was no longer a speech but a collective endeavor, the president and the faithful feeding off each other, just as the eulogy veered into sermon and the Reverend Obama began to preach.

"Ohhhhhhhh"—Obama drew out the word with a tinge of knowing laughter—"but God works in mysterious ways, doesn't He?"

The crowd rose to its feet again.

"God has different ideas. He didn't know he was being *used* by God."

Praise rang down from the second level of the arena.

"Blinded by hatred, the alleged killer could not see the *grace* surrounding Reverend Pinckney and that Bible study group—the light of love that shone as they opened the church doors and invited a stranger to join their prayer circle."

To the lawyers' relief, Obama had added the word "alleged" to each instance.

"The alleged killer could have never anticipated the way families of the fallen would respond when they saw him in court, in the midst of *unspeakable* grief—with words of forgiveness; he couldn't imagine that."

The crowd was on its feet again. I noticed one of the bishops was wearing sunglasses.

"The alleged killer could not imagine how the city of *Charleston*, under the good and wise leadership of Mayor Riley, how the state of *South Carolina,* how the United States of *America* would respond—with not merely revulsion at this evil act, but with bighearted generosity and, more importantly, with a thoughtful introspection and self-examination that we so rarely see in public life."

"Say it, Mr. President!" Each person in the congregation felt they had a part to play.

"Blinded by hatred, he failed to comprehend what Reverend Pinckney so well understood: the power of God's grace."

"Yes, sir." Each outburst felt instinctive, not intentional.

"You know, this whole week, I've been reflecting on this idea of grace."

The crowd responded with knowing laughs and growing applause as if to say, "Here it comes," as if the message they'd been waiting for was just ahead.

"The grace of the families who lost loved ones," Obama continued, "the grace that Reverend Pinckney would preach about in his sermons, the grace described in one of my favorite hymnals; the one we all know."

Obama read the words.

"Amazing grace."

The crowd cheered.

"How sweet the sound."

The crowd cheered louder.

"That saved a wretch like me."

Louder.

"I once was lost, but now I'm found."

The crowd was on its feet.

"Was blind but now I see."

The organ began to play! In the middle of the eulogy! I'd take that over a heckler any day.

Obama then took a gentle path to the hard places.

"For too long," he said, "we were blind to the pain that the Confederate flag stirred in too many of our citizens." After praising Republicans and Democrats who'd called for it to come down in public places, he continued:

"As we all have to acknowledge, the flag has always represented more than just ancestral pride . . ."

He wasn't even halfway through the sentence before the crowd rose again, ready for the president to tell America the truth. The electric guitarist joined in, adding a blues riff in the middle of the eulogy!

". . . for many, Black and white, that flag was a reminder of systematic oppression . . ."

"Yes!"

". . . and racial subjugation . . ."

"Yes!"

"We see that now. Removing the flag from this state's capitol would not be an act of political correctness; it would not be an insult to the valor of Confederate soldiers. It would simply be an acknowledgment that the *cause* for which they fought . . ."

"Yeah!"

". . . the cause of slavery—was wrong." More cheers. "That the imposition of Jim Crow after the Civil War, the resistance to civil rights for all people, was wrong. It would be one step in an honest accounting of America's history. A modest but meaningful balm for so many unhealed wounds. It would be an expression of the amazing changes that have transformed this state and this country for the better because of the work of so many people of goodwill, people of all races striving to form a more perfect union."

It was the second time he'd spoken the phrase "a more perfect union" in a speech that day. But more important, the whole paragraph was quintessential Obama, a sleight of hand that began by denouncing the sins of our past but ended on a redemptive note that offered everyone the chance to join a new story. Taking down the flag wouldn't be an act of surrender but an act of strength.

"By taking down that flag, we express God's grace."

I'd been on the floor of enough arenas with Obama to know when he and the audience were fully joined in a perfect connection that revealed to each what the other needed, when Obama both accepted and directed the crowd's passion and became the conductor of a living orchestra.

I was generally immune to the emotion an audience felt in these moments, my parade of hours spent with the text before each speech rendering me an outside observer, like I was now, watching on television from an idling aircraft ten miles away. But today, with Obama's rewrite offering text that was still novel to me, I felt an unfamiliar excitement to see what came next.

Obama looked into the distance like he was lost in thought, extemporizing: "But I don't think God wants us to stop there." The crowd egged him on.

He returned to the text. "For too long, we've been blind to the way past injustices continue to shape the present."

"That's right!"

"Perhaps we see that now."

There were subtle differences in the way Obama was saying the word "we." When he was talking about the Black Church, "we" made him one of the Black congregation. When he was talking about the flag, or when he would speak about race and guns momentarily, he shifted back into an American "we."

He delved into national self-examination, suggesting *we*—the American *we*—might question how we allow our children to languish in poverty, or study in failing schools, or grow up without prospects for opportunity. How *we* might be teaching our kids to hate; how *we* might seek to reform our criminal justice system and rebuild trust between the police and the communities they serve; how *we* might search our hearts when writing laws intended to make it harder for Black Americans to vote.

He arrived at an addition to the remarks he'd inserted just that morning. "Maybe we now realize the way racial bias can infect us even when we don't realize it. So that we're guarding against not just racial slurs, but we're also guarding against the subtle impulse to call Johnny back for a job interview but not Jamal."

The crowd roared. It was a brilliant piece of speechwriting, a far more eloquent way to show, not tell, that subtle racism creates an unequal playing field from the start, that white names on résumés are interviewed while Black names are ignored. And it was a fascinating insight into Obama's mind that he recalled a several-years-old University of Chicago study that found a 50 percent gap in callback rates between résumés with white-sounding names and those with Black-sounding names—something he'd also alluded to in a commencement speech at Morehouse College two years earlier: "Every one of you have a grandma or an uncle or a parent who's told you that at some point in life, as an African American, you have to work twice as hard as anyone else if you want to get by.

"For too long . . ." He drew it out. The audience played along, shouting it right back at him: *"For too long!"* In the tradition of the Black Church, the eulogy had fully become a call-and-response in which everyone could participate.

"For too long, we've been blind to the unique mayhem that gun violence inflicts upon this nation. Sporadically, our eyes are open, when nine of our brothers and sisters are cut down in a church basement, and twelve in a movie theater . . ."

"Mmm-hmmm!"

". . . and twenty-six in an elementary school."

"Yes!"

"But I hope we also see the thirty precious lives cut short by gun violence in this country *every single day* . . ."

"My Lord!"

". . . the countless more whose lives are forever changed—the survivors crippled; the children traumatized and fearful every day as they walk to school; the husband who will never feel his wife's warm touch . . ."

"Wow!"

"the entire communities . . ."

"Yes, sir!"

". . . whose grief overflows every time they have to watch what happened to them happen to some other place."

"My Lord!"

He remarked that our eyes had been opened to a majority that wants to do something about it, and that "by acknowledging the pain and loss of others, even as we respect the traditions and ways of life that make up this beloved country; by making the moral choice to change, we express God's grace."

It was the one part of the eulogy I believed the least.

"None of us can expect a transformation in race relations overnight . . ." Then he adlibbed again.

"Every time something like this happens, someone says we have to have a conversation about race. We talk a lot about race. There's no shortcut. We don't need more talk."

"Yes!"

". . . None of us should believe that a handful of gun-safety measures will prevent any tragedy; it will not. People of goodwill will continue to debate the merits of various policies, as our democracy requires; it's a big raucous place, America is, and there are good people on both sides of these debates. Whatever solutions we find will necessarily be incomplete."

I was gratified to see that he was generous enough to have kept much of a paragraph I'd worked on earlier in the week, in one of my more cynical moments, when I seethed that a eulogy would let America off the hook, offering absolution without penance. But as was typical of our collaborations, he elevated it in his more mature and merciful way, ultimately offering the chance for redemption yet again:

> But it would be a betrayal of everything Reverend Pinckney stood for, I believe, if we allowed ourselves to slip into a comfortable silence again, once the eulogies have been delivered, once the TV cameras move on, to go back to business as usual. That's what we so often do. To avoid uncomfortable truths about the prejudice that still infects our society; to settle for symbolic gestures without following up with the hard work of more lasting change—that's how we lose our way again. It would be a refutation of the forgiveness expressed by those families if we merely slipped into the old habits, whereby those who disagree with us are not merely wrong but *bad;* where we shout instead of listen, where we barricade ourselves behind preconceived notions or a well-practiced cynicism.
>
> Reverend Pinckney once said, "Across the South, we have a deep appreciation of history—we haven't always had a deep appreciation of each other's history." What is true in the South is true for America. Clem understood that justice grows out of *recognition* of ourselves in each other; that my liberty depends on you being free too; that history can't be a sword to justify injustice, or a shield against progress, but must be a manual for how to avoid repeating the mistakes of the past, how to break the cycle, a roadway toward a better world. He knew that the path of grace involves an open mind, but more importantly, an open heart.

It was less a recitation than a performance. Parked at my laptop for days, I'd done what I could. Armed with a pen over hours, he'd done what I couldn't. It was less him taking the baton to finish the race—that would imply we ran equally impressive legs—than it was me setting up base camp while he climbed the mountain.

Now he'd outdone himself, stepping up to turn the text into a script, a sheet of music, a piece of American art on display in a striking scene. A Black president, backed by Black bishops, eulogizing a Black victim to a crowd of mostly Black mourners. A Black church service on national television. How often did America see something like this? How often was something like this a quintessentially American event?

Obama had delivered a stirring vision of progressive change, religious faith, and American exceptionalism, joined and made indelible through the stately bearing of a president who had the unapologetic cadence of a preacher until they were all one and the same.

He'd long since grown into being president. We were watching him make the presidency bigger in real time. And there was one act left.

"That's what I've felt this week—an open heart. That, more than any particular policy or analysis, is what's called upon right now, I think, what a friend of mine, the writer Marilynne Robinson, calls 'that reservoir of goodness, beyond, and of another kind, that we are able to do each other in the ordinary cause of things.'

"That reservoir of goodness."

"Mmm hmm."

"If we can find *that* grace . . ."

"Uh huh . . ."

". . . anything is possible."

"My my."

"If we can tap *that* grace, everything can change."

Fewer than a dozen people in the world knew what was about to happen.

"Amazing grace."

He paused, then repeated the words for good measure.

"Amazing grace."

Obama looked into the distance, looked down at the text, and shook his head in awe.

Eleven seconds went by. It was a moment of genuine drama. Was he making up his mind? Was he going to take the leap of faith?

I wondered what people who were watching must be thinking: *Had he lost his place?*

Then he began to sing.

After the first two syllables, "Ah-maaaay," one of the bishops laughed in astonishment. But it was too early for most of the world to know for sure what Obama was doing.

Obama leaned into the next two syllables—"ZIIII-iiii-iiiing graaaaaaace"—to make damn sure they knew.

The choir leaped to its feet. One of the bishops tore off the sunglasses he'd been wearing throughout the eulogy. The others, a bit older and slower, followed. Then the entire congregation.

By the time Obama hit "how sweet the sound," the whole arena was singing with him. The organ jumped in at "a wretch like me." The drummer tapped his cymbals with a light touch, but so fast his sticks became a blur, creating a sustained swell of "tssssssssss." The horn section began to blow. The guitarist uncorked another blues riff. Obama's bet, that he wouldn't be left alone, had paid off.

White House staffers in the makeshift office under the bleachers, unaware of the plan Obama had revealed on Marine One, shouted at each other, "Is he *singing*?" then ran to the entrance to the arena floor.

Amazing grace, how sweet the sound, that saved a wretch like me;
I once was lost, but now I'm found; was blind but now I see.

The crowd erupted as Obama finished. The choir members all laughed and hugged each other. Obama continued with the eulogy, remembering every victim.

Clementa Pinckney found that grace.

Cynthia Hurd found that grace.

Susie Jackson found that grace.

Ethel Lance found that grace.

DePayne Middleton-Doctor found that grace.

Tywanza Sanders found that grace.

Daniel L. Simmons Sr. found that grace.

Sharonda Coleman-Singleton found that grace.

Myra Thompson found that grace.

The congregation applauded through it all, saluting each victim with a "Yeah!"

Obama had wisely kept the final paragraph of the eulogy short and tight. He knew people wouldn't return to their seats. The organ kept playing as he spoke, fingers flying over keys.

"May grace now lead them home. And may God continue to shed His grace on the United States of America."

The eulogy complete, Obama hugged the bishops one by one, waved to the crowd, collected his binder, walked back down the stairs, hugged Reverend Pinckney's family along with a Joe Biden still mourning his own son, kissed the First Lady, saluted the audience one last time, then took his seat.

Through it all, the organ never stopped playing "Amazing Grace," the choir never stopped singing, the cymbals never stopped clanging.

The organist, Charles Miller Jr., would later be asked about his contributions to the eulogy.

"As he sang the first word, the first thought in my mind was, *Oh wow, he's really going to sing.* So I'm thinking to myself, *Do we play along?* I just closed my eyes, said a quick word of prayer, because I knew the world was watching, and let the Lord lead me into what to do next."

Obama was a perfectionist. Someone practiced in precision, from the food he consumed to the speeches he delivered. He was a self-proclaimed better speechwriter than his speechwriters; he self-diagnosed as having great comedic timing; he once boasted "I'm LeBron, baby," about his political skill.

But to sing this song, on this occasion, was something different altogether. Women may have fawned over him once when he crooned the opening bars of Al Green's "Let's Stay Together" at a fundraiser. B.B. King and Mick Jagger may have coerced him once to howl "Sweet Home Chicago" at a White House concert broadcast on PBS. But this was a much bigger stage. Millions in a divided country and around the world would be watching.

It was a much bigger leap of faith.

I thought back to something Obama had said in the unusually freewheeling interview he'd recorded for Marc Maron's *WTF* podcast from Maron's Los Angeles garage exactly one week before.

"I was talking to somebody the other day about why I actually think I'm a better president, and would be a better candidate if I were running again, than I have ever been. And it's sort of like an athlete: You might slow down a little bit, you might not jump as high as you used to—but I know what I'm doing and I'm fearless."

"For real," Maron had interjected. "You're not pretending to be fearless."

"Right, you're not pretending to be fearless," Obama had replied. "And when you get to that point . . ."

"Freedom."

"And also part of that fearlessness is, because you've screwed up enough times, that you know that . . . It's all happened. I've been through this . . . I've screwed up. I've been in the barrel tumbling down Niagara Falls. And I emerged and I lived. And that's always a—that's such a liberating feeling, right?"

That's what I saw on that stage. Liberation.

5

ONCE THE MEMORIAL SERVICE ENDED, THE OBAMAS AND BIDENS met privately with each of the families of the Charleston Nine—in a series of offices and training rooms, whatever the advance team had commandeered in the arena—just as the Obamas had at eulogies in

Tucson, Newtown, and a litany of other communities reeling after mass shootings.

I had two hours before everyone arrived back at the plane. My inbox was dinging like a slot machine. My twitter feed was a scrolling spasm of "WHAT" "OMG" "Y'ALL." Even the usual critics were admitting that they were going to miss this guy when he was gone.

A personal favorite reaction came from Ahmir "Questlove" Thompson, producer and drummer for the Roots, who'd shared his pain after Trayvon Martin's killer was acquitted two years earlier in the essay "Trayvon Martin and I Ain't Shit."

Dog, POTUS just went to E Flat like he was collabing w Stevie & Jam/Lewis (for those unaware E flat is THE blackest blues note ever)

Obama would like that one. I reminded myself to show him when he returned.

In the meantime, I texted the tweet to Danielle Gray, who'd responded to that essay and the outcry after the verdict almost two years before not by sitting around a table debating what Obama *should* do, but by grabbing a pen to come up with "My Brother's Keeper" and handing Obama a list of things he *could* do to make a difference.

Danielle replied with a string of exclamation points. "I wish my grandpa were alive to hear POTUS sing 'Amazing Grace' in E flat behind the pulpit. He once explained that if you can't sing E flat in church, you might not be a Black man. 'You definitely ain't saved,' he'd say.

"Seriously, what a week," she continued. "I was so sad last Friday. Amazing, the turnaround."

I knew she hadn't forgotten that it was a memorial service, as Twitter and TV's talking heads seemed to have done. They were still swept up in Obama singing, which I understood—it was an extraordinary moment. But it was still a moment rooted in grief. Danielle was moved by the fact that a Black president—someone she'd called a friend before he was even a senator—had just taken the country and much of the world into the Black church for the first time.

As for me, I hoped that people were as pleasantly surprised by what he'd said—both from the Rose Garden and from a stage in Charleston—as they were with how he sang.

I hoped there were millions of people across America—and the world—who felt better about themselves, who felt as American as anyone else, because of the way their president had talked about them.

I hoped people who were frustrated with politics felt that Obama had taken us above the muddy battlefield of petty tribalism, even if just for a day, offering the chance to see one another anew.

As she had at the beginning of the week, Fiona Reeves, who managed the president's correspondence, sent me a few emails that her team had pulled from the barrage of messages inundating the White House website.

"I think you should see these," she wrote.

Mr. President,

With this supreme court ruling today, I feel as if I can finally breathe. I can finally walk down the street knowing that I am just as deserving and valued as anyone else I may pass by. I know that the Supreme Court made the decision, but without you setting the stage, it would never have happened. I could go on at length, but I will leave it at this: you are my hero, and you very well may have saved me.

Mr. President,

When you came to MacDill AFB I was standing there in the front row when you stated clearly how you depended on us, your military, and how you know you could count on us when called. Well today I know for certain that I can count on you.

You've done a great job against difficult odds and a ton of resistance and yet you continue to fight for us. I'm a medic, but I'm willing to fight and die for the values of this country, to protect and heal peoples suffering all over the world. It's so comforting to know that my commander in chief has our backs and is willing to put it on the line to heal and protect us too. Thank you, Sir!

Dear President Obama,

I thank you for your magnanimous speech this morning after the Supreme Court ruling on same-sex marriage. I got goose bumps—and I'm a conservative! I have struggled with this issue as I have wanted my gay and lesbian friends to be able to do as they please, while also understanding that marriage has always literally meant "between man and woman" since the beginning of recorded history. Thank you so much for stating our greatness as a country in forming a greater Union, and that we are one country with much diversity and that people can believe differently. You also stated the importance of religious freedom, which was deeply appreciated by me. I believe this was your greatest speech, sir. I love my country, and I thank you for your service to it. We will pray for you, and may God continue to bless you!

Mr. President,

While you and I disagree 98 % of the time, I feel that I must give credit where credit is due. Your speech regarding the SCOTUS gay marriage decision was one of the most eloquent speeches that I have heard you or anyone else give. It not only addressed this historical decision, but brought it into perspective as to how this is part of the dynamic that is America. It made me proud to be American. I could tell you were speaking from the heart. You made tears come to my eyes. Good job! Now if you will excuse me, it is time for me to go, Rush Limbaugh is on. :-) God Bless the USA!

Mr. President,

With the ACA, gay marriage, your lack of restraint in condemning congress for not renovating gun laws—to me this is your finest hour. "Change" and "hope" have been given body. I can't thank you enough. It's been a pleasure growing up with you. You've made me proud to be an American.

Dear Mr. President,

I didn't vote for you. One of my biggest regrets in life. Your speech in SC absolutely blew me away. I'm 66 and a product of the 60's where cynical verbiage regarding our politics prevailed. After all of these years you have changed my attitude. For at least one week I'm so proud of being an American. So proud of the real change and direction this wonderful country is going. A lot more work but this last week kicked butt! You, my president, have led us. Just a quick note to thank you.

And finally,

I don't know if the president would really see this or not but it's a shot, I never got to meet you or really ever cared what you had to say only cause I passed judgment for the color of your skin and thought it was wrong you were president, I cursed the fact you took office due to my lack of knowledge of who people are and looking at their skin but not their heart and seeing who they really are, seeing that there is more to this world than judging someone trying to make a better place for me and the rest of us, after seeing the loss of the nine people passing in that church over one man's hate made me see I was being like him full of hate for no reason and I'm sorry I wish nothing but a long healthy life for you and your family and thank you for all you have done, you have made a difference in our lives, God bless.

Each letter gave meaning to what the President had added to the eulogy that morning: "That's what I've felt this week—an open heart."

That pesky lump took shape in my throat again.

The speakers crackled: "Attention on board the aircraft, the president is five minutes out."

I called Kristen before the plane filled with people again. "Well, that was something."

"Everyone here is beyond words," she said. "Today is the most *West Wing* day of all the days."

"This week is too far-fetched for a full *season* of *West Wing,*" I said with a laugh. "And there's more: POTUS and FLOTUS want to come to our wedding." I'd thought about whether to tell her; I knew it would trigger anxiety that would make wedding planning feel more like a job than a joy.

"What! So do we have to get married in D.C. then?"

"Let's talk about it some other time and enjoy today. Speaking of which, you should encourage your team to stick around for a while tonight."

"Why? We're exhausted."

"They're going to light up the front of the White House in rainbow colors."

"Stop it."

"I know, right? But they also want to keep it a bit of a surprise, so Valerie told me to tell my team and yours to head to the vice president's balcony for celebratory beers as a way to keep people around until it's dark enough." The balcony off the vice president's ceremonial office in the Eisenhower Executive Office Building looked out over the West Wing to the North Lawn, where the lights were set up. "And rather than land right away, Marine One is going to loop around the front of the house so the Obamas can see the show. So go out front for that!"

"Amazing! Will you be on the helicopter?"

"Pete's taking my seat so he can get photos. I'll be back about half an hour after they are."

"Oh, boo. Okay, I'll tell the team!"

The motorcade appeared outside the windows at 5:17, only seventeen minutes behind schedule. They'd made up some time.

Thirty seconds later, I heard Obama yell from the front of the plane, "Let's go home!" Denis, Valerie, and Tina piled back into the small cabin I'd had to myself for the past four hours and gave me bearhugs in turn.

Obama soon followed, looking for me. "Cody!" I stood up, and he gave dap, clasping my hand at chest level and slapping my back, punctuated by a fist pound.

"I think that was pretty good," he said.

I laughed. "You need someone to start following you around with an organ." He chuckled.

"And you said you had nothing left to say," Valerie interjected.

"The spirit moved me," he said. "And those people carried me."

"The muse hit," I added.

He concurred. "The muse hit."

"One thing," I said. "You'd already decided you were going to sing."

"I warned you guys!"

"What was with the pause? Dramatic effect?"

"No, man," Obama said. "You know what the thing about 'Amazing Grace' is?"

Obviously, I did not.

He pushed one hand, palm down, toward the floor like he was hushing a crowd. "You gotta start low. Or by the time you get to 'a wretch like me,' you're in trouble. Your voice cracks."

That reminded me to show him Questlove's tweet. He repeated the last part out loud. "The blackest blues note *ever*!" He enjoyed praise like that. Then he straightened his face. "And it was those families that gave us the idea. I just met with them all. That was hard. Some of them were crying. Some of them were still in shock. But they appreciated us being there. They were exactly as kind and loving as you'd hope them to be. I just didn't want to let them down."

Everyone was quiet for a couple seconds. "But you should all feel good," he added. "This was a good day, everybody." He slapped the back of a chair and left the cabin.

Denis was grinning at me with his hands on his hips. "You must be ready to pass out. TGIF, huh?"

"You have no idea, man," I told him. "Don't call me this weekend."

"That's a promise," he replied.

Tanya, the steward who'd been keeping my glass full all afternoon, entered our small cabin to ask each of us if we wanted dinner, then pointed at my empty glass with her eyebrows raised in invitation.

"How 'bout a bourbon," I said.

Valerie overheard my order. "Now we're talking. See, aren't you glad we did that?"

I knew she was kidding, but I groaned to play along.

"I knew you two would get it there," she said, "or I wouldn't have suggested it." I believed that she believed that. But I also knew that she knew the boss better than anybody. She might have had faith in me, but she had unwavering faith in him.

"Valerie, he—"

She cut me off. "I know what he did. I saw him right after the SCOTUS decision this morning and saw how much work he'd put into it. I told you he would. But he couldn't have gotten there without you."

Valerie and Tina left to visit with the rest of the staff onboard. Through the open door of the senior staff cabin, across the aisle of the plane, there was a small side table next to a couch used for impromptu meetings or, for someone quick enough to claim it, a decent night's sleep on an intercontinental flight. A small lamp cast a cone of light on a basket of fruit and a tray of candy and gum. I noticed John Lewis standing there, waiting to see the president. He was quiet, small in stature for someone whose words were once described as having so much weight that they "might as well be carved in granite." I went to shake his hand for the first time. I didn't introduce myself as a speechwriter, just as someone who worked for the president.

He'd seen a lot in his life. "I don't think I've ever seen anything like that," he said.

6

KRISTEN KEPT SENDING ME HAPPY NEWS CLIPS AS WE FLEW BACK from Charleston. Champagne was flowing outside gay bars that fifty years earlier had to keep the blinds closed. Jubilant crowds had grown in the small park opposite the Stonewall Inn in New York City. There had been same-sex weddings at city halls in Denver, New York, and Detroit, where a couple of forty-five years were the first to show up. Mobile, Alabama, had issued its first-ever same-sex marriage license. Senators were already moving to rewrite the tax code to replace "husband and wife" with "married couple" and "spouse." Change was coming fast.

Nightfall, though, wasn't coming as quickly. Not in June, during what were the longest days of the year. By the time Marine One lifted off from Andrews at six forty, sunset was still two hours away, with darkness half an hour after that.

As it turned out, the extra time was a blessing. Because by six thirty, the lights still weren't working.

My suspicion after the president's remarks in the Rose Garden that morning had been correct: Jeff had been rushing from the back to the front of the Residence to start plugging in lights with the vendor and White House electricians.

They tested the lights at midday, in the safety of an hour when the colors wouldn't be bright enough to show on the White House and spoil the surprise. Half of them didn't work. The other half kept flickering. When they opened the supposedly water-resistant black boxes in which the lights were encased, water came pouring out. Jeff told Jen Psaki that they'd keep troubleshooting the problem, but the lights he'd been working on for months might not happen after all.

The crew troubleshooted for hours. Then, shortly after six thirty, all ninety of the LEDs lit up at once—and stayed lit. Jeff fist bumped all the electricians in turn.

He called Jen Psaki. "Jen, they're working. For now. Should we turn them to full power? Once people notice the colors, we can't stop. What should we do?"

"Give 'em full power, Jeff," Jen told him.

White House staffers who'd heard about the scheme had begun to gather on the North Lawn. That caught the attention of the press corps, who spread word to camera crews that began to set up across Pennsylvania Avenue, which in turn attracted a small crowd of tourists hoping they'd be lucky enough to catch a glimpse of the president.

Buzz was building, the lights were at full power, and there was no going back.

But in daylight, the White House façade still appeared . . . white. With nothing to see yet, the Marine One flight plan around the front of the White House was scuttled. The Obamas landed on the South Lawn as usual and held hands as they strolled inside. I arrived back at the West Wing in a van at seven fifteen, dropped my backpack in my office, and walked around the front of the house to peek. I could make out the faintest hint of color, a series of barely pastel bands, but only because I knew to look.

The crowd of tourists and District residents kept growing organically. By eight o'clock, the sills and lintels of the White House windows had begun capturing the colors—red, orange, yellow, green, blue, and violet. By eight thirty, the Portico was fully yellow and green. And by nine thirty, the White House was gleaming in full rainbow, a canvas for a once-in-a-lifetime display.

Photos flooded social media feeds, drawing even bigger throngs of happy people to Lafayette Park. They were every age, race, orientation, class, and creed, all hugging and high fiving and slapping one another on the back. There were no strangers that night. The crowds were just as big as the crowds the night in 2011 when bin Laden met his end, just as loud in their chants of "USA." But there was a lot more kissing. And signs that said LOVE IS LOVE. And a gay men's chorus singing "America the Beautiful."

The gathering in 2011 had felt more like catharsis, an ending, a primal emotional release at the demise of an existential boogeyman. This was exhilarating, like we were breaking free from the burdens of the past. The old limits on America were disappearing, and something new and exciting was possible. A beginning.

It was an expression of joy for all the Americans who'd finally been told their own love was equal to everybody else's, and for the rest of us now that we'd taken another big step together on America's journey to equality. For the millions more who were watching on television, both in the United States and around the world who were wrestling with their identity or their place, it was all a clear symbol that the president of the United States had their back.

Valerie offered a toast to the staff and LGBTQ advocates who'd gathered on the vice president's balcony. She told everyone how proud they should be for helping to make sure the next generation of Americans would grow up knowing that this big, raucous, contradictory country of ours had a place for everybody.

Stephen Goepfert, one of Vice President Biden's young aides, was listening but staring at the colors on the White House. His eyes welled up with tears. He felt as if he hadn't done anything to help make the day a reality. He decided that it would be the last day he walked through the White House gates as a closeted gay man. He left later that night to begin the long journey of letting his family and friends know who he was.

Sarada called her best friend and told him to come meet her in the park, thinking it would be a fitting milestone on the journey they'd taken since the night their sophomore year of college when he quietly came out to her in her dorm room.

At least two women who worked at the White House proposed to their girlfriends on the North Lawn that evening. Two more, Sarah Feldman and Emily Loeb, a young lawyer on the 2008 campaign who ultimately worked as an attorney at the Department of Justice to overturn the Defense of Marriage Act, made plans to scout wedding venues in North Carolina the next day. Kristen made a note to start scouting our own.

The original plan called for turning off the lights at eleven o'clock. But the crowds kept growing; people were showing up singing the national anthem. Jeff Tiller asked Valerie and Tina Tchen if the First Family would be okay with an all-night lightshow. They said yes. He checked with the Secret Service to make sure they wouldn't have any safety concerns. They didn't, citing the vibe out front as positive—but they did require that Jeff stay there all night to help turn the lights off in case of a security breach.

Jeff and his partner Jonny had plans to go to a bar. "Change of plans," Jeff said. "We're in charge of the lights all night. But I know where we can get some lawn chairs and beer. You in?"

"Let's do it," Jonny replied. The two would sit together on the North Lawn until the crowds finally thinned enough to turn off the lights a little before dawn.

I was aware that there were plenty of Americans who didn't share the widespread joy about any of it, who instead of euphoria only saw a further erosion of their own hold on America and people rubbing their noses in it. There would be backlash at some point. There always was. It was like Obama had said a thousand times: For every two steps forward, there was a step back. Or worse. That's the way progress has always been. But for that night, we let ourselves celebrate.

I didn't see any of the celebration, though.

Kristen had gone home before I'd even arrived back at the White House, calling her closest girlfriends and telling them to assemble at our apartment. While they reveled and made plans for the evening, beginning with a stop at the full-color White House, I closed my eyes for what I thought was a minute—only to wake up an hour later to a nuzzle from Kristen, who asked me if I wanted to join them for the party.

I thought about it. It would be a memorable way to mark the fourth anniversary of the day we'd met. Instead, I told her I loved her and said she should go have fun with the girls. My heart was full, but I was running on empty. And I slept until morning.

Kristen and her friends joined the festivities at the White House, where people stayed all night, celebrating one brief, brilliant moment when that dream we had when we were younger came true and, together, we'd done the most extraordinary thing of all: made the world a better place.

Mrs. Obama and Malia snuck out onto the North Lawn to see it all unfold. President Obama, whose presence would require Secret Service to push back the crowds on Pennsylvania Avenue, stayed inside. But I like to think he made a martini and pulled aside the drapes to sneak a peek at the America he'd helped birth into being.

Epilogue

THE DAY BEFORE DYLANN ROOF MURDERED NINE PEOPLE IN Charleston, Donald Trump announced his candidacy for president in a bloviating fusillade of lies asserting that a variety of dark forces had warped the American Dream into a besieged and humiliated nightmare of crime and corruption—and that it was time to take our country back.

For the next year and a half, he waged a campaign based on exploiting the resentment of those susceptible to that argument, pledging to keep America what it was rather than imagine what it could be. At every step, he found societal fault lines to fracture with hostile rhetoric aimed at women, Blacks, Muslims, Asians, Americans with disabilities, and, with some glee, the press and his primary opponents, most of whom assumed Trump's campaign was a joke, a form of entertainment that would go the way of his casinos, his airline, his steaks, his vodka, his mortgage company, and his bottled water—until it was too late.

President Obama saw something more dangerous. Late in 2015, he told me he wanted to make his final State of the Union Address one about the state of our democracy, a theme he'd continue throughout his final year in office in commencement addresses, at the Democratic National Convention, and before the UN General Assembly. In those speeches, he examined the very real challenges facing a changing America and much of the first world—political gridlock, racial division, disinformation and a hostility to facts and reason, and the growing gulf between economic haves and have-nots—challenges that posed a unique threat to the inherent fragility of democracy. He presented a choice between the hard work of harnessing our strengths as a nation to enact actual solutions, or the easy retreat into conflict along lines of race and tribe exploited by the latest model of demagogues peddling distrust and disinformation.

At the 2016 Democratic National Convention in Philadelphia, twelve years to the night when he introduced himself to the world in a speech asking America to choose between a politics of cynicism and one of hope, he again presented the values of liberal democracy as the election's ultimate stakes:

> America has never been about what one person says he'll do for us. It's always been about what can be achieved by us, together, through the hard, slow, sometimes frustrating, but ultimately enduring work of self-government . . .
>
> There's been a lot of talk in this campaign about what America's lost—people who tell us that our way of life is being undermined by pernicious changes and dark forces beyond our control. They tell voters there's a "real America" out there that must be restored.

Obama returned to the lessons he'd learned from people like his Kansas grandparents, who "didn't admire braggarts or bullies."

> They didn't respect mean-spiritedness, or folks who were always looking for shortcuts in life. Instead, they valued traits like honesty and hard work. Kindness and courtesy. Humility; responsibility; helping each other out.
>
> That's what they believed in. True things. Things that last. The things we try to teach our kids . . . They knew these values were

exactly what drew immigrants here, and they believed that the children of those immigrants were just as American as their own, whether they wore a cowboy hat or a yarmulke; a baseball cap or a hijab.

America has changed over the years. But these values my grandparents taught me—they haven't gone anywhere. They're as strong as ever; still cherished by people of every party, every race, and every faith. They live on in each of us. What makes us American, what makes us patriots, is what's in here. That's what matters. That's why we can take the food and music and holidays and styles of other countries and blend it into something uniquely our own. That's why we can attract strivers and entrepreneurs from around the globe to build new factories and create new industries here. That's why our military can look the way it does, every shade of humanity, forged into common service.

That's why anyone who threatens our values, whether fascists or communists or jihadists or homegrown demagogues, will always fail in the end.

Ultimately, that might still be true. But for the next four years, the Trump administration was a nightmare for the idea of a pluralistic democracy, an endless litany of policies and rhetoric aimed at punishing historically marginalized groups of Americans while protecting the cruelty of people who did the same. Underscoring that his brand of economic populism was bullshit, Trump cut taxes for the richest Americans, gutted environmental protections, and held a (premature) victory celebration in the Rose Garden after the House of Representatives voted to repeal the Affordable Care Act and snatch health insurance from millions of working Americans—all while using the powers of the presidency to enrich his own family. For good measure, Trump shredded decades of America's role and responsibility in the world and maintained an embarrassing subservience to the foreign strongmen he admired.

But perhaps most pernicious was his casual and constant undermining of the values, ideals, and institutional conventions that hold a democracy together. He used his bully pulpit to spew a toxic stream of lies, hatred, and paranoia that proved him incapable of the moral imagination required to rally Americans around a common identity or common purpose. And that encouraged America's basest elements to crawl out from under the rocks where they'd been hiding.

In 2017, a gang of white nationalists, right-wing militias, neo-Nazis, and even Klansmen who'd been waiting in the wings for years marched without hoods and with torches on Charlottesville, Virginia (that they were tiki torches added a dash of withering absurdity to what otherwise evoked countless lynch mobs from a darker time). They chanted "White lives matter" and "Jews will not replace us" in protests that ultimately ended with the death of a young woman. In what should have been a presidential moment, Trump instead said, "We condemn in the strongest possible terms this egregious display of hatred, bigotry, and violence on many sides, on many sides." Days later, pushed to clarify, he doubled down: "You had some very bad people in that group, but you also had people that were very fine people, on both sides."

His words equating white nationalist violence with people protesting white nationalism were a dark reflection of Obama after Charleston, not a balm but a bullhorn giving his blessing to far-right elements across the country that political violence would be tolerated. It was as if he'd unleashed something primal, a highly contagious strain of hatred for which he could escape direct blame and wouldn't unequivocally condemn.

Over ten days in October 2018, just before the midterm elections, America was visited by a spree of hate crimes. Outside of Louisville, an armed racist convinced of an epidemic of Black-on-white crime was thwarted from entering a Black church service only to murder two Black shoppers at a grocery store, reassuring a white customer that "whites don't shoot whites." In Tallahassee, a self-professed misogynist complaining that he couldn't find a girlfriend shot up a yoga studio, killing two and wounding five. In south Florida, a man who plastered Trump photos on his van, consumed Fox News, and was steeped in social media conspiracy theories was captured after mailing pipe bombs to CNN headquarters and to a dozen of Trump's political opponents, including President Obama, Joe Biden, and Hillary Clinton. Trump pledged justice, then blamed the media for the rising anger in America. In Pittsburgh, a man obsessed with what he saw as a Jewish conspiracy to replace whites with undocumented immigrants entered a synagogue shouting "All Jews must die" before killing eleven and wounding six in the deadliest attack on the Jewish community in American history. The killer had posted on social media: "I can't sit by and watch my people get slaughtered." Trump suggested that the outcome might have been different if there had been armed guards in the synagogue.

In 2020, when a police officer in Minneapolis killed a Black man named George Floyd by kneeling on his neck for nine minutes despite the man's pleas that he couldn't breathe, Trump called it a "terrible, terrible thing that happened." But he'd also suggested in a speech to police officers three years earlier that they rough up suspects. "Don't be too nice," he'd said. And as the protests over Floyd's murder began, Trump warned of "lawless anarchy and chaos," labeled protesters "thugs," and suggested that "when the looting starts, the shooting starts."

Along with the rule of law, America itself felt like it was coming undone. Trump's animus, falsehoods, and conspiracy theories had infected the body politic like a virus.

And then, in early 2020, the real virus arrived. Trump was caught flat-footed, denying the threat, ducking blame, and decrying experts' recommendations to slow the pandemic's spread. Rather than marshal the American people and our considerable resources to save lives with science, he placed himself at the center of the show, equal parts victim and carnival barker, peddling miracle cures like a snake oil salesman with his eye on his television ratings—even after he was hospitalized with the disease.

By the end of his term in office, the sturdy economy Trump had inherited was in shambles, four hundred thousand Americans were dead from COVID-19, and the lies he'd sowed had grown into an untamable jungle of disinformation that guaranteed people would continue to die for years.

The man who promised to be "the greatest jobs president that God ever created" ended up the first to lose jobs over his term since Herbert Hoover and the first to be impeached not once, but twice—first for trying to blackmail a foreign power into helping him win office, then for inciting a violent insurrection to help him *stay* in office.

Thirty thousand documented lies over one term ended with the biggest lie of all—that he'd won the 2020 election.

In early November, democracy hung for days as cities painstakingly counted ballots, a process that Trump declared a fraud and filed suit after suit to halt. He encouraged his supporters to dismiss the election results and descend on Washington to "stop the steal."

On January 6, 2021, many obeyed, including a mix of white nationalists and right-wing militia groups. At a morning rally on the National Mall, Trump urged them to head to the Capitol to protest the certification of electoral votes, telling them, "You'll never take back our country with weakness. You have to show strength and you have to be strong."

He said he'd go with them. He didn't.

Trump's mob stormed the Capitol, smashing windows, breaking down doors, even assaulting police officers while hunting for the proceedings inside so they could, in their minds, halt the electoral vote certification. Confederate flags were marched through the Capitol, a shocking disgrace to America that hadn't occurred even during the Civil War. The House and Senate chambers were evacuated; Secret Service whisked away Vice President Mike Pence, who refused to indulge Trump's directive to overturn the election results.

Americans still sheltering in place from the pandemic watched on television, horrified, as the symbol of our democracy became the scene of a chaotic and bloody terror attack.

In the months afterward, despite thousands of hours of video from phones and television cameras, the Trump faithful attempted to whitewash the insurrection and gaslight America into believing that the political violence we all witnessed with our own eyes was as quintessentially American as a Norman Rockwell painting.

Even as this book goes to print, Trump persists in peddling the biggest lie, caterwauling at every opportunity that the election was stolen from him. He has admitted that he ordered the election results overturned, considered seizing voting machines, and pledged that, if he wins again, he'll pardon anyone who stormed the Capitol—less an act of mercy than the promise of a future get-out-of-jail free card for anyone who breaks the law on his behalf.

Meanwhile, the rest of his party carries on with efforts to dismantle democracy in broad daylight. Republican senators filibuster any law that might protect voting rights; Republican legislatures push new laws that would make it harder for people of color to register and vote and easier for partisans to overturn a legitimate election result; new Republican officeholders with no interest in governing, only right-wing fame, inspired by Trump and drunk on the megaphone that social media offers, cast political opponents as enemies that must be stopped and elections that don't go their way as rigged invitations to bloodshed. A newly revanchist majority on the Supreme Court—secured when Mitch McConnell, Republican leader of the Senate, took the unprecedented action of refusing to allow President Obama to fill an empty seat before rushing through three of Trump's nominees—set its sights on overturning *Roe v. Wade* along with other hard-earned women's rights and civil rights, including marriage equality.

Even the smallest of men can do outsized damage to the idea of America.

The outcome of the clash of wills, the contest to determine the true meaning of America, is as up for grabs as it has been at any point in my lifetime. And when every day seems small—when every algorithmic invitation to fight *against* some perceived outrage on the battlefields of social media serves as a grating reminder that the people on the other side of that bridge to a better America are louder and angrier—it can feel like our politics are no longer up to the task.

But there's a reason they work so feverishly to lock in minority rule: They know they're the minority. They know they're outnumbered by Americans who know what this country *can* be, a place of equality and diversity and progress and democracy where *all* of us have a role to play. And for all the mileage that remains on that journey, we marched closer to it during those ten days in June 2015 than ever before. We felt it. We lived through it in real time.

After Favs left the White House, he started a company called Crooked Media along with Jon Lovett, Tommy Vietor, and Dan Pfeiffer. In a podcast about the past and future of the Democratic Party, he talked with Rebecca Traister, a political writer and feminist, about Obama's belief that the story of America is each generation trying to turn the founding promise of this country into a reality. At least that was the idea, Favs joked, "back in the hopeful days."

"He was right to have that hope," Traister countered, "because it is possible. It is possible. But the fact that it's possible is precisely what has provoked the punishing pushback that we're living through right now. It's the fact that it's within our grasp to make another huge set of steps toward inclusion and equality and toward the promises, the unfulfilled promises of our founding. It's because we're on the brink of getting to that next place that we are being hit so hard. That's exactly what we're in the midst of right now, and it's not because it's impossible to get to that next step. It's because it's really possible."

For his Farewell Address, in January 2017, President Obama and I tried to stoke that sense of possibility, even when things felt darkest, writing a direct appeal to Americans who may not have felt the urgency to get involved while he was in office to step up and become active citizens in their democracy.

> It falls to each of us to be those anxious, jealous guardians of our democracy; to embrace the joyous task we've been given to continually try to improve this great nation of ours. Because for all our outward differences, we all share the same proud title: Citizen.

> Ultimately, that's what our democracy demands. It needs you. Not just when there's an election, not just when your own narrow interest is at stake, but over the full span of a lifetime. If you're tired of arguing with strangers on the internet, try to talk with one in real life. If something needs fixing, lace up your shoes and do some organizing. If you're disappointed by your elected officials, grab a clipboard, get some signatures, and run for office yourself. Show up. Dive in. Persevere. Sometimes you'll win. Sometimes you'll lose. Presuming a reservoir of goodness in others can be a risk, and there will be times when the process disappoints you. But for those of us fortunate enough to have been a part of this work, to see it up close, let me tell you, it can energize and inspire. And more often than not, your faith in America—and in Americans—will be confirmed.

Eleven days after that speech, on the first day of the Trump presidency, women marched across the country in the largest single-day protest in American history, joined soon after by protesters packing airports in opposition to Trump's "Muslim ban"; by masses of young people organizing marches against gun violence and for climate science; and by a restless new generation of lawmakers, the most diverse and female in history, bounding up the steps of Congress.

One in five Americans claimed participation in at least one protest since the beginning of the Trump administration—many of them following the killing of George Floyd. Without cellphone video, his death might have gone unnoticed, another footnote in a history of state-sponsored violence against Black men. Instead, it ignited more than five thousand protests across the country within a month—not just in diverse metropolises, but in small, rural, mostly white towns where people summoned empathy and common cause, even in cities around the world relieved to see that the America they thought they knew hadn't completely disappeared.

One analysis showed that between 15 and 26 million Americans had joined one of the overwhelmingly peaceful protests in June 2020 alone, masking up and reaching for each other again, even at a point in the pandemic where one thousand Americans were dying every day. As important, perhaps, were the millions more who underwent an active and honest accounting—myself included—as to whether we were as alive as we thought we were to the daily injustices of systemic racism, and how we might do our part to make America better. Some states and cities rekindled Obama-era efforts to reform their police practices. Many corporations changed their business practices. In Mississippi, legislators voted to change the state flag, the only one in America that still incorporated the Confederate banner—just as South Carolina legislators, three weeks after the massacre in Charleston, had voted to remove the Confederate flag from state capitol grounds.

Whether such introspection and empathy will last isn't guaranteed—it's up to us. The 2020 election saw the highest turnout in 120 years. Whether that continues is up to us too.

It will require more than simply massing *against* that darker vision of America. It requires convincing each other, including enough voters who were sympathetic to Trump's argument, that there's a story of America that's worth fighting *for*. One where the most patriotic work of all is the work of changing America for the better. Because there are so many Americans who desperately need all of us to finish that story by making its first sentences—that all of us are created equal, and that We the People can form a more perfect Union—come true.

And after leaving the White House, I found new reasons to believe that we can.

Over the Fourth of July weekend in 2016, Kristen and I got married in Washington, D.C. The Obamas ultimately decided not to attend, citing the disruptions that a twenty-vehicle motorcade and Secret Service would cause. Instead, President Obama invited our wedding party and our families to come celebrate the day in the Rose Garden, and he slipped out of Malia's birthday party to spend time with our guests and offer some words of wisdom about what makes a happy marriage.

That September, he called me into the Oval Office and asked me to stick with him after his presidency ended. Kristen would remain with him too, continuing to serve as his fireproofer even while launching her own research firm with Alex Platkin, her longtime partner from campaigns and the White House.

Obama and I wrote together for four more years, collaborating on campaign speeches, nationwide commencement addresses for students denied in-person graduations, and an emotional eulogy for John Lewis. In the wake of the protests after George Floyd and the dog days of the pandemic, he delivered an intentionally sober 2020 Democratic National Convention address in which he stood alone, with no audience, staring straight into the camera to warn yet again that democracy was more imperiled than ever—but also to remind young people that they were, in so many ways, this country's wildest dreams fulfilled.

"Earlier generations had to be persuaded that everyone has equal worth," he said. "For you, it's a given . . . You can give our democracy new meaning. You can take it to a better place. You're the missing ingredient—the ones who will decide whether or not America becomes the country that finally lives up to its creed."

I believed those words. By then, I'd spent a couple of years teaching at my alma mater, Northwestern University, training a new generation of speechwriters and trying to convince them that public service is worth it. What I didn't expect was that my students would end up teaching me quite a bit in return.

They're more impatient than they are idealistic, challenging my own theory of change. These kids—*my* kids—are twenty years younger than I am, part of a generation that's come of age through two wars and two devastating recessions, the anxiety of active shooter drills in grade school and of a planet that's going to turn inhospitable while they're still alive. They're rightly frustrated by the pace of progress, angry at those who stand in its way, and tired of being told to lower their expectations. They don't want a lecture to vote; they know they have to and they do—but when campaign promises meet the gears of government, when a minority of Republican senators can grind business to a halt or just *one* Democratic senator can block action on a climate that's changing before our eyes, voting becomes a harder, more annoying sell.

Somehow, though, they're not cynical about America and its possibilities. Somehow, they're not as plagued by fear or suspicion as older generations; they're more tolerant of differences between race and culture and gender and orientation, not only comfortable navigating all these different worlds but impatient to make them all fairer, more inclusive, and just plain better.

They're consumed with the idea that they can change things. They just want to do it faster.

I tell them to vote anyway, because not voting plays right into the hands of the enemies of progress who seek their cynicism, who want to exhaust and disengage them. (And because change really is possible and can be durable—I'd be remiss if I didn't mention somewhere that Obamacare is not only still intact; it also now covers more than 30 million Americans.)

But I also tell them that they deserve to vote for something better. And I tell them, regardless of their political views, to create it. To show up. To dive in. To organize. To run. I tell them, here's the baton; take it. Because we will never win full equality, remake our economy, protect ourselves from the worst ravages of climate change, or make any progress on any of the issues they care about without a healthy democracy pumping with the lifeblood of more young people like them—a generation that can redefine and reaffirm what it means to be an American.

I tell them that the words soon to be carved into the stone exterior of the Obama Presidential Center, an excerpt of his speech in Selma, were written for them.

> You are America. Unconstrained by habit and convention. Unencumbered by what is, ready to seize what ought to be. For everywhere in this country, there are first steps to be taken; there is new ground to cover; there are more bridges to be crossed.

> America is not the project of any one person. The single most powerful word in our democracy is the word *We*. We the People. We Shall Overcome. Yes We Can. That word is owned by no one. It belongs to everyone. Oh, what a glorious task *we* are given to continually try to improve this great nation of ours.

I believe in those words. I believe in my students. Because that's the kind of world I want to live in.

At the turn of 2020, Kristen and I moved to New York City to start a new chapter in our lives. Two months into the year, we found out she was pregnant. Two weeks after that, the COVID-19 pandemic shut down New York City. The streets emptied, amplifying the all-night sirens with a haunting echo. We spent much of the next few months grateful to be able to hunker down together in our apartment, taking no chances with the baby, the refrigerated morgue truck across from our bedroom window an awful reminder of the thousands upon thousands of New Yorkers dying around us.

We joined our neighbors every night at seven o'clock, hanging out our windows to clap and whistle, ostensibly to cheer first responders, but also to let each other know we were there, feeling for the first time in a long time like Americans were pulling for each other. As the incessant ambulance wails of spring gave way to the incessant rattle of NYPD helicopters in summer, we masked up and emerged from isolation to join the myriad protest marches that crisscrossed our neighborhood, hopeful that the engines of progress might be starting again.

In the solitude of the pandemic, I realized more acutely than ever that I missed being part of a team of writers, and I told Obama that after nearly fourteen years, it was time for me to move on. I didn't go far, though. I joined Fenway, following Favs all over again, this time to the small firm that he and Tommy had created before leaving to launch Crooked Media. At Fenway, I was once again surrounded by an idealistic team of young speechwriters, half of whom I'd worked with in the White House, all eager to help leaders tell better stories that might shift the country's perception—even the world's perception—of what's possible.

On November 11, 2020, eight days after the election and four days after Joe Biden was proven the victor, we welcomed a healthy baby girl into our lives. Over nine months of pregnancy spent in lonely isolation and surrounded by noisy protest—with every in utero kick, squirm, and spate of hiccups, with every blurry sonogram I was forced to watch over FaceTime from the street outside the doctor's office—she had been a centering presence in an anxious time, a reassurance that something better lay ahead, a blessing we felt we didn't deserve.

We named her Grace.

Acknowledgments

Thank you for spending time with this book.

I've had the privilege to write or edit a whole lot of speeches for others to deliver over the years. To put forward something under my own name has been an exhilarating endeavor—but often a frightening, frustrating, and lonely one too. It was made less so by the wise counsel and patient encouragement of a constellation of people whom I'm extraordinarily fortunate to have in my life.

That list begins and ends with my family, first and foremost, the love of my life, Kristen Bartoloni. To share a New York City apartment with someone who's writing a book is tough enough. To do it through pregnancy, a pandemic, and the first two years of parenthood—all while running your own business—is superhuman. Nobody has been more important to this project or to my life, and I'll always feel foolishly lucky to have spent every moment—literally—of this weird and wonderful time with you.

I've never had to search for support from my parents, Steve and Marilyn Keenan, or my sister Carly Keenan; it's always been a constant. The pandemic agonizingly kept them from their first grandchild and niece for too long, but our vaccinated reunions became a refuge for Kristen and me, and welcome help in raising our daughter when we had to work. The same is true for Kristen's parents, Laurie and Joe Bartoloni, my brother- and sister-in-law Matt and Yanira Bartoloni, and our nanny, Maria Jean, who's become as tightly knit a part of our family as anybody. Nick Ehrmann, who might as well be my brother, pestered me until I finally started writing, and then pestered me throughout. Each of you made this a better book.

So too did the exceptional editorial team that assembled around me like a small army. I'm forever indebted to Todd Shuster, who approached me early in 2017 to ask if I had a story to tell—and who had the patience to wait the five years it took me to finally put it on paper. I'm thankful for him and his whole team at Aevitas Creative Management.

The crew at HMH, Mariner Books, and HarperCollins surprised me with something all too rare: They not only tolerated but encouraged my efforts to be a full-time dad, even as I blew through deadline after deadline. Before Deanne Urmy, the only two editors I'd ever worked with were Barack Obama and Jon Favreau. She was not intimidated; like them, and in some ways surpassing them, she pushed me past my limits, helped me untangle my own mind, and with talent, candor, and no small amount of forbearance, kept me focused on the most important question of all: "What's the story we're trying to tell?" Deanne's heroic efforts were rounded out by the dedication and skill of Deb Brody, Bob Castillo, Andrea DeWerd, Chloe Foster, Ivy Givens, Mark Robinson, and Taryn Roeder, and I've been bolstered from the beginning by the undeniable enthusiasm of Michael Sugar, Angela Ledgerwood, and Ruby Smith at Sugar23.

I often get misty when thinking about the entirety of the Obama universe—the organizers, the experts, the problem solvers, the believers who kept pushing that boulder uphill, no matter what. What a joy to spend a full third of my life serving with you, to watch what you're all doing now, and to have so many of you as friends and colleagues today. You were constantly on my mind while writing this book.

Barack Obama has always been just as good a boss and mentor—professionally and personally—as you'd hope he'd be. He graciously offered his thoughts on this manuscript—and yes, the wait was more harrowing than waiting for him to read any speech draft.

Sara Corbett had every right to a break after working with the Obamas on their books, so I could just pinch myself that she was generous enough to give mine a close read and offer her insightful feedback, as were Sarada Peri, Dan Pfeiffer, and Ben Rhodes.

Anita Decker Breckenridge helped me learn to laugh at the absurdities of life in the White House and helped me navigate the National Archives while writing this book.

Meredith Bohen applied the same indispensable, truly annoying rigorousness to fact-checking this book as she did to President Obama's speeches. I pity the lawyers who find themselves across from her in court someday.

Pete Souza, Lawrence Jackson, Chuck Kennedy, and their team brilliantly captured on film 6 million little moments of the Obama administration, and charitably let me borrow a few of them.

Thanks also to Joshua DuBois, Josh Earnest, Ferial Govashiri, Danielle Gray, Denis McDonough, Brian Mosteller, Joe Paulsen, Fiona Reeves, Eric Schultz, Terry Szuplat, and Jeff Tiller for helping to fill out my memories.

And hats off to my daily therapists and sounding boards who've made the past fifteen years wonderful and toiling on this book bearable: Favs, Dan, Ben, Michael O'Neil, Tommy Vietor, and all my fellow speechwriters from the Obama White House. Nobody should be this lucky.

As I wrote this book, I was also wildly thankful for the people who surrounded me in both of my day jobs. My colleagues at Fenway—the most talented, most fun stable of speechwriters in the world today—were bighearted enough to pick up my slack when I needed to disappear for a bit. My students at Northwestern University gifted me with new lenses with which to view the world and new reasons to believe that we just might make it after all. Don't ever let go of that youthful, idealistic conviction that you can change things for the better. I can't wait to see you do it.

Finally, to my sweet, curious, smarty-pants Gracie—I wrote most of this book while you slept either next to me or in the next room. And I wrote it for you most of all. The years will offer so many reasons to think we can't do any better than the world as it is. But I want you to grow up knowing just how many people are out there trying to make the world into what it should be. I hope you always surround yourself with people like that. And whatever you go on to do, whoever you grow up to be, let me lift one worry from your life right now: I'm *already* so proud of you, and I always will be.

Appendix

The Speeches

REMARKS OF PRESIDENT BARACK OBAMA AS PREPARED FOR DELIVERY

Selma, Alabama
March 7, 2015

It is a rare honor in this life to follow one of your heroes. And John Lewis is one of my heroes.

Now, I have to imagine that when a younger John Lewis woke up that morning fifty years ago and made his way to Brown Chapel, heroics were not on his mind. A day like this was not on his mind. Young folks with bedrolls and backpacks were milling about. Veterans of the movement trained newcomers in the tactics of nonviolence; the right way to protect yourself when attacked. A doctor described what tear gas does to the body while marchers scribbled down instructions for contacting their loved ones. The air was thick with doubt, anticipation, and fear. They comforted themselves with the final verse of the final hymn they sung:

No matter what may be the test, God will take care of you;
Lean, weary one, upon His breast, God will take care of you.

Then, his knapsack stocked with an apple, a toothbrush, a book on government—all you need for a night behind bars—John Lewis led them out of the church on a mission to change America.

President Bush and Mrs. Bush, Governor Bentley, members of Congress, Mayor Evans, Reverend Strong, friends and fellow Americans:

There are places and moments in America where this nation's destiny has been decided. Many are sites of war—Concord and Lexington, Appomattox and Gettysburg. Others are sites that symbolize the daring spirit of the American character—Independence Hall and Seneca Falls, Kitty Hawk and Cape Canaveral.

Selma is such a place.

In one afternoon fifty years ago, so much of our turbulent history—the stain of slavery and anguish of civil war; the yoke of segregation and tyranny of Jim Crow; the death of four little girls in Birmingham; and the dream of a Baptist preacher—met on this bridge.

It was not a clash of armies, but a clash of wills; a contest to determine the meaning of America.

And because of men and women like John Lewis, Joseph Lowery, Hosea Williams, Amelia Boynton, Diane Nash, Ralph Abernathy, C.T. Vivian, Andrew Young, Fred Shuttlesworth, Dr. King, and so many more, the idea of a *just* America, a *fair* America, an *inclusive* America, a *generous* America—that idea ultimately triumphed.

As is true across the landscape of American history, we cannot examine this moment in isolation. The march on Selma was part of a broader campaign that spanned generations; the leaders that day part of a long line of heroes.

We gather here to celebrate them. We gather here to honor the courage of ordinary Americans willing to endure billy clubs and the chastening rod; tear gas and the trampling hoof; men and women who despite the gush of blood and splintered bone would stay true to their North Star and keep marching toward justice.

They did as Scripture instructed: "Rejoice in hope, be patient in tribulation, be constant in prayer." And in the days to come, they went back again and again. When the trumpet call sounded for more to join, the people came—Black and white, young and old, Christian and Jew, waving the same American flag and singing the same anthems full of faith and hope. A white newsman, Bill Plante, who covered the marches then and who is with us here today, quipped at the time that the growing number of white people lowered the quality of the singing. To those who marched, though, those old gospel songs must have never sounded so sweet.

In time, their chorus would reach President Johnson. And he would send them protection, echoing their call for the nation and the world to hear:

"We shall overcome."

What enormous faith these men and women had. Faith in God—but also faith in America.

The Americans who crossed this bridge were not physically imposing. But they gave courage to millions. They held no elected office. But they led a nation. They marched as Americans who had endured hundreds of years of brutal violence, and countless daily indignities—but they didn't seek special treatment, just the equal treatment promised to them almost two hundred years before.

What they did here will reverberate through the ages, never to be undone. Not because the change they won was preordained; not because their victory was complete; but because they proved that nonviolent change is *possible;* that love and hope can conquer hate.

As we commemorate their achievement, we are well-served to remember that many in power condemned rather than praised them. Back then, they were called Communists, half-breeds, outside agitators, sexual and moral degenerates, and worse—everything but the name their parents gave them. Their faith was questioned. Their lives were threatened. Their patriotism was challenged.

And yet, what could be more American than what happened in this place?

What could more profoundly vindicate the idea of America than plain and humble people—the unsung, the downtrodden, the dreamers not of high station, not born to wealth or privilege, not of one religious tradition but many—coming together to shape their country's course?

What greater expression of faith in the American experiment than this, what greater form of patriotism is there, than the belief that America is *not* yet finished; that we are *strong* enough to be self-critical; that each successive generation can look upon our imperfections and decide that it is in our power to remake this nation to more closely align with our highest ideals?

That's why Selma is not some outlier in the American experience. *That's* why it's not just a museum or static monument to behold from a distance. It is instead the manifestation of a creed written into our founding documents:

"*We* the People . . . in order to form a more perfect union."

"*We* hold these truths to be self-evident, that all men are created equal."

These are not just words. They are a living thing, a call to action, a roadmap for citizenship and an insistence in the capacity of free men and women to shape our own destiny. For founders like Franklin and Jefferson, for leaders like Lincoln and FDR, the success of our experiment in self-government rested on engaging *all* our citizens in this work. *That's* what we celebrate here in Selma. That's what this movement was all about, one leg in our long journey toward freedom.

The American instinct that led these young men and women to pick up the torch and cross this bridge is the *same* instinct that moved patriots to choose revolution over tyranny. It's the *same* instinct that drew immigrants from across oceans and the Rio Grande; the *same* instinct that led women to reach for the ballot and workers to organize against an unjust status quo; the *same* instinct that led us to plant a flag at Iwo Jima and on the surface of the Moon.

It's the idea held by generations of *citizens* who believed that America is a constant work in progress; who believed that loving this country requires more than singing its praises or avoiding uncomfortable truths. It requires the occasional disruption, the willingness to speak out for what's right and shake up the status quo.

That's what makes us unique and cements our reputation as a beacon of opportunity. Young people behind the Iron Curtain would see Selma and eventually tear down a wall. Young people in Soweto would hear Bobby Kennedy talk about ripples of hope and eventually banish the scourge of apartheid. Young people in Burma went to prison rather than submit to military rule. From the streets of Tunis to the Maidan in Ukraine, this generation of young people draws strength from *this* place, where the powerless could change the world's greatest superpower, and push their leaders to expand the boundaries of freedom. They saw that idea made real in Selma, Alabama. They saw it made real in America.

Because of campaigns like this, a Voting Rights Act was passed. Political, economic, and social barriers came down, and the change these men and women wrought is visible here today: African Americans who run boardrooms, who sit on the bench, who serve in elected office from small towns to big cities; from the Congressional Black Caucus to the Oval Office.

Because of what they did, the doors of opportunity swung open, not just for African Americans, but for *every* American. Women marched through those doors. Latinos marched through those doors. Asian Americans, gay Americans, and Americans with disabilities came through those doors. Their endeavors gave the entire South the chance to rise again, not by reasserting the past, but by transcending the past. What a glorious thing, Dr. King might say.

What a solemn debt we owe.

Which leads us to ask: Just how might we repay that debt?

First and foremost, we have to recognize that one day's commemoration, no matter how special, is not enough. If Selma taught us anything, it's that our work is never done—the American experiment in self-government gives work and purpose to each generation.

In teaches us too that action requires us to slough off cynicism. When it comes to the pursuit of justice, we can afford neither complacency nor despair.

Just this week, I was asked whether I thought the Department of Justice's Ferguson report shows that, when it comes to race, nothing has changed in this country. I understand the question, for the report's narrative was woefully familiar. It evoked the kind of abuse and disregard for citizens that spawned the civil rights movement. But I cautioned against suggesting that this was proof nothing's changed. Ferguson may not be unique, but it's no longer endemic or sanctioned by law and custom; and before the civil rights movement, it was.

We do a disservice to the cause of justice by intimating that bias and discrimination are immutable, or that racial division is inherent to America. If you think nothing's changed in the past fifty years, ask somebody who lived through Selma whether nothing's changed. Ask the female CEO who once might have been assigned to the secretarial pool if nothing's changed. Ask your gay friend if it's easier to be out and proud in America now than it was thirty years ago. To deny this progress—*our* progress—would be to rob us of our own agency; our responsibility to do what we can to make America better.

Of course, an even more common mistake is to suggest that racism is banished, that the work that drew men and women to Selma is finished, and that whatever racial tensions remain are a consequence of those seeking to play the "race card" for their own purposes. We don't need the Ferguson report to know that's not true. We just need to open our eyes, and ears, and hearts, to know that this nation's racial history still casts its long shadow upon us. We know the march is not yet over, the race is not yet won, and that reaching that blessed destination where we are all truly judged by the content of our character requires admitting as much.

"We are capable of bearing a great burden," James Baldwin wrote, "once we discover that the burden is reality and arrive where reality is."

This is work for all and not just some. Not just whites. Not just Blacks. If we want to honor the courage of those who marched that day, then all of us are called to possess their moral imagination. All of us will need to feel, as they did, the fierce urgency of now. All of us need to recognize, as they did, that change depends on our actions, our attitudes, the things we teach our children. And if we make such effort, no matter how hard it may seem, laws can be passed, and consciences can be stirred, and consensus can be built. We can do that. Yes we can.

With such effort, we can make sure our criminal justice system serves all and not just some. Together, we can raise the level of mutual trust that policing is built on—the idea that police officers are members of the communities they risk their lives to protect, and citizens just want the same thing young people here marched for—the protection of the law. Together, we can address unfair sentencing, and overcrowded prisons, and the stunted circumstances that rob us of too many boys before they become men, and too many men who could be good dads.

With effort, we can roll back poverty and the roadblocks to opportunity. Americans don't accept a free ride for anyone, nor do we believe in equality of outcomes. But we do expect equal opportunity, and if we really mean it, if we're willing to sacrifice for it, then we can make sure *every* child gets an education suitable to this new century, one that expands imaginations and lifts their sights. We can make sure every person willing to work has the dignity of a job, and a fair wage, a real voice, and sturdier rungs on that ladder into the middle class.

And with effort, we can protect the foundation stone of our democracy for which so many marched across this bridge—and that is the right to vote. Right now, in 2015, fifty years after Selma, there are laws across this country *designed* to make it harder for people to vote. As we speak, more of such laws are being proposed. Meanwhile, the Voting Rights Act, the culmination of so much blood and sweat and tears, the product of so much sacrifice in the face of wanton violence, stands weakened, its future subject to partisan rancor.

How can that be? The Voting Rights Act was one of the crowning achievements of our democracy, the result of Republican *and* Democratic effort. President Bush signed its renewal when he was in office. More than a hundred members of Congress have come here today to honor people who were willing to die for the right it protects. If we want to honor this day, let these hundred go back to Washington, and gather four hundred more, and together, pledge to make it their mission to restore the law this year.

Of course, our democracy is not the task of Congress alone, or the courts, or the president. If every new voter suppression law was struck down today, we'd still have one of the lowest voting rates among free peoples. Fifty years ago, registering to vote here in Selma and much of the South meant guessing the number of jellybeans in a jar or bubbles on a bar of soap. It meant risking your dignity, and sometimes your life. What is our excuse today? How do we so casually discard the right for which so many fought? How do we so fully give away our power, our voice, in shaping America's future?

Fellow marchers, so much has changed in fifty years. We've endured war, and fashioned peace. We've seen technological wonders that touch every aspect of our lives, and take for granted conveniences our parents might scarcely imagine. But what has *not* changed is the imperative of citizenship, that willingness of a twenty-six-year-old deacon, a Unitarian minister, or a young mother of five, to decide they loved this country so much that they'd risk everything to realize its promise.

That's what it means to *love* America. *That's* what it means to *believe* in America. *That's* what it means when we say America is *exceptional*.

For we were *born* of change. We *broke* the old aristocracies, declaring ourselves entitled not by bloodline, but *endowed* by our Creator with certain unalienable rights. We secure our rights and responsibilities through a system of self-government, of and by and for the people. That's why we argue and fight with so much passion and conviction. That's why, for such a young nation, we are so big and bold and diverse and full of contradictions: because we know our efforts matter. We know America is what we make of it.

We are Lewis and Clark and Sacajawea—pioneers who braved the unfamiliar, followed by a stampede of farmers and miners, entrepreneurs and hucksters. That's our spirit.

We are Teddy Roosevelt, who charged up that hill with the Rough Riders, and invited Booker T. Washington to dinner to hear his implausible vision of things to come. That's what we do.

We are Sojourner Truth and Fannie Lou Hamer, women who could do as much as any man and then some; and we're Susan B. Anthony, who shook the system until the law reflected that truth. That's our character.

We're the immigrants who stowed away on ships to reach these shores, and the hopeful strivers who cross the Rio Grande because they want their kids to know a better life. That's how we came to be.

We're the slaves who built the White House and the economy of the South, and we're the countless laborers who laid rail, and raised skyscrapers, and organized for workers' rights.

We are the millions of volunteer warriors who leave no one behind and risk everything to save one of our own. We're the fresh-faced GIs who fought to liberate a continent, and we're the Tuskeegee Airmen, Navajo code-talkers, and Japanese Americans who fought for this country even as their own liberty had been denied.

We are the huddled masses yearning to breathe free—Holocaust survivors, Soviet defectors, the Lost Boys of Africa.

We are the gay Americans whose blood ran on the streets of San Francisco and New York, just as blood ran down this bridge.

We are storytellers, writers, poets, and artists who abhor unfairness, and despise hypocrisy, and give voice to the voiceless, and tell truths that need to be told.

We are the inventors of gospel, jazz and the blues, bluegrass and country, hip-hop and rock and roll, our very own sounds with all the sweet sorrow and dangerous joy of freedom.

We are Jackie Robinson, enduring scorn and spiked cleats and stealing home plate in the World Series anyway.

We are the people Langston Hughes wrote of, who "build our temples for tomorrow, strong as we know how."

We are the people Emerson wrote of, "who for truth and honor's sake stand fast and suffer long"; who are "never too tired, so long as we can see far enough."

That's what America is. Not stock photos or feeble attempts to define some as more American than others. We respect the past, but we don't pine for it. We don't fear the future; we grab for it. America is not some fragile thing; we are large, in the words of Whitman, containing multitudes. We are boisterous and full of energy, perpetually young in spirit. That's why someone like John Lewis at the ripe age of twenty-five could lead a mighty march.

And that's what the young people here today and listening all across the country must take away from this day. You *are* America. Unconstrained by habits and convention. Unencumbered by what *is,* and ready to seize what *ought to be*. For everywhere in this country, there are first steps to be taken, and new ground to cover, and bridges to be crossed. And it is you, the young and fearless at heart, the most diverse and educated generation in our history, who we are waiting to follow.

Because Selma shows us that America is not the project of any one person.

Because the single most powerful word in our democracy is the word *we*. *We* the People. *We* Shall Overcome. It is owned by no one. It belongs to everyone. Oh, what a glorious task we are given, to continually try to improve this great nation of ours.

Fifty years from Bloody Sunday, our march is not yet finished. But we are getting closer. Two hundred and thirty-nine years after this nation's founding, our union is not yet perfect. But we are getting closer. Our job's easier because somebody already got us through that first mile. Somebody already got us over that bridge. When it feels that the road is too hard, when the torch we've been passed feels too heavy, we will remember these early travelers, and draw strength from their example, and hold firmly the words of the prophet Isaiah: "Those who hope in the Lord will renew their strength. They will soar on wings like eagles. They will run and not grow weary. They will walk and not be faint."

We honor those who walked so we could run. We must run so our children soar. And we will *not* grow weary. For we believe in the power of an awesome God, and we believe in the promise of America.

May He bless those warriors of justice no longer with us, and may He bless our precious United States.

REMARKS OF PRESIDENT BARACK OBAMA AS PREPARED FOR DELIVERY ON THE SUPREME COURT'S RULING ON THE AFFORDABLE CARE ACT

The White House

June 25, 2015

Five years ago, after nearly a century of talk, decades of trying, and a year of bipartisan debate—we finally declared that in America, health care is not a privilege for a few, but a right for all.

Over those five years, as we've worked to implement the Affordable Care Act, there have been successes and setbacks. But as the dust has settled, there can be no doubt this law is working. It has changed, even saved, American lives. It has set this country on a smarter, stronger course.

And today, after more than fifty votes in Congress to repeal or weaken this law; after a presidential election based in part on preserving or repealing this law; after multiple challenges to this law before the Supreme Court—the Affordable Care Act is here to stay.

This morning, the Court upheld a critical part of this law—the part that has made it easier for Americans to afford health insurance regardless of where you live. If the partisan challenge to this law had succeeded, millions of Americans would have had thousands of dollars' worth of tax credits taken from them. For many, insurance would have become unaffordable again. Many would have become uninsured again. Ultimately, everyone's premiums could have gone up.

America would have gone backward. And that's not what we do. We move forward.

Today is a victory for hard-working Americans all across this country whose lives will continue to become more secure in a changing economy because of this law.

If you're a parent, you can keep your kids on your plan until they turn twenty-six—something that has covered millions of young people so far. That's because of this law.

If you're a senior, or an American with a disability, this law gives you discounts on your prescriptions—something that has saved 9 million Americans an average of $1,600 so far.

If you're a woman, you can't be charged more than anybody else—even if you've had cancer, or your husband had heart disease, or just because you're a woman. Your insurer has to offer free preventive services like mammograms. They can't place annual or lifetime caps on your care.

Because of this law, and because of today's decision, millions of Americans will continue to receive the tax credits that have given about eight in ten people who buy insurance on the new marketplaces the choice of a health care plan that costs less than $100 a month.

And when it comes to preexisting conditions—someday, our grandkids will ask us if there was really a time when America discriminated against people who get sick. Because that's something this law has ended for good.

As the law's provisions have gradually taken effect, more than 16 million uninsured Americans have gained coverage so far. Nearly one in three Americans who were uninsured a few years ago is insured today. The uninsured rate in America is the lowest since we began to keep records. That's something we can all be proud of.

The law has helped hold the price of health care to its slowest growth in fifty years. If your family gets insurance through your job, you're paying about $1,800 less per year on average than you would be if we hadn't done anything. By one leading measure, what business owners pay out in wages and salaries is now growing faster than what they spend on health insurance for the first time in seventeen years—which is good for workers and good for the economy.

The point is, this is not an abstract thing. This law is working exactly as it's supposed to—and in many ways, better than we expected it to. For all the misinformation campaigns and doomsday predictions; for all the talk of death panels and job destruction; for all the repeal attempts—this law is helping tens of millions of Americans. As many have told me poignantly, it has changed their lives for the better. And it's going to keep doing just that.

Five years in, this is no longer just about a law. This isn't just about the Affordable Care Act, or Obamacare.

This is health care in America.

Unlike Social Security or Medicare, a lot of Americans still don't know what Obamacare is beyond the political noise in Washington. Across the country, there remain people who are directly benefiting from the law but don't even know it. There's no card that says Obamacare when you enroll. And that's okay.

For this has never been a government takeover, despite cries to the contrary. This reform remains what it always has been—a set of fairer rules and tougher protections that have made health care in America more affordable, more attainable, and more about you.

With this case behind us, we still have work to do to make health care in America even better. We'll keep working to provide consumers with all the tools you need to make informed choices about your care. We'll keep working to increase the use of preventive care that avoids bigger problems down the road. We'll keep working to boost the steadily improving quality of care in hospitals, and bring down its cost. We'll keep working to get people covered. We'll keep working to convince more governors and state legislatures to expand Medicaid and cover their citizens.

But we are not going to unravel what has now been woven into the fabric of America. My hope is that rather than keep refighting battles that have been settled again and again, I can work with Republicans and Democrats to move on, and make health care in America even better.

Three generations ago, we chose to end an era when seniors were left to languish in poverty.

Two generations ago, we chose to end an age when Americans in their golden years didn't have the guarantee of health care.

This generation of Americans chose to finish the job. To turn the page on a past when our citizens could be denied coverage just for being sick. To close the books on a history where tens of millions of Americans had no hope of finding decent, affordable health care, and hung their chances on fate. To write a new chapter, where in a new economy, we can change our jobs, chase that new idea, and raise a family, free from fear, and secure in the knowledge that portable, affordable health care is there for us, and always will be.

That's when America soars—when we look out for one another. When we take care of each other. When we root for one another's success. When we strive to do better, to *be* better, than the generation that came before us, and try to build something better for generations to come.

This was a good day for America. Let's get back to work.

REMARKS OF PRESIDENT BARACK OBAMA AS PREPARED FOR DELIVERY ON THE SUPREME COURT'S RULING ON MARRIAGE EQUALITY

The White House

June 26, 2015

Good afternoon. Our nation was founded on a bedrock principle: that we are all created equal.

The project of each generation is to bridge the meaning of those founding words with the realities of changing times—a never-ending quest to ensure those words ring true for every single American.

Progress on this journey often comes in small increments, often two steps forward for every step back, propelled by the effort of persistent, dedicated citizens.

But sometimes, there are days like this—days when that slow, steady effort is rewarded with justice that arrives like a thunderbolt.

This morning, the Supreme Court recognized that the Constitution guarantees marriage equality. In so doing, they've reaffirmed that all Americans are entitled to the equal protection of the law. That all people should be treated equally, regardless of who they are or who they love. This decision will end the patchwork system we currently have. It will end the uncertainty hundreds of thousands of same-sex couples face from not knowing whether their marriage, legitimate in the eyes of the law in one state, will remain that way if they decide to move to or even visit another. And it will strengthen all of our communities by offering to all loving same-sex couples the dignity of marriage across this great land.

In my second inaugural address, I said that if we are truly created equal, then surely the love we commit to one another must be equal as well. So I am very pleased to see that principle enshrined into law by this decision. This ruling is a victory for Jim Obergefell and the other plaintiffs in the case. It's a victory for gay and lesbian couples who have fought so long for their basic civil rights. It's a victory for their children, whose families will now be recognized as equal to any other. It's a victory for the allies and friends and supporters who have spent years, even decades, working and praying for change to come.

And this ruling is a victory for America. This decision affirms what millions of Americans already believe in their hearts: When all Americans are treated as equal, we are all more free.

My administration has always been guided by that idea. It's why we stopped defending the so-called Defense of Marriage Act, and why we were pleased when the Court finally struck down a central provision of that discriminatory law. It's why we ended Don't Ask, Don't Tell. From extending full marital benefits to federal employees and their spouses to expanding hospital visitation rights for LGBT patients and their loved ones, we have made real progress in advancing equality for LGBT Americans—in ways that were unimaginable not too long ago.

Change, for many of our LGBT brothers and sisters, must have seemed so slow for so long. But compared to so many other issues, America's shift has been so quick. I know that Americans continue to hold a wide range of views on this issue, based on sincere and deeply held beliefs. All of us who welcome today's news should be mindful of that fact. We respect different viewpoints and revere our deep commitment to religious freedom.

But today should also give us hope that on the many issues with which we grapple—often painfully—real change is possible. A shift in hearts and minds is possible. And those who have come so far on their journey to equality have a responsibility to reach back and help others join them.

Because for all our differences, we are one people, stronger together than we could ever be alone. That's always been our story. We are big and vast and diverse, a nation of people with different backgrounds and beliefs, each with our own experiences and stories—but bound by our shared ideal that no matter who you are, what you look like, how you started out, or who you love, America is a place where you can write your own destiny. We are a people who believe that every single child is entitled to life and liberty and the pursuit of happiness.

There is so much work to be done to extend the full promise of America to every American. But today, we can say in no uncertain terms that we have made our union a little more perfect.

Thank you, and may God bless this country we love.

REMARKS OF PRESIDENT BARACK OBAMA

Charleston, South Carolina

June 26, 2015

The Bible calls us to hope. To persevere, and have faith in things not seen.

"They were still living by faith when they died," Scripture tells us. "They did not receive the things promised; they only saw them and welcomed them from a distance, admitting that they were foreigners and strangers on Earth."

We are here today to remember a man of God who lived by faith. A man who believed in things not seen. A man of service who persevered, knowing full well that he would not receive all those things he was promised, because he believed his efforts would deliver a better life for those who followed.

To Jennifer, his beloved wife; to Eliana and Malana, his beautiful daughters; to this Mother Emanuel family and the people of Charleston:

I did not have the good fortune to know Reverend Pinckney very well. But I did have the pleasure of meeting him, here in South Carolina, back when we were both a little bit younger. The first thing I noticed was his graciousness, his smile and reassuring baritone, his deceptive sense of humor—all qualities that helped him wear so effortlessly a heavy burden of expectation.

Friends of his remarked this week that when Clementa Pinckney entered a room, it was like the future arrived; that even from a young age, folks knew he was special. Anointed. He was the progeny of a long line of the faithful—a family of preachers who spread God's word, and protesters who sowed change to expand voting rights and desegregate the South.

Clem heard their instruction and did not forsake their teaching. He was in the pulpit by thirteen, pastor by eighteen, public servant by twenty-three. He did not exhibit any of the cockiness of youth, nor youth's insecurities; instead, he set an example worthy of his position, wise beyond his years, in his speech, his conduct, his love, faith, and purity.

As a senator, he represented a sprawling swath of the Lowcountry, a place that has long been one of the most neglected in America. A place still wracked by poverty and inadequate schools; a place where children can still go hungry and the sick too often go without treatment. A place that needed someone like Clem. His position in the minority party meant the odds of winning more resources for his constituents were often long. His calls for greater equity were too often unheeded, the votes he cast sometimes lonely. But he never gave up; stayed true to his convictions; would not grow discouraged. After a full day at the capitol, he'd climb into his car and head to the church to draw sustenance from his ministry, and from the community that loved and needed him; to fortify his faith, and imagine what might be.

Reverend Pinckney embodied a politics that was neither mean nor small, conducting himself quietly, and kindly, and diligently. He encouraged progress not by pushing his ideas alone, but by seeking out yours, and partnering with you to make it happen. He was full of empathy, able to walk in someone else's shoes, see the world through their eyes. No wonder one of his senate colleagues remembered Senator Pinckney this week as "the most gentle of the forty-six of us—the best of the forty-six of us."

Clem was often asked why he'd choose to be a pastor *and* a public servant. But as our brothers and sisters in the AME Church know well, they're one and the same. "Our calling," Clem once said, "is not just within the walls of the congregation, but . . . the life and community in which our congregation resides." It's the idea that our Christian faith demands deeds and not just words; that the "sweet hour of prayer" actually lasts the whole week long; that to put our faith in action is about more than our individual salvation, but about our collective salvation; that to feed the hungry and clothe the naked and house the homeless is not merely a call for isolated charity but the imperative of a just society.

Preacher by thirteen. Pastor by eighteen. Public servant by twenty-three. What a life Clementa Pinckney lived. What an example he set. What a model for his faith.

And to lose him at forty-one—slain in his sanctuary with eight wonderful members of his flock, each at different stages in life but bound together by a common commitment to God.

Cynthia Hurd. Susie Jackson. Ethel Lance. DePayne Middleton-Doctor. Tywanza Sanders. Daniel L. Simmons Sr. Sharonda Coleman-Singleton. Myra Thompson.

Good and decent people, so full of life, and kindness, and perseverance, and faith.

To the families of these fallen, the nation shares in your grief. Our pain cuts that much deeper because it happened in church. The church is and always has been the center of African American life—a place to call our own in a too often hostile world, a sanctuary from so many hardships. Over the course of centuries, Black churches served as "hush harbors" where slaves could worship in safety; praise houses where their free descendants could gather; rest stops for the weary along the Underground Railroad; and bunkers for the foot soldiers of the civil rights movement. They have been and are community centers where we organize for jobs and justice; places of scholarship and networking; places where children are loved and kept out of harm's way and told that they are beautiful and smart; taught that they matter.

That's what the Black church means. Our beating heart; the place where our dignity as a people is inviolate. There is no better example of this tradition than Mother Emanuel—a church built by Blacks seeking their liberty, burned to the ground because its founder sought to end slavery, only to rise up again, a phoenix from these ashes. When there were laws banning all-Black church gatherings, services happened here, in defiance of unjust laws. When there was a righteous movement to dismantle Jim Crow, Dr. King preached from its pulpit, and marches began from its steps. A sacred place, this church, not just for Blacks or Christians, but for every American who cares about the steady expansion of human rights in this country; a foundation stone of liberty and justice for all.

We do not know whether the killer of Reverend Pinckney and eight others knew all this history. But he surely sensed the meaning of his violent act—an act that drew on a long history of bombs and arson and shots fired at churches as a means to terrorize and control and oppress; an act that could only incite fear and recrimination; violence and suspicion; an act that could only deepen divisions that trace back to our nation's original sin.

Oh, but God works in mysterious ways, doesn't He?

Blinded by hatred, the alleged killer could not see the *grace* surrounding Reverend Pinckney and that Bible study group—the light of love that shone as they opened the church doors and invited a stranger to join their fellowship circle. The alleged killer could have never anticipated the way families of the fallen would respond when they saw him in court, in the midst of unspeakable grief—with words of forgiveness. The alleged killer could not imagine how the city of Charleston under the wise leadership of Mayor Riley, and the state of South Carolina, and the United States of America would respond—with not merely revulsion at this evil act but with a bighearted generosity and, more important, a thoughtful introspection and self-examination so rarely seen in our public life.

Blinded by hatred, he failed to comprehend what Reverend Pinckney so well understood: the power of God's grace.

This whole week, I've been reflecting on this idea of grace—the grace of the families who lost loved ones, the grace Reverend Pinckney would preach about in his sermons; the grace described in my favorite hymnal; the one we all know:

Amazing grace, how sweet the sound, that saved a wretch like me;
I once was lost, but now I'm found; was blind but now I see.

According to Christian tradition, grace is not earned. It is not merited; not something we deserve. Rather, grace is the free and benevolent favor of God, as manifested in the salvation of sinners and the bestowal of blessings.

As a nation, out of terrible tragedy, God has visited grace upon us. For He has allowed us to see where we've been blind. He has given us the chance, where we've been lost, to find our best selves. We may not have earned it, this grace, with our rancor and complacency and shortsightedness and fear of each other—but we got it all the same. He's once more given us grace—but it is up to us now to make the most of it, to receive it with gratitude, and prove ourselves worthy of the gift.

For too long, we were blind to the pain that the Confederate flag stirred in too many of our citizens. It's true—a flag didn't cause these murders. But as people from all walks of life, Republicans and Democrats now acknowledge—including Governor Haley, whose recent eloquence on the subject is worthy of praise—the flag has always represented more than just ancestral pride. For many, Black and white alike, it has been a reminder of systematic oppression and racial subjugation. We see that now. Removing the flag from the state capitol isn't an act of political correctness or an insult to the valor of Confederate soldiers. It is an acknowledgment that the cause for which they fought—the cause of slavery—was wrong. That the imposition of Jim Crow and the resistance to civil rights for all was wrong. It is one step in an honest accounting of America's history, and a modest but meaningful balm for so many unhealed wounds. It is an expression of the amazing changes that have transformed this country for the better because of the work of so many people of goodwill, people of all races striving to form a more perfect union. By taking down that flag, we express God's grace.

For too long, we've been blind to the way past injustices continue to shape the present. Perhaps we see that now. Perhaps this tragedy causes us to ask some tough questions about how we can permit so many of our children to languish in poverty, or attend dilapidated schools, or grow up without prospects for a job or career. Perhaps it causes us to examine what we are doing to cause some of our children to hate. Perhaps it softens hearts toward those lost young men, tens and tens of thousands caught up in the criminal justice system, and leads us to make sure it is not infected with bias; that we embrace changes in how we train and equip our police so that the bonds of trust between law enforcement and the communities they serve make us all safer and more secure. It's possible that we now realize the way racial bias can infect us even when we don't realize it, so that we guard against not just racial slurs, but also guard against the subtle impulse to call Johnny back for a job interview but not Jamal; so that we search our hearts when considering laws that make it harder for some of our fellow citizens to vote. By recognizing our common humanity, by treating every child as important, regardless of the color of their skin or the station into which they were born, and do what is necessary to make opportunity real for all, we express God's grace.

For too long, we've been blind to the unique mayhem that gun violence inflicts upon this nation. Our eyes open when nine of our brothers and sisters are cut down in a church basement, and twelve in a movie theater, and twenty-six in an elementary school. But maybe we will now also see the thirty precious lives cut short by gun violence in this country every single day, as well as the countless more whose lives are forever changed: the survivors crippled with permanent pain; the children traumatized and fearful every day as they walk to school; the husband who will never again feel his wife's warm touch; the entire communities whose grief overflows every time they have to watch what happened to them happen again somewhere else. The vast majority of Americans, the majority of gun owners even, want to do something about this. We see that now. By acknowledging the pain and loss of others, even as we respect the traditions and various ways of life that make up this beloved country; by making the moral choice to change if it will save even one precious life, we express God's grace.

We don't earn grace, but we choose how to receive it. We decide how to honor it. None of us can expect a transformation in race relations overnight; none of us should believe that a handful of gun-safety measures will prevent any tragedy. People of goodwill will continue to debate the merits of various policies, as our democracy requires, and whatever solutions we find will necessarily be incomplete.

But it would be a betrayal of everything Reverend Pinckney stood for, I believe, if we allowed ourselves to slip into a comfortable silence again, once the eulogies have been delivered and the TV cameras have moved on. To avoid uncomfortable truths about the prejudice that still infects our society; to settle for symbolic gestures without following up with the hard work of more lasting change—that's how we lose our way again. Likewise, it would be a refutation of the forgiveness expressed by those families if we merely slipped into the old habits, whereby those who disagree with us are not merely wrong but bad; where we shout instead of listen, and barricade ourselves behind our preconceived notions, or a well-practiced cynicism.

Reverend Pinckney once said, "Across the South, we have a deep appreciation of history—we haven't always had a deep appreciation of each other's histories." What is true in the South applies to America. Clem understood that justice grows out of recognition, of ourselves in others; that my liberty depends on my respect for yours; that history must not be a sword to justify injustice, or a shield against progress, but must be a manual for how to avoid repeating the mistakes of the past, and a roadway toward a better world. He knew that the path to grace involves an open mind, but more important it requires an open heart.

That's what I've felt this week—an open heart. That, more than any particular policy or analysis, is what's called upon right now, I think, what a friend of mine, the writer Marilyn Robinson, calls "that reservoir of goodness, beyond, and of another kind, that we are able to do each other in the ordinary cause of things."

If we can find *that* grace, anything is possible. If we can tap *that* grace, everything will change.

Amazing grace, how sweet the sound, that saved a wretch like me;
I once was lost, but now I'm found; was blind but now I see.

Clementa Pinckney found that grace.
Cynthia Hurd found that grace.
Susie Jackson found that grace.
Ethel Lance found that grace.
DePayne Middleton-Doctor found that grace.
Tywanza Sanders found that grace.
Daniel L. Simmons Sr. found that grace.
Sharonda Coleman-Singleton found that grace.
Myra Thompson found that grace.

Through the example of their lives, they have now passed it on to us. May we find ourselves worthy of this precious and extraordinary gift, as long as our lives endure. May grace now lead them home, and may God continue to shed His grace on the *United* States of America.

Index

ABOUT

MARINER BOOKS

MARINER BOOKS traces its beginnings to 1832 when William Ticknor cofounded the Old Corner Bookstore in Boston, from which he would run the legendary firm Ticknor and Fields, publisher of Ralph Waldo Emerson, Harriet Beecher Stowe, Nathaniel Hawthorne, and Henry David Thoreau. Following Ticknor's death, Henry Oscar Houghton acquired Ticknor and Fields and, in 1880, formed Houghton Mifflin, which later merged with venerable Harcourt Publishing to form Houghton Mifflin Harcourt. HarperCollins purchased HMH's trade publishing business in 2021 and reestablished their storied lists and editorial team under the name Mariner Books.

Uniting the legacies of Houghton Mifflin, Harcourt Brace, and Ticknor and Fields, Mariner Books continues one of the great traditions in American bookselling. Our imprints have introduced an incomparable roster of enduring classics, including Hawthorne's *The Scarlet Letter,* Thoreau's *Walden,* Willa Cather's *O Pioneers!,* Virginia Woolf's *To the Lighthouse,* W.E.B. Du Bois's *Black Reconstruction,* J.R.R. Tolkien's *The Lord of the Rings,* Carson McCullers's *The Heart Is a Lonely Hunter,* Ann Petry's *The Narrows,* George Orwell's *Animal Farm* and *Nineteen Eighty-Four,* Rachel Carson's *Silent Spring,* Margaret Walker's *Jubilee,* Italo Calvino's *Invisible Cities,* Alice Walker's *The Color Purple,* Margaret Atwood's *The Handmaid's Tale,* Tim O'Brien's *The Things They Carried,* Philip Roth's *The Plot Against America,* Jhumpa Lahiri's *Interpreter of Maladies,* and many others. Today Mariner Books remains proudly committed to the craft of fine publishing established nearly two centuries ago at the Old Corner Bookstore.